Bilingual Education in China

PEFC
PEFC/16-33-111
CATG-PEFC-052
www.pefc.org

BILINGUAL EDUCATION AND BILINGUALISM
Series Editors: Professor Colin Baker, *University of Wales, Bangor, Wales, Great Britain* and Professor Nancy H. Hornberger, *University of Pennsylvania, Philadelphia, USA*

Recent Books in the Series
Negotiation of Identities in Multilingual Contexts
   Aneta Pavlenko and Adrian Blackledge (eds)
Beyond the Beginnings: Literacy Interventions for Upper Elementary English Language Learners
   Ángela Carrasquillo, Stephen B. Kucer and Ruth Abrams
Bilingualism and Language Pedagogy
   Janina Brutt-Griffler and Manka Varghese (eds)
Language Learning and Teacher Education: A Sociocultural Approach
   Margaret R. Hawkins (ed.)
The English Vernacular Divide: Postcolonial Language Politics and Practice
   Vaidehi Ramanathan
Bilingual Education in South America
   Anne-Marie de Mejía (ed.)
Teacher Collaboration and Talk in Multilingual Classrooms
   Angela Creese
Words and Worlds: World Languages Review
   F. Martí, P. Ortega, I. Idiazabal, A. Barreña, P. Juaristi, C. Junyent, B. Uranga and E. Amorrortu
Language and Aging in Multilingual Contexts
   Kees de Bot and Sinfree Makoni
Foundations of Bilingual Education and Bilingualism (4th edn)
   Colin Baker
Bilingual Minds: Emotional Experience, Expression and Representation
   Aneta Pavlenko (ed.)
Raising Bilingual-Biliterate Children in Monolingual Cultures
   Stephen J. Caldas
Language, Space and Power: A Critical Look at Bilingual Education
   Samina Hadi-Tabassum
Developing Minority Language Resources
   Guadalupe Valdés, Joshua A. Fishman, Rebecca Chávez and William Pérez
Language Loyalty, Language Planning and Language Revitalization: Recent Writings and Reflections from Joshua A. Fishman
   Nancy H. Hornberger and Martin Pütz (eds)
Language Loyalty, Continuity and Change: Joshua A. Fishman's Contributions to International Sociolinguistics
   Ofelia Garcia, Rakhmiel Peltz and Harold Schiffman
Bilingual Education: An Introductory Reader
   Ofelia García and Colin Baker (eds)
Disinventing and Reconstituting Languages
   Sinfree Makoni and Alastair Pennycook (eds)
Language and Identity in a Dual Immersion School
   Kim Potowski

For more details of these or any other of our publications, please contact:
Multilingual Matters, Frankfurt Lodge, Clevedon Hall,
Victoria Road, Clevedon, BS21 7HH, England
http://www.multilingual-matters.com

BILINGUAL EDUCATION AND BILINGUALISM 64
Series Editors: Colin Baker and Nancy H. Hornberger

Bilingual Education in China
Practices, Policies and Concepts

Edited by
Anwei Feng

MULTILINGUAL MATTERS LTD
Clevedon • Buffalo • Toronto

To Jing, Jennifer, and Angela
with whom I converse in different languages,
from whom I draw motivation and inspiration.

Library of Congress Cataloging in Publication Data
Bilingual Education in China: Practices, Policies and Concepts/Edited by Anwei Feng.
Bilingual Education and Bilingualism: 64
Includes bibliographical references and index.
1. Education, Bilingual–China–Cross-cultural studies. 2. Bilingualism–China–
Cross-cultural studies. I. Feng, Anwei
LC3737.C6B35 2007
370.1170951–dc22   2007000086

British Library Cataloguing in Publication Data
A catalogue entry for this book is available from the British Library.

ISBN-13: 978-1-85359-992-7 (hbk)
ISBN-13: 978-1-85359-991-0 (pbk)

Multilingual Matters Ltd
UK: Frankfurt Lodge, Clevedon Hall, Victoria Road, Clevedon BS21 7HH.
USA: UTP, 2250 Military Road, Tonawanda, NY 14150, USA.
Canada: UTP, 5201 Dufferin Street, North York, Ontario M3H 5T8, Canada.

The policy of Multilingual Matters/Channel View Publications is to use papers that
are natural, renewable and recyclable products, made from wood grown in
sustainable forests. In the manufacturing process of our books, and to further support
our policy, preference is given to printers that have FSC and PEFC Chain of Custody
certification. The FSC and/or PEFC logos will appear on those books where full
certification has been granted to the printer concerned.

Typeset by TechBooks Ltd.
Printed and bound in Great Britain by MPG Books Ltd.

Contents

Foreword

Much is known about bilingual education in North America and in Western Europe. The world knows very little about bilingual education in China. That is why this book is so important. It opens up, almost for the first time, varieties of bilingual education in China and the practices and ideology that surrounds bilingual education in this large and growingly important region of the world.

It has often been stated that there are more speakers of Mandarin Chinese than of English in the world. One estimate is that there are 1200 million speakers of Chinese Mandarin as a first or second language in the world, compared with 750 million speakers of English as a first or second language. One favorite question from students that follows this remark is "what is the future of Mandarin Chinese relative to English in the remainder of this century?" Language prediction is difficult if not impossible, witness the death of Latin and the life of English. But the question subtly suggests that the numbers of speakers of any language and its future status and power are not separate issues.

As this book reveals, English and Mandarin Chinese cannot be kept separate. This book engages the relationship between Mandarin Chinese and English in its additive relationship. Various chapters focus on bilingual education as a site for these two eminent languages to be combined. The book throws light on the history, philosophy, politics, policy, provision, and practice of the combination of these two world languages within education in China.

Apart from recent developments in bilingual education using English and Mandarin Chinese, this book also examines minority language education experiences in China where bilingual education concerns Mandarin Chinese plus one of the many lesser-used languages in China.

There is a wonderful variety of voices in this book that adds to the novel nature of its contents. Such a variety of voice includes not only pedagogical understandings but also important historical and political contextualization. Such multidisciplinary viewpoints indicate that bilingual education in China is a fast developing, politically and economically important, and educationally significant activity.

This eagerly awaited book shares Eastern viewpoints and understandings that are sometimes varied from the dominant Western writings on bilingual education. Conceptualizations naturally differ as there is an historical legacy from centuries of Chinese philosophy, politics, and policy that frame bilingual education in a way that is valuably fresh and challenging for Western readers.

Colin Baker

Acknowledgement

This volume for the first time puts two strands of studies side by side on bilingualism and bilingual education in China, one for the minority nationality groups and the other for the majority, and examines the relationship between the two. In the whole process of compiling this volume, I owe a great deal to two internationally respected scholars in bilingual education. Since the very initial stage when this initiative was formulated, Professor Colin Baker has always supported it in all ways spiritually, technically, and academically. Without his vision and support, this volume would never be possible. An equally significant role is played by Professor Mike Byram, a colleague and a lifetime mentor. He reviewed the drafts of many of the chapters included and gave not only useful comments on the drafts but more importantly insightful suggestions for the compilation of the whole volume. From these two scholars, I have witnessed true qualities of prolific and efficient academics who are at the same time generous in offering time and help to others.

In writing this, I would also like to express my gratitude for all the contributors to this volume, not only for the insights, views, research, and experiences they share in their individual chapters but their readiness to cooperate in every way to make this volume a quality one. It was sheer pleasure and honour for me to work with such an agreeable and mutually supportive team consisting of a diversity of authors in terms of cultural background, academic interest, and expertise in bilingualism and bilingual education.

Thanks also go to Dr Mike Fleming, Director of the Research Office in the School of Education of Durham University, who is always there to support staff research and publication and to respond to requests for assistance. My gratitude also goes to the Centre for Contemporary China Studies, Durham University, for the financial support I received for a related bilingual education project the findings of which benefit the last chapter of this volume. Last but not least, I sincerely thank Ms Lihong Wang and Miss Jennifer Feng for their efforts to translate or retranslate some chapters from Chinese to English.

The Contributors

Dr Bob Adamson is an Associate Professor in the Department of Curriculum and Instruction at Hong Kong Institute of Education, where he is coordinator of the Doctor of Education programme. He has published in the fields of English language teaching, teacher education, comparative education, curriculum studies, and higher education. His books include *China's English*, a study of the official English Language textbooks and syllabuses for secondary schools in China since 1949; *Higher Education in Post-Mao China* (coedited with Michael Agelasto); and *Changing the Curriculum* (coedited with Tammy Kwan and Chan Ka Ki).

Dr Ben Jiao is a Tibetan from the Tibetan Autonomous Region. He earned his doctorate in Anthropology at the Case Western Reserve University in the United States. He is Senior Research Fellow, Institute for Contemporary Tibet Studies, Tibet Academy of Social Science, Lhasa, Tibet.

Professor Yanyan Cheng teaches and supervises MA students in linguistics in the College of Minority Languages and Literature at the Central University for Minorities in Beijing. She is secretary-general of International Bilingual Society, vice secretary-general of Chinese Minority Languages Studies Society. Her major research interests include studies of modern Hazak and contrastive studies of modern Hazak and Mandarin Chinese. She has published books, book chapters, and articles in these areas. She is now in charge of "the Contrastive Studies of Modern Hazak and Mandarin Chinese Verbal Clauses Based on the Second Language Teaching and Learning" project.

Heidi Cobbey works for the East Asia Group of SIL International and has lived in China for 10 years. Her focus is on researching needs of minority language speakers in China and implementing programs that focus on mother tongue education. She currently works in Xishuangbanna Prefecture in Yunnan Province, managing a bilingual education project among the Dai minority people group.

Professor Qingxia Dai teaches and supervises PhD students and postdoctoral fellows in linguistics in the College of Minority Languages and

Literature at the Central University for Minorities in Beijing. He is the chairman of International Bilingual Society, vice president of Chinese Linguistic Society, vice president of Chinese Minority Languages Studies Society, and honorary member of American Linguistic Society. His major research interests include Chinese minority languages studies and sociolinguistics. He has published books, book chapters, and articles in these areas. At present, he is engaged in studies of language use in Chinese minority areas, bilingualism, and endangered languages in China. He now is in charge of "the Chinese Minority Languages Reference Grammar Series" project.

Dr Anwei Feng works in the School of Education of Durham University teaching and supervising Education Doctorate and PhD students. His research interests include bilingual education, intercultural studies, international education, and TESOL. He has published book chapters and journal articles in all these areas. A recent book titled *Living and Studying Abroad* that he coedited with Mike Byram deals with many issues relevant to these areas. He is now leading a research project on the impact of English–Chinese bilingual education on minority nationality students in China.

Professor Zengjun Feng teaches and supervises Education Doctorate and PhD students in the School of Education at South China Normal University, in the School of Education at Nanjing Normal University, and in the Institute for Studies in Education at Sun Yat-Yet University. His research interests include comparative education, bilingual education, modernization of education, educational anthropology, moral education, higher education, and educational management. He has published about 40 books, more than 250 journal articles, and has led more than 10 national research projects in these areas.

Guangwei Hu holds a PhD and teaches postgraduate courses on language education and research at the National Institute of Education, Nanyang Technological University, Singapore. His main research interests include bilingualism and bilingual education, language policy, language teacher education, language learning strategies, and second language acquisition. His recent papers have been published in *Asian Englishes, Asian Journal of English Language Teaching, ELT Journal, International Journal of Educational Reform, Journal of Multilingual and Multicultural Development, Language and Education, Language, Culture and Curriculum, Language Teaching Research, Language Policy, Studies in Second Language Acquisition, TESOL Quarterly,* and *Teachers College Record.*

Dr Binlan Huang, Professor of English, has been teaching and supervising MA students of foreign linguistics and applied linguistics at College of

Foreign Languages of Guangxi University, China. She read and obtained her Doctor of Education from the University of Hull, UK. Her research interests cover applied linguistics, second language acquisition, intercultural studies, and bilingual education. She has published books and journal articles in the above-mentioned areas. She is now leading two provincial research projects on bilingual education.

Dr. Qiuxia Jiang is Professor and Dean of College of Foreign Languages and Literature, Northwest Normal University. She teaches and supervises EFL education doctoral students. Her academic fields are EFL education and translation studies. She has a lot of publications in both fields. The Commercial Press in China has published her book entitled *Aesthetic Progression in Literary Translation: Image-G Actualization* in 2002. Her paper entitled *Aesthetic Progression in Literary Translation* has been broadcasted in *Meta* (Vol. 1, 2004, A&HCI) to be published. She is currently the Director of the National Association for Education, and President of the Association for EFL Education Gansu Branch.

Born in Hong Kong, **Agnes Lam** did her BA (Hons) and MA in Singapore and her PhD and TESOL Certificate at the University of Pittsburgh. An Associate Professor at the University of Hong Kong, she has held visitorships awarded by Fulbright, the British Council, ASAHIL, and Universitas 21 among others. Her research interests include multilingualism, language education, and Asian poetry in English. Her recent publications include *Language education in China: Policy and experience from 1949* (2005), "Defining Hong Kong poetry in English: An answer from linguistics" in *World Englishes* (2000), and a poetry collection, *Water Wood Pure Splendour* (2001).

Quanguo Liu is a lecturer and doctoral student at College of Foreign Languages and Literature, Northwest Normal University. His research interests are mainly in applied linguistics and EFL education for ethnic minority learners. He is now leading two national research projects on the mechanism of trilingual transference and trilingual contact for ethnic minority learners who learn English as their third language. He is now a dean of a research institute and the secretary-general of the Association for EFL Education Gansu Branch.

Caiqin Ma, an associate professor, is working as an English teacher in Lanzhou Polytechnic College. Her research interests are mainly in the applied linguistics and language teaching methodology. Since 1999, she has published six articles, most of which are about college English teaching method. Her main publications are English textbooks, such as, *A Basic Course for English Writing (in English edition)* and *College English Reading* (three volumes). She is now the deputy dean of the English department of the college.

Manlaji is a Tibetan from Qinghai Province. She has been on the staff of Qinghai Normal University in Qinghai, China. She earned her Master's degree at Columbia University and is working toward her doctorate at the University of Hong Kong.

Prof. Jiazhen Pan works in the School of Mechanical and Power Engineering, East China University of Science and Technology, and is Chairman of the Committee of Academic Degrees in mechanical engineering. In the school, he is the team leader of an English–Chinese bilingual course offered to students of the school and, as Deputy Director of Teaching Guiding Committee of the Process Equipment and Control Engineering appointed by the Ministry of Education, he organized a national seminar on bilingual education in that specialized area in 2003. His research interests include fracture and fatigue of pressure vessels, experimental mechanics, ultra-high pressure technique, R & D for process equipment especially for chemical engineering and pharmaceutical industries, and bilingual education.

Gerard A. Postiglione is Professor, Faculty of Education, University of Hong Kong. His research focuses on the social and cultural underpinnings of reform and development in China. His books include *Education and Social Change in China: Inequality in a Market Economy, China National Minority Education: Culture, Schooling and Development, Education and Society in Hong Kong: Toward One Country and Two Systems: Hong Kong's Reunion with China, Asian Higher Education, and Ethnicity and American Social Theory: Toward Critical Pluralism*. He is the coeditor of the journal *Chinese Education and Society* and was the Director of Hong Kong University's Centre of Research on Education in China from 2000 to 2005.

Xiaohui Quan is an associate professor of College of Foreign Languages and Literature, Northwest Normal University. He now teaches and supervises postgraduates of EFL education. His research interests include EFL education and translation studies. He has participated as a key member in several research projects related to EFL education. He is now Deputy Dean of the International Corporation and Exchange Division, Northwest Normal University.

Minggang Wan is the professor and dean of Research Center for the Educational Development of Minorities at Northwest Normal University in China. He is the secretary of the minority nationality council of the Social Psychology Association of China. Wan Minggang specializes in minority nationality education research and has written many articles and books in this field. His books include Tibetan cultural book of readings and the pedagogy of minority nationality, and his new book is *Multi-culture View: Research on Values and Nationality Self-identity*, which was published by the Ethnic Publishing House of China in May 2006.

Dr Jinjun Wang once taught English in the Air Force Engineering University. He is now responsible for a national research project on Integrated English in primary schools and kindergartens. His interests include bilingual education, intercultural studies, comparative education, and TEFL.

Shanxin Zhang is the assistant researcher of Research Center for the Educational Development of Minorities at Northwest Normal University in China. His research interests are basic theory of education and minority education. At present, he has published several papers on minority education, and their contents refer to minority education, rural education in west area, education investment, and so on. He is now participating in a case research named Educational Policy of Gansu in China.

Ellen Yuefeng Zhang received her PhD in curriculum studies from the University of Hong Kong in 2005. She is currently working as a Teacher Development Consultant in the Hong Kong Institute of Education. She publishes in the field of English language teaching and language policies in China. Her teaching and research interests include language-teaching methodology, curriculum studies, learning studies, and public speaking skills.

Chapter 1
Introduction

ANWEI FENG

While the subtitle, 'practices, policies and concepts', suggests the main themes of this book, the use of the plural forms of these terms indicates the diverse and complex reality and differing conceptions of bilingualism and bilingual education in China. Indeed, the complexity and diversity of the linguistic situations, practices, policies and theories of bilingual education can hardly be overestimated in a country with a population of some 1.3 billion people consisting of 56 officially recognised indigenous nationalities speaking more than 80 languages (Dai *et al.*, 2000; Zhou, 2001). Coupled with forces of globalisation, overt or hidden, and the vigorous promotion of English and other foreign languages in China's schools and society, the country faces an unprecedented situation where massive financial and human resources are being invested in different forms of bilingual education, whether for minority nationalities or for the majority *Han* nationality.

The literature on bilingual education in China shows that the concepts of bilingualism and bilingual education have had a long association with minority groups. There is a large bank of literature on the history of bilingualism, bilingual educational practices, policies and research projects, particularly in the last three decades when the country has opened up to the world. This literature consists of a large number of publications accessible both in Chinese (Dai, 1992; Dai *et al.*, 1997; He, 1998; Xie & Sun, 1991) and in English (Bass, 1998; Hansen, 1999; Lee, 1986; Lee, 2001; Lewin & Wang, 1994; Postiglione, 1999; Zhou, 2004 – to list only a few). The main body of this literature records history, policies, approaches, experiences and challenges of teaching and learning Mandarin Chinese (or Putonghua[1]) in ethnic minority regions and of maintaining minority linguistic and cultural heritages. To the *Han* majority nationality that comprises 92% of the total population of the country, bilingualism and bilingual education remained largely remote notions as they speak the language of majority status and power (Feng, 2005). The literature on foreign language provision to this majority has rarely referred to bilingual education because foreign language education was traditionally taken as an area in applied linguistics, which is usually seen as having little to do with bilingualism.

In the last two decades, however, foreign language education, particularly English as a foreign language, has been increasingly perceived by Chinese policy makers and other stakeholders as crucial for the economic development of the country and individual advancement in the society. Using English as well as Chinese as media of instruction (Chinese–English bilingual education) has attracted much attention among policy makers and academics as it is believed to be a 'way out' of the dilemma long experienced in the 'much time spent but little achieved' foreign language education (Wang & Wang, 2003). To meet the challenge of globalisation and economic growth, the country longs for *Zhuanye Waiyu Fuhexing Rencai* (human resources who possess both knowledge in specialised areas and strong competence in a foreign language) or *Guojixing Rencai* (international talents). Particularly in major metropolitan areas, such as Beijing, Shanghai, and Guangzhou, and special economic zones, such as Shenzhen, a school system is being rapidly developed in which a foreign language, in most cases English, and Mandarin Chinese are used as the languages for teaching school subjects. From nurseries to tertiary institutions, bilingual schooling has become part of the everyday vocabulary not only of educationists but also of ordinary people. Catalytic factors, such as China's 'open-door' policy, its successful bid for the 2008 Olympic Games in 2001 and membership of the World Trade Organisation in the same year, have all played important roles in promoting Chinese–English bilingual education, which looks certain to reshape China's education system as a whole. This large-scale Chinese–English bilingual education is a brand-new phenomenon and discussions about it are mainly accessible in Chinese (e.g. Feng, 2003; Qiang & Zhao, 2001; Wang, 2003). One important purpose of this book is, therefore, to make this literature accessible to international readers, and thereby to update existing sources on Chinese bilingual education.

The book is unprecedented as a comprehensive study of issues in bilingual education for both minority and majority nationalities in China and as a text to explore the links between the two major forms of bilingual education. It includes the authentic voices of many 'insiders' from China as well as 'outsiders' writing about China while abroad and voices of key Chinese and international researchers and practitioners[2] who work and research in educational institutions and organisations located in various parts of China and the world. The chapters in this book deal with a range of topics including overviews and critical analyses of policies, practical models and concepts related to language provisions, empirical studies into perceptions of bilingualism and bilingual education and effectiveness of different models in various settings; they also report personal engagement in projects and reflections on bilingual education provision and examine interrelationships between bilingual provisions for the majority and minority nationality groups. Through varied and divergent analyses by this group of local and international education researchers and practitioners, a coherent and holistic picture emerges, a picture that contributes to current international considerations of bilingual education.

Educators and researchers tend to make clear distinctions between the two parallel conceptions of bilingualism for the minority and majority nationality groups (Feng, 2005) by arguing that they differ in terms of aims and practices: one for transitioning to the mainstream education system to develop balanced bilinguals who identify with both minority and majority groups and the other for adding to students' knowledge repertoire linguistic competence in a foreign language. Many commentators have hitherto used the term 'additive bilingual teaching' to refer to language provision for the majority group indicating that there will be no displacement of learners' mother tongue and culture (Wang, 2003) and 'transitional bilingual education' for minority nationality groups to spell out an educational process that aims for developing ethnic and more importantly national identities. This book shows that behind the differences with regard to terminology, aims and approaches, there are common sociocultural, political and pedagogical factors that characterise all forms of bilingual education. It is through comparison and contrast of these contextual factors and their consequences that we gain a better understanding of the terminology and the multifaceted nature of bilingual education in China.

There are potentially many ways to group the chapters of this book. One natural and plausible way would be to categorise them according to the major forms of bilingual education such as those written for minority nationality groups, those for the majority and those on the interrelationship between the two. Such categorisation may however do a disservice to the aim of this book as it leads to an internal division of bilingual education provisions for minority and majority nationality groups. To better achieve the purpose, the chapters are placed under four main sections to reflect major themes of the book namely, (1) policy, curriculum and ideology; (2) models and approaches; (3) projects and their underpinning principles; and (4) English provision for minority nationality pupils. Under each theme, discussions and analyses of the two types of language provisions are placed side by side and readers can easily compare the two types of bilingual education in terms of policies, concepts and practices and bring them into relationship. The book concludes with a critical analysis of the aims of bilingual education in China with a focus on the cultural dimension. Brief synopses of the chapters in each section now follow.

Part 1 consists of three chapters with a focus on policies and ideological orientations in bilingual education. With an emphasis on language and cultural rights in the last few decades, the chapter by Agnes Lam considers models to enhance bilingualism or multilingualism that have been developed and implemented in various countries. Her chapter examines how the language education model in China compares with those in the research literature. The analysis covers both the circumstances of the Han Chinese, the majority nationality group, who are expected to acquire competence in *Putonghua*, the national language, and in English, and the expectations for the ethnic minorities to become bilingual in their own language and *Putonghua* (and sometimes to learn English as well). The chapter makes reference to the findings from the Language Education in China project and focuses on the appropriateness of the current model in China. It ends with recommendations in terms of policy goals as well as curricular implementation to enhance efficacy in learning without detriment to the development of cultural identity in learners and national coherence.

The chapter by Bob Adamson centres on the political dimension of English curricula since 1949. He argues that the English curriculum since then has reflected different degrees of politicisation at different times, as manifested in the ideological messages transmitted in the syllabus documents and official textbooks. In recent years, the shifts in orientation have ceased to resemble a pendulum and a process of increasing depoliticisation has taken place. He identifies the nature of these shifts and the reasons behind them. The chapter concludes by suggesting that new issues have emerged to replace the former debates concerning political orientations – namely, that the high value ascribed to English in modern China and the uneven availability of appropriate resources to teach the language in schools raise questions of social equality. This chapter provides a much needed background for later discussions on the ever-growing popularity of Chinese–English bilingual education.

In the chapter by Postiglione, Ben Jiao and Manlaji, a very special programme, run in many major cities throughout China in the last two decades for secondary students from Tibet, is analysed and evaluated with empirical data. This programme, called *Neidiban* (Inland Boarding Schools), is unique in that it takes Tibetan children away from their home environment to live and study in inland cities for secondary school education with the aim to 'create a class of Tibetans that can bring Tibet into the national fabric'. Though the programme is ambitious in all aspects, cultural, political or linguistic, language is the focus of evaluation. Empirical evidence shows that many graduates have failed to become *Zang-Han Jiantong* bilinguals with native-speaker competence in their home language, Tibetan, and in *Putonghua,* the standard Chinese. Thus they find it difficult to meet the linguistic needs in their workplace when they return to Tibet.

Part 2 is made up of three chapters that offer descriptions and analyses of typologies of bilingual education for both minority and majority nationalities. Dai and Cheng's chapter provides a comprehensive typology of bilingualism and models of bilingual education in Chinese minority nationality regions. It summarises the experience of bilingual education for Chinese minority nationalities in the past half century and puts forward suggestions on how to develop bilingual education for Chinese minority nationalities in the era of globalisation. Towards the end, Dai and Cheng present an argument for a multidisciplinary perspective for developing the research and teaching in minority bilingual education.

In contrast to Dai and Cheng's comprehensive description of bilingual education for minority nationality groups, Guangwei Hu presents a critical analysis of the Chinese–English bilingual education 'craze' sweeping across major economic centres in China. Hu's chapter first offers an overview of the historical background for the promotion of bilingual education as a major reform initiative, describes its current scale, outlines the various instructional models in use and discusses the major constraints on Chinese–English bilingual education in the country. The overview is illustrated with two case studies. The chapter then examines the driving forces behind the bilingual education 'craze'. Drawing on Bourdieu's sociological theory, the chapter concludes with a critique of the consequences of bilingual education in China.

In Wan and Zhang's chapter on Tibetan–Chinese bilingual education, bilingualism is seen as a common sociolinguistic phenomenon and bilingual education an important reflection of a societal aspiration for bilingualism in an educational setting. They state that after many years of implementation, Tibetan–Chinese bilingual teaching, one of the teaching forms in regions of Zang nationality, has achieved remarkable success. The chapter summarises and reflects on two bilingual teaching models used in Zang minority regions, namely the 'Tibetan plus Chinese' model and the 'Chinese plus Tibetan' model, and the 'alternative priority' approach adopted in Gannan, Gansu where small Tibetan compact communities live side by side with the Han majority group. At the end, they offer a review of the reform and the significance of Tibetan–Chinese bilingual teaching.

In Part 3, four chapters discuss important research projects and portray themes of practitioners working at the forefront of bilingual education. It has become apparent that bilingual education is a feasible and potentially successful option to attain the dual goals of providing for minority learners a better opportunity for learning the national language effectively, as well as developing and maintaining their ethnic minority language. Heidi Cobbey presents the backgrounds, experiments and challenges faced by bilingual educationists in four different bilingual education projects in four different minority language communities – Dongxiang, Dong, Bai and Dai – across three provinces. As a promoter of minority language and Chinese bilingual education in minority regions, she draws from her experience of living and working among minority nationality groups in underdeveloped areas, to develop feasible models within the education system of China.

Feng and Wang's work is a contrast to Heidi Cobbey's in that it is situated in a well-developed region in China that promotes Chinese–English bilingual education. The model they have experimented with over the years is called Integrated English (IE), which is developed to suit the context of well-developed regions such as Guangdong. IE is in principle an approach that bears a resemblance to a content-based language learning models. It differs slightly from the latter in that IE is more language-driven with less pressure on mastery of content on the part of the students. IE is characterised by six beliefs in bilingual education: starting to offer English to pupils at an early age; teaching totally in English; focusing on listening and speaking skills first; developing strategies to help pupils acquire English naturally; developing pupils' overall abilities and integrating content learning with language learning. Over the past 5 years, IE appears to have been effective in developing pupils' bilingual competence in English and Chinese and popular with all stakeholders involved in experiments.

To produce a bilingual workforce, Zhang and Adamson note that at the national level task-based language teaching (TBLT) was adopted in the national English curriculum in 2001 in an attempt to replace the teacher-dominated, knowledge-transmitting and grammar-based methods prevailing in primary English language teaching. However, Zhang and Adamson observe that contextual factors in schools distort and dilute the intentions of policy makers. Research shows that there is very limited dissemination and promotion of TBLT by top-level change agents and a vacuum at the mid-level of school adoption. Teachers at the grassroots have a limited understanding and make little deliberate use of TBLT. Their chapter raises questions about the effectiveness of China's language policy in schools in its current top-down form.

There are few detailed discussions around the world on bilingual education at higher education level. Jiazhen Pan's chapter is thus a valuable contribution to this literature. Pan describes the background, the status quo and the development of bilingual education in universities and presents an overview of practices and strategies adopted in high-profile universities in China. A valuable part of the chapter is the case study of a bilingual programme to illustrate how this new development impacts on a particular university, its staff and students. Towards the end, the chapter also presents a critical examination of Chinese–English bilingual education programmes at the university level.

Part 4 consists of two chapters that report empirical findings concerning teachers' perceptions of Chinese–English bilingual education and minority pupils' experiences in learning English as a foreign language. Both empirical studies were conducted in areas dominated by minority students. Bin-lan Huang's chapter adds further insights to Jiazheng Pan's discussion on Chinese–English bilingual education at the tertiary level by providing interview data to show how Chinese–English bilingual education is seen by practitioners in tertiary institutions. It should be noted, however, that the context of her research differs greatly from Pan's. Guangxi, where Huang's work was carried out, is one of the least developed provinces with the biggest minority group (the *Zhuang* nationality) in China. The findings of her research indicate that though practitioners generally hold a positive attitude towards Chinese–English bilingual teaching, they face difficulties and obstacles caused by serious lack of resources. One of the notable findings in Huang's research is that bilingual educators in Guangxi universities do not seem to take the Zhuang language into account, as they believe that it has little to do with Chinese–English bilingual education. This raises the important question for bilingual or trilingual education in minority regions: does the minority language have a role to play at all for minority students in this drive for Chinese–English bilingual education? If yes, what role?

The empirical study reported in the chapter by Jiang, Liu, Quan and Ma is based on a large sample of English learners selected from remote areas dominated by minority nationality groups. The survey was conducted to identify issues and challenges that the ethnic minority pupils face in English as a foreign language (EFL) education. Compared with their majority peers, ethnic minority learners were characterised by lower motivation and weaker cultural awareness. Their EFL learning was found to be often negatively affected by their L2, Mandarin Chinese. EFL teachers in those regions were found less qualified in terms of education background and language teacher training but eager to be further educated. On the basis of these findings, they make recommendations with a view to pedagogical development, teacher training improvement and appropriate use of available resources.

In the concluding chapter, Anwei Feng offers a critical analysis of the aims of bilingual education and explores how the culture of the desired

language can be dealt with in bilingual education in China. Most researchers and policy makers seem to agree that the notion of *Min-Han
Jiantong* as an aim of minority bilingual education entails bicultural identities as well as native-speaker competence in both languages. Feng argues
that this is a goal beyond reach for many, if not all, minority students. In
majority bilingual education that aims for Chinese–English bilinguals, the
relationship between home and target languages and cultures is fervently
debated. The notion of additive bilingual education as is currently interpreted suggests tensions between globalisation and political agendas of
the nation state and between various ideological and cultural forces, hidden or overt, which strongly impact on academic discussions and Chinese–
English bilingual education practice in the country. Feng's chapter explores
the underpinning factors of these notions through an analysis of the current academic discourse, evaluates their effects on bilingual education and
argues for a reinterpretation of the two notions by injecting an intercultural
perspective into the aim statements.

As stated before, this is the first compilation that aims to present a holistic, coherent and comprehensible picture of contemporary bilingual education in the most populous country in the world. Among the key features
we present in this book, the following are worth highlighting. The first is
the important issue of contextualising case studies and conceptual analysis
of bilingual education. Byram (1997) points out that language education
always takes place in a particular context. In this compilation, it is through
a thorough and comprehensive analysis of sociopolitical, economical, geographical, cultural and historical factors that impact on bilingual education for both majority and minority groups that we make better sense of
the complex, ambivalent and even self-contradictory phenomena which
we encounter in our studies of bilingual education. In this connection, a
second issue we deal with is the interrelationships among different forms
of bilingual education practice. Although bilingual education differs from
one nationality group to another in terms of policy, approach, history, geography, resource and so forth, a holistic and comparative approach adopted
in this book to examining bilingual education is effective for seeing the
interplay between different forms being offered simultaneously in China
and gaining new insight into issues and challenges faced by stakeholders
of a particular form of bilingual education. This is especially the case when
we examine a bilingual education programme for a minority nationality
group because any change in education for the majority has an impact
on it.

A final feature is the wide range of original and authentic voices we
include in this book. Various key issues in bilingual education in China are

presented, interpreted and analysed by authors whose voices are 'emic' or 'etic', local or international, and who work at the forefront of bilingual education or in the development of theory. All these voices are needed as different and divergent perspectives represent a reality and help make sense of phenomena that may otherwise look ambivalent and even self-contradictory.

Notes

1. I wish to clarify a terminology issue here regarding the spoken and written forms of Chinese. Strictly speaking, in China, *Putonghua* (literally 'common speech') refers to the official Chinese spoken language the phonology of which is based on that of the Beijing dialect, while *Mandarin Chinese* is a category of related Chinese dialects spoken across most of northern and southwestern China. The standard written form of Chinese is referred to as *Vernacular Chinese*. Though some linguists and writers still make a distinction between these terms in their writings, many use Mandarin Chinese and Putonghua interchangeably to refer to both spoken and written forms of contemporary Chinese. This is evident in this compilation. For some readers in the west, it is also worth pointing out that Putonghua or Mandarin Chinese differs from *Cantonese* in that the former is promoted as *the* lingua franca all over China whereas the latter, though also one of the major spoken languages, is mainly spoken in southern Mainland China, Hong Kong, Macau and by numerous overseas Chinese who originally came from those regions.
2. As this book aims at different and divergent perspectives, a deliberate effort was made at the planning stage to include both well-established researchers in this area of study and practitioners who are actively engaged in bilingual education programmes in different contexts. I am aware that categorisation of this type might be seen as over-simplistic because of the heterogeneous and dynamic identities of the authors. However, differing styles of writing and unique views and observations made by individual authors as demonstrated in this book suggest that to achieve the set objective it is worth the effort.

References

Bass, C. (1998) *Education in Tibet: Policy and Practice Since 1950*. London; New York: St. Martin's Press.

Byram, M. (1997) *Teaching and Assessing Intercultural Communicative Competence*. Clevedon: Multilingual Matters Ltd.

Dai, Q.X. (1992) *Hanyu yu Shaoshuminzu Yuyan Guanxi Gailun* (An Outline of the Relationships between Mandarin Chinese and Minority Nationality Languages). Beijing: Zhongyang Minzu Daxue Chubanshe (Central University for Nationalities Press).

Dai, Q., Cheng, Y., Fu, A. and He, J. (2000) *Applied Studies of Chinese Minority Nationality Languages and Orthographies*. Kunming: Yunnan Minzu Chubanshe (Yunnan Nationalities Publishing House).

Dai, Q.X., Teng, X., Guan, X.Q. and Dong, Y. (1997) *Zhongguo Shaoshu Minzu Shuangyu Jiaoyu Gailun* (Introduction to bilingual education for China's ethnic minorities). Shenyang: Liaoning Minzu Chubanshe (Liaoning Nationalities Publishing House).

He, J.F. (1998) *Zhongguo Shaoshuminzu Shuangyu Yanjiu* (Studies of Bilingualism in Chinese Minority Nationality Regions). Beijing: Zhongyang Minzu Daxue Chubanshe (Central University for Nationalities Press).

Feng, A.W. (2005) Bilingualism for the Minor or for the Major: An evaluative analysis of parallel conceptions in China. *International Journal of Bilingual Education and Billingualism* 8(6), 529–551.

Feng, Z.J. (2003) *Shuang Yu Jiao Yu Yu Zong He Ying Yu* (Bilingual Teaching and Integrated English). Guangzhou: Zhongshan Daxue Chubanshe (Sun Yat-Sen University Press).

Hansen, M.H. (1999) *Lessons in Being Chinese: Minority Education and Ethnic Identity in Southwest China*. Seattle: University of Washington Press.

Lee, C.J. (1986) *China's Korean Minority: The Politics of Ethnic Education*. Boulder, Colorado: Westview.

Lee, M. (2001) *Ethnicity, Education and Empowerment: How Minority Students in Southwest China Construct Identities*. Aldershot: Ashgate.

Lewin, K.M. and Wang, Y.K. (1994) *Implementing Basic Education in China: Progress and Prospects in Rich, Poor and National Minority Areas*. Paris: UNESCO International Institute for Education Planning.

Postiglione, G.A. (ed.) (1999) *China's National Minority Education Culture, Schooling, and Development*. New York; London: Falmer Press.

Qiang, H.Y. and Zhao, L. (2001) *Zhongwei Dier Yuyan Chengqinshi Jiaoxue Yanjiu* (A study of immersion models of second language learning in China and abroad). Xi'an: Xi'an Jiaotong Daxue Chubanshe (Xi'an Jiaotong University Press).

Wang, B.H. (ed.) (2003) *Shuangyu Jiaoyu Yu Shuangyu Jiaoxue* (Bilingual education and bilingual teaching). Shanghai: Shanghai Jiaoyu Chubanshe (Shanghai Education Press).

Wang, H.H. and Wang, T.X. (2003) Shuangyu Jiaoxue yu Gonggong Yingyu Jiaoxue de Jiekou Wenti (Interfaces between bilingual teaching and EFL teaching). *Wai Yu Jie* 1, 26–31.

Xie, Q. and Sun, R. (1991) *Zhongguo Minzu Jiaoyu Fazhan Zhanglue Juece* (Strategies for the development of minority education in China). Beijing: Zhongyang Minzu Daxue Chubanshe (Central University for Nationalities Press).

Zhou, M.L. (ed.) (2004) *Language Policy in the People's Republic of China: Theory and Practice Since 1949*. Boston: Kluwer Academic Publishers.

Zhou, M.L. (2001) Language policy and illiteracy in ethnic minority communities in China. *Journal of Multilingual and Multicultural Development* 21(2), 129–148.

Part 1

Policy, Curriculum and Ideological Orientations

Chapter 2

Bilingual or Multilingual Education in China: Policy and Learner Experience

AGNES S. L. LAM

Introduction

Since the declaration of "fundamental freedoms for all without distinction as to race, sex, language, or religion" in the United Nations Charter in 1945 (some articles of which are reprinted in Skutnabb-Kangas & Phillipson, 1994: 372), the call for recognition of language and cultural rights, particularly for minority or nondominant groups (Nunan & Lam, 1998: 118) within a country, has attracted more and more support in various domains in different countries. Salient in such endeavors are models of education that aim at facilitating the development of bilingual or multilingual competence among learners. In spite of its political seclusion from the West in the early decades of its history, the People's Republic of China (hereafter referred to as the PRC or China) has also not neglected such issues in its language education policy; this should not be surprising because communist ideology also requires an egalitarian respect for all ethnic groups in a classless society. This chapter briefly reviews the models of bilingual and multilingual education as practiced in other parts of the world so as to compare them to the policy model in China before discussing the actual learner experience of such policy in China. The discussion of learner experience covers both the circumstances of Han Chinese learners, the majority ethnic group, as well as those of the minority ethnic groups. The chapter ends with recommendations on how to enhance the efficacy of the existing model in China and highlights the need to ensure a good balance between maintaining each learner's native language and culture and helping learners to participate in the mainstream life of the nation or the more global culture of the international community.

Language Dominance and Bilingual or Multilingual Models

In any society, there are dominant groups, those with political or economic power, and nondominant groups, those with little power. Dominant groups may not always be the majority in terms of numbers (Nunan & Lam, 1998: 118). In a colonial society, for example, the colonizers may actually be in the minority though they tend to come from a country that has greater political or economic power in the international arena than the colonized. Dominant languages in a country also tend to be official or national languages either by law or in practice. At the time of finalizing this chapter, May 2006, the United States is trying to pass a bill to make English the national language of America, a move considered by some as a racist act against Spanish speakers and other immigrants in America and not in line with the hitherto multicultural rhetoric in America (South China Morning Post, 2006); this circumstance might appear surprising to most people outside America, who are likely to have thought of English as America's official language even prior to such legislation.

The national language issue in America illustrates well the tension between having a unifying language and respecting the language rights of nondominant groups in a country. Essentially, what statuses and functions a government ascribes to the languages or dialects used in a country by law or in practice have a direct bearing on the educational opportunities provided for teaching and learning such languages to the degrees necessary for the language use patterns of the citizens to support the language policy decisions made by the state. Hence, if a state upholds a bilingual or multilingual policy, meaning that more than one language or dialect can be used in government, law, education, or other official circumstances, then its educational system has to provide opportunities to facilitate the development of such competence. The effects are two-way since the state also has to take into account the language use patterns of its citizens at any one time in its policy making.

Governments and educators around the world have been faced with the choice that America is faced with and educational models that support the development of bilingual or multilingual competence have been developed (Baetens Beardsmore, 1993b; Cenoz & Genesee, 1998; Garcia & Baker, 1995; Hoosain & Salili, 2005; Oudin, 1996; Skutnabb-Kangas, 1995b; Wright, 1994). It should be pointed out here that even if several languages are used in a country, it is possible for individual learners to be just bilingual or even monolingual, especially if they know one of the official or dominant languages in a country. Baker's (2006: 215–216) comprehensive typology, for example, includes various possibilities in terms of language outcomes: monolingual forms of education for bilinguals, weak forms of bilingual education for bilinguals, and strong forms of bilingual education for bilingualism and biliteracy. The outcomes aimed at in these three categories are, respectively, monolingualism, limited bilingualism, and bilingualism and/or biliteracy.

In relation to language dominance, bilingual or multilingual education models can be largely categorized according to the following two dimensions (Nunan & Lam, 1998: 120–126):

(1) Whether a nondominant language is valued as a *target language* (a language that one aims to acquire competence in) and
(2) whether a nondominant language is used as a medium of instruction.

Models that value the learning of a nondominant language in itself and hence encourage speakers of that language to continue to use it are known as *language maintenance* programs. Those models that do not are known as *language shift* programs because the nondominant group is likely to slowly shift to using the dominant language and the nondominant language will eventually not be used at all. This may even lead to linguistic genocide (Skutnabb-Kangas, 2000).

Language maintenance models emphasize the enrichment aspects of bilingualism or multilingualism, even for learners from the dominant language groups—that to know more than one language is desirable for a learner's development. Prominent among them are the Canadian Immersion Model (Cummins, 1995; Genesee, 1998), the European School Model (Baetens Beardsmore, 1993a; Baetens Beardsmore, 1995; Hoffmann, 1998), and the Californian Two-way Bilingual Immersion Model (Dolson & Lindholm, 1995).

(1) *The Canadian Immersion Model*: In this model, Canadian children from English-speaking homes learn French, the nondominant language in Canada, through being taught other subjects in French.
(2) *The European School Model*: European Schools aim at maintaining the learner's first language as well as developing in the learner multilingual competence. Every learner is taught subject matter in at least two European languages and is also required to learn a third language and encouraged to learn a fourth (Baetens Beardsmore, 1993a: 122).
(3) *The Californian Two-way Bilingual Immersion Model*: This model aims at "proficient bilingualism and multiculturalism for *all* participants" (Dolson & Lindholm, 1995: 70). All learners, whether they are from dominant language groups or nondominant language groups, are taught subject matter and given language lessons both in their first language and a second language.

Language maintenance models that have been found to be generally successful tend to use the nondominant language(s) as a medium/media of instruction for at least a part of the curriculum. An example of a model that aims at language maintenance but does not use the nondominant language as a medium of instruction in the regular school program is the Heritage Language Model, in which a learner from a nondominant group learns his/her ethnic language outside the regular school curriculum, often as an extra-curricular activity or as a voluntary program in community centers or religious establishments. The competence thus acquired tends to be not impressive but is still worthwhile as it contributes in some way to the development of a learner's cultural identity.

Language shift models attribute little functional value to the nondominant languages, either overtly or covertly. Some examples of models that do not aim at language maintenance are Submersion (Cummins, 1984: 75; Hamers & Blanc, 1989: 189), Dominant Language Intensive Programmes (Nunan & Lam, 1998: 122), and Transitional Bilingualism (Cummins, 1984: 75; Hamers & Blanc, 1989: 189; Nunan & Lam, 1998: 123).

(1) *Submersion*: When learners speaking a nondominant language as their first language are required to undergo all education in a dominant language, it is known as submersion, akin to throwing learners into deep water and expecting them to learn to swim on their own; more often than not, they sink. The educational rhetoric is often presented as follows: The earlier the learners from nondominant groups are exposed to the target language necessary for their educational success, the better for them; having them learn other subjects in the target language from the start is therefore beneficial to them. (See Cummins (1994: 177) for a similar observation.)

(2) *Dominant Language Intensive Programs*: Such programs are intended to help learners from nondominant language groups learn the dominant language intensively so that they do not have to sink when they study other subjects in the dominant language. These programs may be offered in parallel with a regular curriculum using the dominant language as a medium of instruction or at the transition point between an early period of learners being taught in their native language (for example, primary school) and a later period of their being taught in a second language (for example, secondary school).

(3) *Transitional Bilingualism*: In such programs, a nondominant language is used as a medium of instruction for all or some subjects over a period of time, usually for a few years in primary school, to help learners from the nondominant language group make the transition to being taught entirely in the dominant language.

Language shift models tend not to use the nondominant language(s) as a medium/media of instruction. Even if used as a medium/media of instruction for a period of time, as in Transitional Bilingualism, the nondominant language(s) is/are often not learnt as ends in themselves.

Of the two types of models summarized above, language maintenance and language shift models, moral issues of language rights for nondominant groups aside, from the point of view of linguistic ecology, it has been argued that language maintenance is the only humanly viable option, because linguistic diversity and the associated cultural diversity are as necessary for humankind to have a future as maintaining biodiversity in the natural world (Skutnabb-Kangas, 1995a: 17–18; Skutnabb-Kangas, 2000). This range of models will be referred to in the discussion of learner experience below.

The Implicit Trilingual Model in China

China, a land with many languages and many dialects, is an interesting case in the study of multilingual education. The majority ethnic group, the Han Chinese, speaks a host of Chinese dialects, which can be categorized into two main groups: the northern dialects and the southern dialects. The northern dialects can be subdivided into seven subgroups and the southern dialects into six subgroups (Huang, 1987: 33–45). Chinese dialects (particularly the southern dialects) differ from each other in pronunciation, vocabulary, and some aspects of syntax. They share one writing script of about 3500 years old. The national language, Chinese, is also known as Hanyu (Han Language). The standard dialect for oral interaction is Putonghua (common language), a northern dialect mapping well onto Baihua, the written variety of Modern Standard Chinese propagated from around 1920. Among the ethnic minorities (106,430,000 people constituting about 8.4% of the total population in China) (National Bureau of Statistics of the People's Republic of China, 2001), 55 groups of whom are officially recognized, over 80 to 120 languages are spoken (State Language Commission, 1995: 159; Zhou, 2003: 23).

To unify and modernize the nation, soon after China entered into the PRC era in 1949, it embarked on a campaign to enhance literacy. For the Han Chinese, the move was to standardize and propagate a national dialect, Putonghua, and a simplified script. The PRC also recognized that, in line with the classless political ideology adopted and for the sake of social stability, it was necessary to respect the language and cultural rights of the minority or nondominant groups within its national borders. A major initiative to describe the minority languages was begun in the 1950s. In addition to the codification work on domestic languages, because China's initial desire was to align with the Soviet Union, Russian was promoted as a foreign language. Only when relations with the Soviet Union did not develop as hoped for did China replace the learning of Russian with the learning of English from the late 1950s. All language education work, however, was interrupted by the outbreak of the Cultural Revolution (1966 to 1976), during which formal education suffered a severe setback. University admissions resumed in 1978 and work on all three language policies also recommenced (Lam, 2005: 8–10). In 1991, the disintegration of the Soviet Union provided the political space for China to ease its way into the international arena through initiatives such as joining the World Trade Organization in 2001 and hosting the Olympics in 2008. This international orientation makes it necessary for China to include in its policy agenda the objective to prepare its citizens to communicate with the world, as mentioned in the latest 2003 English syllabus for the schools (Wang & Lam, 2006) or the College English Curriculum Requirements publicized in 2004 (Lam *et al.*, 2006).

The national language policy goals of China are three-fold: to enhance literacy, to assure internal stability, and to strengthen the nation with the acquisition of scientific knowledge and economic progress so as to withstand foreign aggression. Such an agenda requires societal, if not individual, trilingualism: competence in Putonghua and English as well as a local/home Chinese dialect, if Putonghua is not normally spoken in the learner's locale/home (for the Han Chinese) or a minority language (for the minorities). In terms of literacy, since all Chinese dialects map onto one Chinese script, Han Chinese learners only need to be biliterate, while the minority learners may need to be triliterate if their minority language has a written form. At the moment, just over 40% of the officially recognized minority groups (24 out of the 55 groups) still do not have officially codified scripts for their languages. While national needs seem to call for societal trilingualism, the public rhetoric tends to emphasize only bilingualism: Putonghua and English for the Han Chinese and Chinese and a minority language or, at least, a minority culture for the minorities.

The implicit trilingual and biliterate/triliterate model in China is only partially supported by explicit legislation. The *Zhonghua Renmin Gongheguo Guojia Tongyong Yuyan Wenzi Fa* (The Law on Language Use of the People's Republic of China), announced on October 31, 2000, and effective from January 1, 2001, reaffirms the official position since the mid-1950s—that Putonghua and standardized characters are the speech and the script to be used throughout the nation (Article 2), though minority groups still have the freedom to use and develop their own languages and scripts (Article 8) (Editorial Committee, China Education Yearbook, 2001: 813).

Although Putonghua has been required as a medium of instruction for all Han Chinese schools, the law does not forbid the use of other Chinese dialects at home or in other informal circumstances. In other words, it neither encourages nor discourages the informal maintenance of other Chinese dialects in certain domains of use. Likewise, the teaching of English as a compulsory subject at school from around Primary 3 to both the Han Chinese and minority learners (wherever teaching conditions permit) is only supported by recommendations in the syllabus and various policy announcements from the Ministry of Education (Lam, 2005: 191) but not by legislation. In any case, the learning of foreign languages is seldom overtly provided for in the legislation of most countries. Therefore, China is not unusual in this regard. Because the law is silent on the promotion of English, the official rhetoric concerning language learning for both the Han Chinese and the minorities emphasizes bilingualism, not trilingualism. The Han Chinese are encouraged to become bilingual in Putonghua and English, while the minorities are encouraged to become bilingual in their own minority language and Putonghua, (in actual practice, the minorities have to learn English as well if they wish to succeed in education). The official call for bilingualism in Chinese and a minority language on the part of the minorities is already a major change from the policy position in the 1950s and has become more overt only from around 1991 when the Soviet Union disintegrated. In the early years of the PRC, the minorities were largely left autonomous; there was little concerted effort to overtly assimilate them into the Greater Han culture then. The late 1950s and early 1960s marked a period of an unstable policy toward minority languages. During the Cultural Revolution, the minorities and their languages were suppressed. From around 1977, the positive official policy toward minority groups was restored. But after 1991, it was almost as if China was concerned that the minorities within its own borders should be more integrated into the national culture so that they would not develop separatist tendencies like the various ethnicities in the former Soviet Union (Lam, 2005: 123–130). Hence, while the Chinese constitution still supports minority language rights, the realities nowadays are very complex and greatly depend on the stance taken by local authorities, which vary from promotion to permission to tolerance (Zhou, 2005).

The Experience of Learners in China

How has the overtly bilingual but covertly trilingual model in China been experienced by learners in China? This question will be answered with reference to some of the findings from the Language Education in

China (LEDChina) Project reported more fully in Lam (2005). The LED-China project was designed to track how policy changes in China from 1949 had been experienced by different cohorts of learners through the analysis of survey statistics and interview transcripts. The survey questionnaire was presented in Chinese to 415 Han Chinese respondents and 60 minority learners. One-hour interviews aimed at eliciting learning biographies were also conducted in Putonghua for 35 Han Chinese learners and 17 minority learners. All learners participating in the study were university graduates; the findings may therefore be less readily generalizable to non-university graduates. In the presentation of the six interview excerpts below, only pseudonyms are used. Where necessary, explanations have been inserted in square brackets. (More data is available in Lam, 2005.)

Han Chinese learning Putonghua

As a whole, Han Chinese learners seem to have adjusted well to the propagation of Putonghua from the mid-1950s though those from the south are likely to begin learning Putonghua a little later. In the LEDChina project, southern dialect speakers in the interior began learning Putonghua latest; 47.4% of them learnt it from primary school, 5.3% from secondary school, and 31.6% only when they entered university or started working. University education seems to guarantee the acquisition of Putonghua if it was not acquired earlier. In the schools, more northern dialect respondents used Putonghua more often. This is not surprising because Putonghua is a northern dialect. At university level, Putonghua was frequently used by most respondents (around 85%) from both dialect backgrounds. At home, while learning Putonghua, northern dialect respondents also enjoyed more conversational support from family members (Lam, 2005: 47). Over the years, however, even speakers speaking a southern dialect from birth have become more open to learning Putonghua. Compare, for example, the attitude of Tian, an older southern dialect speaker, with that of Danny, a younger one, in the following interview excerpts:

Tian: I was born in 1962 in Jiangxi [in the southern interior]. . . . At school, we were taught in Kejiahua [a southern Chinese dialect]. What the teachers spoke was closer to written Chinese but it was not Putonghua. In pronunciation, it still seemed like a dialect. After classes, my classmates and I conversed in Kejiahua. In junior secondary school, we had a very young music teacher from the local region. . . . She could speak very standard Putonghua. In her first lesson, she tried to teach in Putonghua; the whole class laughed because we were not used to being spoken to in such standard Putonghua. . . . In our region at that time, there was no market for Putonghua. Unless you were from another province, if you spoke

Putonghua, people would think you were trying to *da³guan¹qiang¹* [speak like an official] and would laugh at you.... Kejia people have a saying 'Rather sell the land of the ancestors than change the speech from the ancestors.' (Lam, 2005: 55)

Tian eventually learnt how to speak Putonghua well at university because the university was in a big city with many people coming from different provinces, making it necessary to use Putonghua as a common code for interdialectal communication. Even during his university days though, when he was with friends from his home village, he would continue to speak his home dialect, Kejiahua. In contrast, the younger interviewee, Danny, was more open to learning and using Putonghua from the very beginning.

Danny: I was born in Gulangyu [an island off Xiamen in the southern coastal region] in 1972.... I speak Minnanhua [a southern dialect] and Putonghua equally well. I learnt Minnanhua from my grandmother....Putonghua was not used at home. When I was four, I went to kindergarten and was taught in Putonghua. Outside the classroom, my classmates and I still conversed in Minnanhua but we spoke Putonghua with the teachers. In [the same southern coastal city], we have a lot of visitors from other provinces. In a group of three or four people, if one does not speak Minnanhua, we immediately switch to Putonghua. This is a kind of respect for that person. (Lam, 2005: 56)

Danny did not begin learning Putonghua at home but received his education in Putonghua from kindergarten. It is worth noting that the variation in the use of Putonghua as a medium of instruction experienced by Tian and Danny still exists. In the big cities, Putonghua is more used as a medium of instruction but in the rural areas, it is still not uncommon for learners to be taught Chinese first in a local Chinese dialect before switching to Putonghua. What is interesting to note is that although the maintenance of their first dialect has not been provided for in the official policy guidelines, most Han Chinese learners seem to have succeeded in maintaining some use of it either at home or in informal situations with friends even after switching to instruction in Putonghua. As Putonghua becomes more widely used, particularly in the cities and in families with parents from different dialect groups, more and more young Han Chinese learners may even begin to speak Putonghua at home but, because of the cultural pride in their native dialect, it is unlikely that all knowledge of that dialect will be lost, provided that it is still used in some domains in the community.

If we are trying to categorize the modes of education Tian and Danny went through, Tian's would be a type of Transitional Bidialectalism (from the use of Kejiahua as a medium of instruction to the use of Putonghua), while Danny's would be Submersion (being taught entirely in Putonghua, the dominant dialect, from kindergarten). However, since Danny himself looked upon his experience positively, he himself might categorize it as Immersion with its enrichment connotations. That Tian's and Danny's first dialects are still maintained in spite of the use of models which traditionally result in language shift argues that models developed in some countries may not entirely apply to circumstances in a different country because of different sociolinguistic circumstances and attitudes. In China, because of the invasion by various nations and civil instability prior to the PRC era, most young Han Chinese learners are more willing to learn Putonghua as support for the national cause, whatever their dialectal pride. The emergence of China as a nation to be reckoned with in the international arena and the increasing interest in learning Chinese in the international community (Lam, 2005: 189) also reinforce this readiness. At the same time, it is also important to note that certain dialects (such as Shanghainese and Cantonese) also have economic power attached to them and can also be conceived of as dominant dialects, though not as predominant as Putonghua.

Minority learners learning Putonghua

In general, the minority learners in China tend to have a more difficult time learning Putonghua, the dominant language. Many of them learn written Chinese first through another regional/local Chinese dialect and have to invest a lot of time and energy into learning Putonghua outside the classroom. Here is an excerpt from He, a learner from the Hui minority, to illustrate this.

He: I . . . was born in a village in the Ningxia Autonomous Region in 1972. . . . Before I went to school, I learnt a little Arabic at home and mostly at the Muslim temple. . . . At home, most of the time, we spoke the local northern Chinese dialect. I also spoke it with my friends and classmates or buying things. I started learning Putonghua only when I went to school at nine or ten. . . . Almost all the teachers taught in Putonghua . . . I felt my Chinese dialectal pronunciation was a hindrance to my learning of Putonghua; because my pronunciation was not accurate, I could not figure out the words. . . . Learning Chinese was very, very painful for me . . . . I often failed my Chinese. In junior secondary school, I spent about two years reading books of folktales and fairytales in our town library. Then I could link up the words into sentences and the sentences into texts. . . . When I went to university, my Chinese dialect became Putonghua by and by. . . . My best language now is Chinese. (Lam, 2005: 164–165)

Although the Hui minority has as a whole converted to the use of Chinese, He's story still gives an indication of what minority learners who want to succeed academically have to come to terms with. He knew only a little of his ethnic language and had to learn Putonghua through another local Chinese dialect, which made his learning process more strenuous. The mode of education he went through could even be named Double Submersion, though it could be argued that what he underwent is not different from that of many northern Han Chinese learners since he usually spoke a northern Chinese dialect at home in any case. As Putonghua becomes more and more used in the Chinese educational system, more minority learners may have a slightly easier time acquiring Chinese because they may then be taught Putonghua along with written Chinese from the beginning. Perhaps then, they will have more learning resources to acquire their own minority language at home. But it will take time for Putonghua to pervade the entire educational system, particularly in the rural areas where most minority learners come from (Lam, 2005: 153–154).

Minority learners learning their own ethnic language

Where the learning of his ethnic language is concerned, He's case is one of language shift, as he hardly managed to retain Arabic. His case also illustrates that language shift is ultimately not an individual matter since the entire Hui minority has shifted to using Chinese and few Hui people retain any knowledge of Arabic after learning it at the Muslim temple, a mode classifiable as a Heritage Language program. Minority learners from groups with a small population or without a written language are particularly vulnerable to language shift as many of them will end up in a Submersion program (being taught in a local Chinese dialect or another minority language before being taught in Putonghua) or a Transitional Bilingualism program (being taught for a short period in their own language, then in a Chinese dialect, and finally in Putonghua) (see Lam (2005: 155–173) for other examples.)

There are of course minority learners who manage to maintain their minority language. Mei, from the Yao minority, is an example. She learnt her ethnic language successfully and became a teacher of that language.

Mei: I was born in Lingui in Guangxi in 1963. . . . I started learning the Yao language at home from the time I was born. . . . I grew up in the Yao region and went to a primary school in a village where some Han Chinese lived. I did not have any Yao language classes in primary school, secondary school or university. I only learnt the written form of the Yao language when I started working. In primary school, some of the lessons for other subjects were taught in the Yao language. During primary school, I often used the Yao language to speak with my classmates; in secondary school,

I still did so sometimes. But at university, I did not use the Yao language with my classmates because my classmates came from several different regions. . . . Ever since I was young, I have felt very proud that I can speak my own language. . . . After I started working, I found that there are also Yao people residing in countries outside China. I can communicate with them using our language. I often do interpretation. So I feel my language can cross national boundaries. (Lam, 2005: 160)

Mei's success is what most educators would like to see. She manages to learn the dominant language (Chinese) well and also retains the use of her minority language, largely learnt through informal interaction at home and in the community, though her minority language was used as a medium of instruction for some subjects in primary school. The fact that she learnt the written form of the Yao language only after she started working is particularly encouraging in that even at such a late stage, it is possible to become literate in a language if a learner already knows the oral form, provided of course that there is sufficient motivation. In Mei's case, her ethnic pride could have been the basis for such motivation though her motivation could also have been enhanced by her professional need as a minority language teacher. Mei's circumstances also show that for successful learning of a nondominant language, there needs to be a domain of use for that language, such as communication in the immediate community or a wider one. In all likelihood, that was also why Tian and Danny managed to retain their native Chinese dialects and the Canadian Immersion and European School models could be successful. The positive connotations attached to Mei's learning of the Yao language are not unlike those associated with ethnic Chinese born in America learning Chinese in Modern Languages or Asian Languages departments in American universities.

The learning of English by Han Chinese and minority learners

The learning of English by both Han Chinese learners and minority learners is mostly a story of learning hardship. Both groups of respondents in the LEDChina project (88.2% of the minority learners and 88.9% of the Han Chinese learners on the average) felt that their competence in their foreign language (mostly English) was not good enough at the point of completing secondary school (Lam, 2005: 152). On a more positive note though, younger cohorts of respondents from both groups of learners seemed slightly more confident of their foreign language competence. This could partly be due to the increase in awareness that foreign language learning requires learners to invest learning time and energy beyond the classroom setting. In their interviews, many learners from both groups mentioned how they tried to listen to broadcasts or campus radio, speak to each other in English in the university dormitory at certain times, go to the English Corner (usually an open space on campus where learners can gather informally on Friday nights to talk to others in English), memorize sentences from books, and so forth. Those that succeed tend to have engaged a lot more in such activities (Lam, 2005: 97–99) and exhibit a tremendous amount of motivation.

Hua, a young Northern Han Chinese who started learning English from Secondary 1, exemplifies what can be achieved if a learner decides to take advantage of learning opportunities.

Hua: I grew up in a city in Guangxi.... When I was in Secondary 1, conditions for exposure to English were not very good.... At university, the English material I was exposed to enabled me to become more aware of my learning. The only time I really felt I wanted to learn English was when I was a graduate student.... Around me, many classmates had very good English. Many of them wanted to go overseas and had to prepare for the TOEFL [Test of English as a Foreign Language] and the GRE [Graduate Record Examination]. So their English was very good. I felt I should also try harder. When I first went to university, I tried going to the English Corner but I was too shy. I cared very much about whether people would laugh at me. When the other person spoke, she too was very nervous. So after going twice, I stopped. But as a graduate student, I felt I should go to the English Corner because it was meaningless to learn English if I could not speak or understand it. So I went and I spoke. (Lam, 2005: 107–109)

Likewise, the story of Ma, a minority learner from the Dong minority, illustrates well the need to have an intrinsic interest to succeed in learning a foreign language and the importance of teachers in cultivating this interest.

Ma: I was born in a mountain village in Guangxi in 1975.... I started learning English from Junior Secondary 1 in the *xian*[4] [county]. I learnt it well mainly because I was very interested. At that time, I did not think I wanted to become an interpreter or something instrumental like that. I just felt it was good to learn so I wanted to learn it well. For example, when I read the books and there were some pictures and I wondered, 'Why does this person have yellow hair?' So I became interested and wanted to learn their language.... I think the influence of teachers is very important. When I was in junior secondary school, my first English teacher was able to develop our interest in learning English. At university too, the teacher's English was very good. He had been to America and he was never tired and very hardworking. He affected me a lot. So I set my heart on learning English well. (Lam, 2005: 167–169)

Ma eventually learnt English well enough to become a foreign language graduate student. His repertoire includes the Dong language (his native language), the Zhuang language (another minority language), the Guiliu dialect (a Chinese dialect spoken in his region), Putonghua, English, Japanese, and German. Ma's multilingual achievement is certainly not that of the typical learner (whether from a Han Chinese or minority background) in China.

Nowadays, for most learners in China not majoring in English, English is taught only as a subject and not used as a medium of instruction for other subjects. The shortage of English teachers makes it difficult to think of increasing the use of English as a medium of instruction. In a primary school in the southern interior that I visited, there was only one young teacher teaching English to the whole school. The recent move at university level to include, for non-English majors, a course from their discipline (such as law or engineering) taught in English as a type of English for Specific Purposes (ESP) program (Lam, 2005: 192–193) or to include, for English majors, related knowledge of a profession such as foreign relations, trade, law, management, journalism, education, technology, culture, and military affairs (Lam, 2005: 192) is an attempt to use English as a medium of instruction for teaching other subjects. It is not easy to provide the teaching resources needed for the implementation of such policies.

An adjusted model for China

A comparison of the learning circumstances of the majority ethnic group, the Han Chinese learners, and those of the ethnic minorities shows that the former, particularly those speaking a northern Chinese dialect and growing up in the coastal region, are educationally more advantaged than the minority learners. Among the Han Chinese, those speaking a southern Chinese dialect as their home language also have slightly greater difficulty than those speaking a northern dialect as their home language. This is because Putonghua, the standard Chinese dialect, is much closer to the northern dialects. The learners facing the greatest linguistic challenge are those from the small ethnic minorities living among the Han Chinese, because, in addition to or in lieu of learning their own minority language used at home, they usually have to first learn a Chinese dialect for everyday communication in their locale or even for classroom interaction in their early years before they are taught in Putonghua.

To redress this imbalance in educational advantage in a realistic manner, the current implicit trilingual model in China needs to be adjusted.

If trilingualism or multilingualism is considered a desirable educational objective for all, irrespective of ethnicity or first language, then the targets for competence in the languages to be learnt must be achievable. Some operational principles that may be useful are as follows:

(1) Promote trilingualism/multilingualism as enrichment rather than as educational compulsion.
(2) Provide minority learners with the choice to receive basic education in their mother tongue or Putonghua, the official language, whenever resources permit.
(3) Use the official language, Putonghua, as the medium of instruction beyond basic education for most learners.
(4) Provide all learners with the choice to study an additional language (which could be either English, another foreign language, or even a minority language in China) as a subject at specific points in the educational system.
(5) Create a special educational stream or a group of institutions to enable learners to become bilingual or multilingual from a young age so as to ensure that a certain percentage of the population in China will be highly competent in Putonghua and another language to meet China's national needs to communicate with the rest of the world.

Multilingualism as enrichment

This basic principle requires a change of attitude. Rather than perceive language learning as a series of hurdles to cross to achieve educational success, learners can be encouraged to consider multilingual competence as personal enrichment. That is the attitude taken among the elite or cultured groups in various countries (Skutnabb-Kangas, 1995a: 7). The case of English-speaking children learning French with such an attitude in the Canadian Immersion Model is a much-quoted example of success. The European School Model is also based on cultural enrichment. For this attitude to be inculcated in China, those having to learn fewer languages at the moment could be strongly encouraged to undergo the experience of learning an additional language, whether domestic or foreign. Hence, at some point in their education, the Han Chinese learners speaking a northern dialect as their native dialect can be given the opportunity to choose to learn a southern dialect or a minority language, even if the learning is only for a semester, because this will enhance their cultural openness to the other dialect/ethnic groups. This is in line with the egalitarian ethos in the Californian Two-way Model and can also be considered a measure to protect the language rights of northern dialect speakers not to lose out on the advantage of enrichment through learning another language, because it has even been claimed that only by studying another language or culture can one understand one's own (Veit, 1992: 130).

Choice of language for basic education

Respecting language rights does not mean that learners must study in their own mother tongue but they need to be provided with the opportunity to choose to do so. Hence, ideally, there should be two streams in primary schools in locations where there is a sizable population of minority learners: one teaching in Putonghua and one teaching in the minority language. Many minority learners (or their parents in reality) may actually choose to receive their basic education in Putonghua, the official language, rather than their minority language. As more and more Han Chinese use Putonghua as their home dialect as a result of interdialectal marriage or the general rise in educational level among the parents, it is to be expected that Putonghua will be more fully used as a medium of instruction in schools for Han Chinese children in any case. But in communities where there is a high minority population, the use of Putonghua as a medium of instruction in the Chinese stream even at the primary level needs to be more strictly enforced or supported with well-trained teachers of Chinese. Then, if minority children choose to receive their basic education in Chinese, they do not have to undergo Double Submersion, that is, to learn through the medium of another regional Chinese dialect first before switching to Putonghua in secondary school or later. If there are not enough teachers who are able to teach in the minority language stream for all 6 years in primary school, then the use of the minority language as a medium of instruction can at least be implemented for the first 2 or 3 years. In actual practice, it is likely that only minority learners from large populations and who already have writing scripts for their language can have such an option. Those from small minority populations or speaking languages without a writing form are likely to choose to receive their basic education in Putonghua.

These minority learners should be provided with the opportunity for oral instruction in their own language as a subject in the Heritage Language mode, wherever possible, to assure their cultural integrity. One important aspect to be addressed before this principle can be implemented is the issue of examinations. It is not possible to implement this recommendation if there are no corollary changes in the examination system.

The official language

If we bear in mind that linguistic human rights include not only the right to identify positively with one's mother tongue and to receive basic education in it but also the right to learn "at least one of the official languages in one's country or residence" (Skutnabb-Kangas, 1995a: 7), then the learning of Putonghua cannot be compromised for any of the groups in China, regardless of their first language or dialect, not just because all of them will need Putonghua to participate in the national life but because it is their right to be provided with the opportunity to achieve high competence in such a language. Hence, even if minority learners choose to receive their basic education in their own language, they still need to be given the opportunity to study Putonghua as a subject throughout their basic education. Beyond basic education, it will be necessary for Putonghua to be used as a medium of instruction for all learners to ensure that they can achieve a high level of competence in various domains for their further development.

Learning an additional language

At the moment, all learners in China need to learn English and most of them cannot manage to achieve high competence in it. The rationale among policy makers is that English is useful for the learners' future career and necessary for the international positioning of China as a major player in the global arena. A bold move will be to provide all learners with the opportunity to learn English but not to require them to achieve a pass in English for admission to university. For example, learners can all be given the opportunity to acquire basic competence in English (or another foreign or minority language) but can be allowed to opt out of this and study another language or another subject at a certain point in their education, for example, after Junior Secondary 3. In other words, the recommendation is to allow learners to choose to continue to study English at a higher level. This is because unless learners choose to invest their learning time and energy outside the classroom into learning a foreign language, it is not possible, given the classroom circumstances and the lack of opportunity for interactive practice, for unmotivated learners to achieve high competence in a foreign language. In actual practice, it is most likely that parents will choose for their children to study English. But if choice is provided, those who do not wish to study English can choose to study another foreign language such as Japanese, French, Spanish or Russian, or, if they are from the ethnic minorities, their own minority language. It is useful to remember that several of the minorities in China speak languages with various degrees of similarity to languages with sizable populations beyond Chinese borders. Hence, if allowed to develop their languages, some minority learners may actually be well disposed to become future Foreign Service personnel or interpreters.

Bilingual/multilingual streams, programs, or institutions

If university-level competence in English is not required for all learners in China, to ensure that the country will still have a core of highly competent bilinguals or multilinguals, more truly bilingual or multilingual institutions targeting bilingual or multilingual competence for their students can be established to develop such competence in a core group of learners from a young age. In such institutions, Putonghua and another foreign language can be used as alternate media of instruction either for different days or for different subjects, similar to the European School Model. It is likely that such institutions can only be established in the major cities with a growing international population, such as Beijing, Shanghai, Guangzhou, or even Hong Kong, where learners will be sufficiently motivated to become multilingual because there will be genuine opportunities for them to use the languages learnt. These institutions will also emphasize multicultural understanding. At the school level, the 1979 restoration of the fourteen foreign language schools (first established in 1964) (Lam, 2005: 79) was already a step in this direction and the more recent increase of international schools in China will also add to this impetus. At the university level, the foreign language universities and the institutions for ethnic minorities can be augmented with programs for certain disciplines bilingually taught in Putonghua and a foreign language or a minority language. Scholarships can also be offered as incentives and very strict language competence requirements can be enforced for midway admission such as at Junior Secondary 1, Senior Secondary 1, or University Year 1. In a way, the new syllabus for English majors at university level is a program already in line with this mode of thinking. It is possible for universities to experiment more with bilingual teaching for certain university programs which have a strong international focus. The student numbers for such bilingual streams, programs, or institutions can be adjusted according to the pace of China's internationalization or parents' or learners' growth in awareness of the enrichment inherent in the development of bilingual or multilingual competence.

Conclusion

In this chapter, the models to enhance bilingual or multilingual competence in various parts of the world have been summarized and the implicit trilingual policy model in China has been outlined and illustrated with learner experience. The chapter ends with a proposal for an adjusted trilingual model in China, which maintains some competence in the learner's first language or dialect and requires the development of high competence in Standard Chinese (Putonghua) but makes the learning of a third language (English or another foreign or domestic language) optional at a certain point in the educational system. The main thrust of the recommendations is to allow a little more flexibility in language education requirements or curricular modes so that learners can have a certain degree of choice in how bilingual or multilingual they wish to become, not just because choice is central to the concept of language rights (and intercultural harmony as a result of those rights being respected), but even more because it is most essential for learners to choose to invest learning time and energy into learning before they can succeed in learning a language not widely used in their environment.

Acknowledgment

This chapter draws upon the findings in the Language Education in China project, which was fully supported by a grant from the Research Grants Council of the Hong Kong Special Administrative Region, China (Project No. HKU7175/98H).

References

Baetens Beardsmore, H. (1993a) The European School Model. In H. Baetens Beardsmore (ed.) *European Models of Bilingual Education* (pp. 121–154). Clevedon: Multilingual Matters.

Baetens Beardsmore, H. (ed.) (1993b) *European Models of Bilingual Education*. Clevedon: Multilingual Matters.

Baetens Beardsmore, H. (1995) The European School experience in multilingual education. In T. Skutnabb-Kangas (ed.) *Multilingualism for All* (pp. 21–68) Lisse: Swets & Zeitlinger B. V.

Baker, C. (2006) *Foundations of Bilingual Education and Bilingualism* (4th edn). Clevedon: Multilingual Matters.

Cenoz, J. and Genesee, F. (eds) (1998) *Beyond Bilingualism: Multilingualism and Multilingual Education*. Clevedon: Multilingual Matters.

Cummins, J. (1984) The minority language child. In S. Shapson and V. S'Oyley (eds) *Bilingual and Multilingual Education: Canadian Perspectives* (pp. 71–92). Clevedon: Multilingual Matters.

Cummins, J. (1994) The discourse of disinformation: The debate on bilingual education and linguistic rights in the United States. In T. Skutnabb-Kangas and R. Phillipson (eds) *Linguistic Human Rights: Overcoming Linguistic Discrimination* (pp. 159–177). Berlin: Mouton de Gruyter.

Cummins, J. (1995) The European Schools Model in relation to French Immersion Programs in Canada. In T. Skutnabb-Kangas (ed.) *Multilingualism for All* (pp. 159–167) Lisse: Swets & Zeitlinger B. V.

Dolson, D. and Lindholm, K. (1995) World class education for children in California: A comparison of the Two-way Bilingual Immersion and European School Models. In T. Skutnabb-Kangas (ed.) *Multilingualism for All* (pp. 69–102) Lisse: Swets & Zeitlinger B. V.

Editorial Committee, China Education Yearbook. (2001) *China Education Yearbook 2001.* Beijing: People's Education Press.

Garcia, O. and Baker, C. (eds) (1995) *Policy and Practice in Bilingual Education: A Reader Extending the Foundations.* Clevedon: Multilingual Matters.

Genesee, F. (1998). A case study of multilingual education in Canada. In J. Cenoz and F. Genesee (eds) *Beyond Bilingualism: Multilingualism and Multilingual Education* (pp. 243–258). Clevedon: Multilingual Matters.

Hamers, J.F. and Blanc, M.H.A. (1989) *Bilinguality and Bilingualism.* Cambridge, U.K.: Cambridge Univ. Press.

Hoffmann, C. (1998) Luxembourg and the European Schools. In J. Cenoz and F. Genesee (eds) *Beyond Bilingualism: Multilingualism and Multilingual Education* (pp. 143–174). Clevedon: Multilingual Matters.

Hoosain, R. and Salili, F. (eds) (2005) *Language in Multicultural Education.* Greenwich, CT: Information Age.

Huang, H.-H. (1987) *Hanyu Fangyanxue* [Chinese Dialectology]. Xiamen: Xiamen University Press.

Lam, A.S.L. (2005) *Language Education in China: Policy and Experience from 1949.* Hong Kong: Hong Kong University Press.

Lam, A.S.L., Lu, Z.-S. and Wu, Y.-A. (2006) English-medium instruction in higher education in China: Two case studies. Manuscript in preparation.

National Bureau of Statistics of the People's Republic of China. (2001) Communique on Major Figures of the 2000 Population Census (No. 1). On WWW at http://www.stats.gov.cn/english/newrelease/statisticalreports/200204230084.htm. Accessed 11.10.03.

Nunan, D. and Lam, A. (1998) Teacher education for multilingual contexts: Models and issues. In J. Cenoz and F. Genesee (eds) *Beyond Bilingualism: Multilingualism and Multilingual Education* (pp. 117–140). Clevedon: Multilingual Matters.

Oudin, A.-S. (1996) *Immersion and Multilingual Education in the European Union: Inventory of Bilingual Educational Systems in which Teaching is Provided Partly or Entirely through the Medium of a Regional or Minority Language.* Brussels: European Bureau for Lesser Used Languages.

Skutnabb-Kangas, T. (1995a) Introduction. In T. Skutnabb-Kangas (ed.) *Multilingualism for All* (pp. 7–20). Lisse: Swets & Zeitlinger B. V.

Skutnabb-Kangas, T. (ed.) (1995b) *Multilingualism for All.* Lisse: Swets & Zeitlinger B. V.

Skutnabb-Kangas, T. (2000). *Linguistic Genocide in Education – or Worldwide Diversity and Human Rights?* Mahweh, NJ: Lawrence Erlbaum.

Skutnabb-Kangas, T. and Phillipson, R. (eds) (1994) *Linguistic Human Rights: Overcoming Linguistic Discrimination*. Berlin: Mouton de Gruyter.

South China Morning Post (Daily newspaper, Hong Kong) (May 20, 2006) Vote backs English as US national language, p. A10.

State Language Commission (1995) *Yuyan Wenzi Gongzuo Baiti* [100 Questions in Language Orthography Work]. Beijing: Yuwen Chubanshe.

Veit, W. (1992) 'In Australia, we read it differently . . .': Interculturality and the theory of literary criticism. In S. Gunew and K.O. Longley (eds) *Striking Chords: Multicultural Literary Interpretations* (pp. 129–145). Sydney: Allen & Unwin.

Wang, W.-F. and Lam, A.S.L. (2006) The English language curriculum for secondary school in China from 1949. Manuscript in preparation.

Wright, S. (with Kelly, H.) (ed.) (1994) *Ethnicity in Eastern Europe: Questions of Migration, Language Rights and Education*. Clevedon: Multilingual Matters.

Zhou, M.-L. (2003) *Multilingualism in China: The Politics of Writing Reforms for Minority Languages 1949–2002*. Berlin: Mouton de Gruyter.

Zhou, M.-L. (2005) Legislating literacy for linguistic and ethnic minorities in contemporary China. *Current Issues in Language Planning* 6(2), 102–121.

Chapter 3
Depoliticisation in the English Curriculum

BOB ADAMSON

Introduction

This chapter identifies the political orientations of the English curriculum in junior secondary schools in the People's Republic of China (PRC) since the 1949 revolution, by analysing curriculum documents, such as the centrally approved syllabuses and textbooks. English has, historically, been a highly controversial subject in the school curriculum – Ross (1992) argues that the role and status of English language (and other foreign languages) in the school curriculum make it a weathervane of the prevailing socio-political climate. The language, with its connotations of Western imperialism, capitalism and even barbarianism (Dzau, 1990), is viewed by some national leaders as a useful tool for the development of the economy but a negative force culturally and politically. Indeed, at various stages in the history of the PRC, English speakers were victimised for 'worshipping things foreign' (Tang, 1983) and the subject was dropped from the secondary school curriculum.

It is undeniable that official pressure has been brought to bear on the political orientation of school subjects in the PRC. The publishing wing of the Ministry of Education, the People's Education Press (PEP), was responsible for the design of syllabuses and of recommended textbooks for nationwide use for several decades, although these functions have been increasingly decentralised since the education reforms of 1985 (Lewin *et al.*, 1994). As a state agency, the PEP has had the job of interpreting general policy decisions made by the nation's leaders and producing syllabuses and textbooks that are acceptable politically to Party officials and pedagogically to teachers. In this chapter, 'political' orientations refer to the transmission of values and messages that are linked to the prevailing ideology or doctrine promoted by the state. Prefaces to syllabuses have regularly alluded to political slogans, policies or speeches by national leaders, suggesting that these provided the motivational force or genesis for curriculum change. The English curriculum was not the only subject to be influenced by the vagaries of the socio-political climate. Similar phenomena have been identified, for example, in the geography curriculum (Leung, 1989, 1991) and the Chinese Language curriculum (Lai, 1991, 1994). However, while this chapter highlights the political influences, the detailed nature and content of the English curriculum was not simply a result of top-down transmission of centrally determined political messages, but was the product of a more sophisticated process involving a variety of stakeholders (Adamson & Morris, 1997). Nonetheless, the linkage between the orientations of macro-level state policies and those of education reforms has proved a matter of academic debate.

Much of the literature on curriculum innovation in China has posited a causal link between changes in national policies and subsequent educational reforms (e.g. Chen, 1981; Löfstedt, 1980). These portrayals emphasise strong linkages between the oscillations of national politics from predominantly economic orientations to predominantly political orientations, and the hegemonic role of the state in defining the nature of school curricula through its bureaucratic, centralised and power coercive mechanisms. The changes to the school curriculum since 1949 have been described in terms of a pendulum swinging between 'academic' (i.e. related to citizenship training and human resource development for economic modernisation) and 'revolutionary' (i.e. ideologically oriented) education (Chen, 1981) or 'moderate' and 'radical' (Ruyen, 1970, cited in Löfstedt, 1984) trends. Thus, for instance, the Cultural Revolution was viewed as a period when the 'revolutionary' model (a primary emphasis on politics with production and development as secondary) was predominant, but the post-Mao era was characterised by the 'academic' model (a primary emphasis on development and modernisation with politics and ideology secondary). Shen (1994) adopts a political influence perspective and identifies two groups as the key actors in causing the pendulum to swing: the 'radical' group, under the leadership of Mao Zedong, and the 'moderate' group, represented by Liu Shaoqi, Deng Xiaoping and others.

This pendulum model, with oscillations between two lines, has been challenged (e.g. Nathan, 1976; Sautman, 1991), as shown in Figure 3.1, which also shows (for reference and comparison) a periodisation of the English curriculum (Adamson, 2004) that links changes in the curriculum to socio-political shifts. Nathan (1976) prefers a linear development of distinct phases, some of which revisited previous policies, while Sautman (1991) identifies three groups or policy currents: the 'bureaucratic' current, which seeks to inculcate set political ideas while maintaining the political order

Date	Pendulum Ruyen (1970)	Three strands Sautman (1991)	Linear periodisation Nathan (1976)	Trends in the English curriculum Adamson (2004)
1949	Radical	Bureaucratic & radical	Pragmatic/moderate	**Soviet influence** Initial neglect, then English promoted to some degree Strong political content
1952				
1953				
1954				
1957	Moderate	Radical	Leftist	
1958			Rightist	
1959	Radical		Mobilisation	
1961		Reform	Rightist	
	Moderate			**Towards quality in education** English popularised Although still strong, political content de-emphasised
1966				
1969				
1976	Radical	Radical	Radical	**The Cultural Revolution** English in disrepute Only taught as a political vehicle
1977				
1980			Pragmatic/moderate	
		Bureaucratic		**Modernisation under Deng Xiaoping** English flourishes Political content declines
1993		Reform		
				Integrating with globalisation Rapid expansion of English provision Absence of political content

Figure 3.1 Views of shifts in socio-political climate and general education policy in the PRC and the English curriculum

and economic development; the 'radical' current, which promotes hyperpoliticisation at the expense of all other goals of education and the 'reform' current, which seeks depoliticisation in favour of the goals of economic development. According to Sautman, the 'bureaucratic' current coexisted with the 'radical' current in the 1950s and held sway briefly in the late 1970s. It was essentially concerned with ensuring political stability through centralised control but allowing for the development of expertise. In other words, the bureaucrats had to tread a wary line between promoting 'redness' and 'expertise'. The 'radical' current predominated during the Great Leap Forward (1958–1959) and the Cultural Revolution (1966–1976). The 'reform' current had its origins in the early sixties and became dominant when Deng Xiaoping's modernisation drive gained momentum from the eighties onward. Sautman's identification of the bureaucratic trend is useful for the present study, as the work of the PEP is essentially bureaucratic, with a long-standing objective of balancing the competing political, economic and educational pressures when developing the English curriculum (Adamson, 2004).

This study of the orientations of the English syllabus and textbook series at different times suggests that the pendulum model, while useful for a general description of education policy in the earlier stages of the history of the PRC, does not provide an adequate model to account for more contemporary trends. The chapter identifies a process of increasing depoliticisation as the state's priorities have shifted to economic imperatives. It employs the periodisation developed by Adamson (2004), as this was concerned specifically with the English curriculum and key triggers of reforms to the junior secondary school curriculum. After relative neglect in the first 12 years since the founding of the PRC, English received a boost in the early sixties with a greater allocation of curriculum time and an openness to new pedagogical trends. Virtually abandoned during the Cultural Revolution, English became a cornerstone of the Four Modernisations campaign that started in the late seventies, and its stock continued to rise at the turn of the millennium as China became a powerful political and economic force internationally.

Soviet Influence: 1949–1961

The aftermath of the Communist victory in the civil war and the founding of the PRC in 1949 was a period of state-building. In terms of language education, the initial priority was mother tongue teaching to enhance literacy rates especially amongst the peasants (who had proved the staunchest supporters of the Chinese Communist Party). This move formed part of the government's strategy as expressed in the Common Programme established in 1949, which sought to eradicate the influence of pre-revolutionary ideas and inculcate socialist ideology, as well as to provide an educated work force for national construction. The Common Programme thus balanced political and economic goals, and this was also reflected in the choice of foreign languages. Russian was adopted as the main foreign language in the school curriculum as the USSR was providing aid and advice to the PRC based on that nation's own experience of revolution and developing a socialist economy. However, English was neglected primarily for political reasons. Leading English-speaking countries refused to recognise the PRC. The United States, which had backed the opponents of the Commuist Party in the civil war, imposed an economic blockade on the PRC, which created a strong anti-American backlash, and hence it 'became somehow unpatriotic to study the language of our enemies' (Tang, 1983: 41).

Economic forces – namely the industrial expansion of the mid-fifties – brought about a reconsideration of the role and status of English in the PRC. The language was perceived as a valuable conduit for accessing technological information. There was also an element of political will, as China's foreign policy shifted towards a state of *détente* with the West and with non-aligned nations in Asia. From 1956, English was introduced in the curriculum of secondary schools in major cities, such as Beijing, Shanghai and Tianjin, where resources permitted (Tang, 1983). The textbooks were heavily influenced by Russian approaches to pedagogy (often teacher-centred mastery of a defined body of linguistic knowledge) and contained a significant proportion of political texts, many denouncing the foreign policy and internal social injustices of United States and Britain. The latter feature was even more obvious in new editions of the textbooks that were produced at times of political movements such as the Anti-Rightist Campaign and the Great Leap Forward (which aimed at achieving economic strength through political activism) in the late 1950s (Adamson, 2004).

During this first phase, education policy was driven by economic and political motives. English was initially neglected but gradually seen as a positive contributor to the economic well-being of the nation and introduced into classrooms. However, it was politically suspected – hence the orientation of the English curriculum was characterised by political rhetoric.

Towards Quality in Education: 1961–1966

In the early 1960s, the internal political movements died down and more attention was paid to the PRC's role in international affairs and to developing the nation's economy, which had suffered during the turmoil of the Great Leap Forward. Proficiency in English was seen as an important means for international engagement for the economic development, particularly after the schism between the PRC and the USSR. The relative depoliticisation of this time was demonstrated by the receptivity to Western pedagogical approaches (in response to dissatisfaction with the Soviet style pedagogy previously promoted) and the employment of British teachers as curriculum consultants in the PEP. More time was devoted to English in secondary schools, and there were experiments in extending the provision to primary schools, whereby Primary 4 or 5 classes could study the junior secondary school textbooks (Qun & Li, 1991).

Changes were introduced to curriculum development in English at this time. An official syllabus that covered the junior secondary school curriculum was produced for the first time in 1963. Textbook writing became an in-house rather than an outsourced activity for the PEP, and quality assurance measures (such as the panel of consultants and the trialling of draft versions of textbooks) were introduced. The political orientation of the curriculum was muted. According to the leader of the curriculum development project, Tang Jun, the PEP stressed pedagogical rather than political concerns:

> In structuring the textbooks, the need to nurture the students step by step in their ability to read, speak and write was the guiding factor. The basic components of phonetics and grammar, and the selection of vocabulary and passages were designed to take students' ability to learn into consideration, and were organised from simple to complex. (Tang Jun, cited in Adamson, 2004)

The textbooks produced between 1961 and 1965 contained fewer anti-Western references than their predecessors, but there remained a political edge to the curriculum. The preamble to the syllabus, which appeared in May 1963, identifies anti-imperialism as a curricular goal:

> Foreign language learning is an important tool to develop cultural and scientific knowledge, to carry out international interaction, to foster cultural exchanges, and to increase the understanding between peoples of different countries. English is commonly used throughout the world. A good grasp of English enables us to absorb the aspects of science and technology which will help socialist construction; to introduce our experience to friendly countries and people; to strengthen our relationship with people in different countries; and to unite people in different countries to combat imperialism. (People's Education Press, 1963: 1, in translation)

According to the syllabus, reading passages should include

> ones about class struggle and the struggle over production in English speaking countries, the life, customs, culture and historical traditions of these countries, and there should also be some passages introducing our own country. Some passages about popular science and socio-political issues can also be chosen. (People's Education Press, 1963: 5, in translation)

However, the syllabus cautions against overemphasising the political purposes of the curriculum, but advocates that teachers should keep a weather-eye on the socio-political climate:

> We should not have a one-sided view that foreign language study serves proletarian politics, make inappropriate political connections, or over-emphasise the ideas and contents of the reading passages. However, as textbooks are fixed but the social situation is changing, teachers should use the textbooks flexibly according to the prevailing climate, should some passages not be compatible with the times. (People's Education Press, 1963: 11, in translation)

This second phase is characterised by relative depoliticisation. In terms of the 'red and expert' interaction between political and economic goals, the English curriculum was promoted to develop the nation's expertise, while the 'redness' faded in comparison to the previous period. That is not to say that there was a large swing of the pendulum: rather there was a shift in emphasis towards economic aims that did not, at the same time, repudiate political goals.

The Cultural Revolution: 1966–1976

This relative depoliticisation lasted until 1966, when the Great Proletarian Cultural Revolution was launched. This was a mass political movement that lasted for a decade and impacted very strongly on education, with the mobilisation of schoolchildren as *hong weibing* ('Red Guards') at the vanguard of political struggles. The aims of the Cultural Revolution were to re-establish class struggle as the main thrust of policy and social action, to eradicate feudal customs, culture and ideas, and to place the country under the supreme leadership of Mao Zedong. For a while, schools were closed down so that students could participate in revolutionary activities that quickly veered to anarchy. The English curriculum was, for much of the period, a victim of the campaign. The teaching of English was suspended in most schools at least until 1972, and the English section of the PEP was closed from 1968 until 1977 (Liu, 1988). English teachers, because of their perceived affiliation with Western nations, were particularly vulnerable to violent attacks (Adamson, 2004).

The new phase of *détente* that emerged with the visit by US President Richard Nixon in 1972 led to a partial restoration of English in schools. The curricula were locally produced, in the form of textbooks without an accompanying syllabus. The writers of these textbooks were aware that they were treading on dangerous political ground. The preface to a series produced in Shanghai states:

> Editing new teaching materials for the proletariat is a difficult and long-term mission which requires continuous trial-and-error and adjustments. Regarding the problems that exist in these materials, we hope you comrades will put forward your valuable suggestions and criticisms. (Shanghai Secondary and Primary Teaching Materials Editing Team, 1973, in translation)

Similarly, the writers of another series defend themselves against political attack:

> Since we do not claim to have a thorough comprehension of the revolutionary educational thought of our Great Leader Chairman Mao, this teaching material is bound to have many mistakes and shortcomings. We hope the worker-peasant-soldier masses and the revolutionary teachers and students will point them out and criticise them. (Beijing Municipal Education Office Teaching Materials Editorial Team, 1974, in translation)

The textbooks published during the Cultural Revolution were heavily politicised. For instance, a series that was written for schools in Sha'anxi province introduces the Communist symbols of the hammer and sickle as vocabulary items at the beginning of Book 1. In subsequent lessons, the students are encouraged to engage in revolutionary activities in their daily lives, such as by helping on a farm or by studying the works of Mao, Marx and Lenin. The series produced in major cities such as Beijing and Shanghai were more moderate in this respect, but nevertheless were more politicised than the textbooks of the early 1960s (Adamson, 2004).

There was a dramatic swing in the education policy regarding English during the Cultural Revolution, which can only be ascribed to political events. The swift abolition of the language – hitherto increasingly promoted by the state – from the school curriculum resulted from the desire to eradicate values that were deemed antithetical to those of the political campaign. The partial, tentative and circumspect restoration of English to the curriculum after 1972 was motivated by the defrosting of relations with the United States. This represented a minor readjustment in policy orientation, but one that started a trend that has continued to the present day.

Modernisation Under Deng Xiaoping: 1977–1993

The Cultural Revolution ended with the death of Mao Zedong and the arrest of the 'Gang of Four', the major proponents of the political movement, in 1976. The shift in the policies of the government of the PRC, which had started in 1972, became much more pronounced: where once 'politics to the fore' was the watchword, whereby political ideology dictated the governance of state and local affairs, the new policies under Deng Xiaoping, most notably his 'Four Modernisations' Programme (of industry, science and technology, agriculture and defence), brought enormous social changes and economic growth. To a large extent, this programme was accompanied by the depoliticisation of many aspects of life in the PRC. Foreign companies were encouraged to invest in the country. Foreign tourism became a major industry. On a mundane level, public parks, which were shorn of 'bourgeois' grass during the Cultural Revolution, became home to money-spinning fairgrounds and amusement arcades.

From 1977 onwards, order was restored in schools, the national educational framework was reconstituted (based on the model of the early 1960s) and efforts were undertaken to improve the academic quality of the school curriculum. The PEP was re-established in 1978 and charged with the task of developing materials for schools. The legacy of the Cultural Revolution was a country in economic shambles, with the added complication that young, qualified personnel were in short supply because of 10 years' disruption to their education. Given the hysterical savagery of attacks on English teachers during the Cultural Revolution, it is not surprising to find the discourse of the first curriculum documents in its aftermath to be politically circumspect, despite the emphasis of Dengist policies on economic rather than political goals. For instance, the introduction to the English syllabus produced in 1978 states

> English is a very widely used language throughout the world. English is a very important tool for international class struggle; for economic and trade relationships; for cultural, scientific and technological exchange; and for the development of international friendship.
>
> We have to raise Chairman Mao Zedong's glorious flag, and carry out the policies initiated by the Party under Hua Guofeng's leadership, so that by the end of this century, we can achieve the Four Modernisations of industry, science and technology, agriculture and defence and make

China a strong socialist country. To uphold the principle of proletarian internationalism and to carry out Chairman Mao's revolutionary diplomacy effectively, we need to nurture a large number of "red and expert" people proficient in a foreign language and in different disciplines. That is why we have to strengthen both primary and secondary teaching. (People's Education Press, 1978)

This circumspection could be due to the power struggle during the interregnum (when Hua Guofeng nominally held the reins) between Mao's death in 1976 and Deng's assumption of paramount leadership, as well as to the caution needed for handling a highly politicised subject. The purposes defined for English in the 1978 syllabus included international exchange. The textbooks include positive portrayals of foreigners (especially those involved in improving social justice), but there were also passages attacking human rights in the United States. The 1978 curriculum was not strongly reformist. It revisited many ideas current in the fifties and sixties, mainly through pressure of time, the experience of those involved in the design process and the uncertain political climate. The circumspection of the political elements is indicative of the initial tentativeness of the reform programme. While foreign influence was not strong, the restoration of English to the curriculum and some of the pedagogy of the textbooks was indicative of the PRC's opening to the outside world.

As the rate of reforms accelerated, with the Open Door policy in particular being emphasised, the political content was reduced in the 1982 revision of the curriculum. The new syllabus did not mention leading political figures in its introduction; instead, it concentrated on the economic benefits accruing from the study of English:

A foreign language is important for learning cultural and scientific knowledge, acquiring information in different fields from around the world; and developing international communication. "Education must be oriented towards modernisation, the outside world and the future" [a slogan instigated by Deng Xiaoping]. Our country has adopted the Open Door Policy; the reforms of our country's economics, politics, technology and education are being wholeheartedly implemented; throughout the world, new technological reforms are booming. In order to construct our country as a modern socialist nation, with a high level of civilisation and democracy, we have to raise the cultural and scientific quality of all people in the country. We need to nurture a large number of experts who are goal-oriented and ethical, possessing culture, discipline and, to different extents, competence in foreign languages. (People's Education Press, 1983, in translation)

In tune with the Open Door policy, the new textbooks published by the PEP concentrated less on giving a bad impression of foreign countries and included more passages that presented aspects of Western culture and biographies of influential scientists and musicians (Adamson, 2004).

The change of direction in the English curriculum after the Cultural Revolution can be attributed to the policy changes instigated by Deng Xiaoping, which emphasised economic goals. Suddenly, English became highly desirable for trade, careers, study and overseas travel. Learning English became a necessity for the ambitious people and a hobby for many, and the political contents of the English curriculum for secondary schools diminished. The thrust of these reforms was sustained over time, despite the vagaries of political events. The biggest crisis for the PRC in this period was the demonstrations for reform and the subsequent crackdown against protestors in and around Tiananmen Square in 1989. This event, unlike the Cultural Revolution, had no significant impact upon the English curriculum.

Integrating with Globalisation: 1993 Onwards

China became increasingly influential on the international stage as it grew as an economic power and as the USSR disbanded. This growing stature is reflected in the PRC's entry into the World Trade Organisation in 2001 and the success of the bid to host the Olympic Games in Beijing in 2008 (Lam, 2005). Economic reforms increased the demand for English competence, and it became a requirement for civil service jobs, university entrance, taxi drivers and other facets of life. Opportunities to travel overseas for work, study or tourism multiplied. Chinese cities were transformed by the influx of multinational businesses, retail outlets and advertisements. Modern technology became available to the increasingly affluent sections of the populace.

These changes were reflected in the 1993 curriculum, which had its origins in the state educational policies of 1985 that targeted universal provision of 9 years' schooling and various measures to enhance the quality of education, including decentralisation of decision-making and the opening up of the textbook market. The textbooks published by the Ministry of Education were innovative in that they were produced by a joint venture with a Western publisher, Longman International. The syllabus emphasises the role of English in the nation's modernisation:

> In order to turn our country into a modern socialist nation with a high level of civilisation and democracy, education must implement the guiding principle of all-round development—moral, intellectual and

physical—and be oriented towards modernisation, the outside world, and the future so that students can develop into socialist citizens with ideals, moral qualities, culture, and discipline, thus raising the ideological, ethical, scientific, and cultural quality of the Chinese people. A foreign language is an important tool for international interaction. In accord with our nation's reform and Open Door policy and to meet the needs of speeding up socialist modernisation, efforts should be made to enable as many people as possible to acquire a certain command of one or more foreign languages. (People's Education Press, 1993, in translation)

According to the PEP, the English curriculum should

... develop [students'] thinking ability; help them acquire more knowledge of foreign culture; strengthen international understanding; arouse their interest in study and form correct methods and good habits of study so that an initial foundation can be laid for their further study of English as well as future work. (People's Education Press, 1989, in translation)

As a result, political content (other than texts arousing national pride) was absent from the textbooks designed by the PEP. Students were introduced to American football, fish and chips, stories from daily life from around the world and other cultural aspects (Adamson, 2004). The revision of the curriculum in 2000 brought in an innovative pedagogical approach for China – the task-based approach – that had been adopted by other countries, while the PEP produced different sets of textbooks to cater for the differing needs of various regions of the PRC. These textbooks included a revised version of a series originally produced overseas, indicating that the textbook market in China had become part of the globalised educational publishing business (Adamson, 2004).

A number of factors contributed to the depoliticisation of the English curriculum in this period. The freedom granted to Shanghai, Guangdong and other selected areas of China to develop their own curriculum created opportunities for innovation. These areas took the lead in importing foreign textbooks and in collaborating with overseas publishers – a trend that the PEP was compelled to follow. Furthermore, the desire to incorporate 'state of the art' pedagogy (with a preference for imported rather than indigenous methods) such as the task-based approach and information technology in the English curriculum together with the growing implementation of 'bilingual education' (teaching various subjects through the medium of English – see Chapter 6) means that more attention is given to educational quality in terms of international standards rather than overtly political goals to suit domestic agenda. A third factor is the general de-politicisation of life in China as economic reforms gathered pace and the Chinese leadership devoted more attention to such issues. Communist ideology has waned; more stress is placed upon the development of 'Asian values' (such as a strong work ethic and social harmony) and patriotism.

Discussion

There is clearly a link between the PRC's priorities in terms of the 'redness' versus 'expertise' debate and the nature of the English curriculum in junior secondary schools. After the 1949 revolution, ideological education was high on the state's agenda as a cornerstone of nation-building. Political campaigns were viewed by Mao and his close supporters as a means of achieving social and economic ends, and the contents of the English curriculum reflected the prevailing politicised climate. There was a brief period of depoliticisation in the early 1960s that allowed the English curriculum to concentrate more on developing the linguistic expertise of students rather than their political ideology, before the turmoil of the Cultural Revolution reversed the trend. The post-Mao era picked up from where the early sixties left off by reintroducing and expanding the economic modernisation drive, and soliciting the support of overseas agents to assist the nation's efforts. As a result, the later curriculum innovations have emphasised economic and academic goals and fostered international understanding through the cultural contents. Politically charged issues in textbooks have gradually been replaced by passages that cover academic and ethical themes, and which are open-minded with regard to foreign countries. In the current period, political rhetoric has disappeared from curricular content, other than lip-service to 'socialist modernisation' in the syllabus introduction in 1992. Market forces have opened the textbook business to international competition (albeit with local adjustments), and economic prerogatives rather than socialist ideology are now the firm drivers of the English curriculum in the PRC.

There is some superficial support for a pendulum view of the fortunes of English in the PRC, given that the role and status of the language as a school subject have gone from low to high to low and back to high again, but the circumstances of each phase were different – official attitudes and policies towards the role of English in the fifties and during the Cultural Revolution were not the same, for instance. Furthermore, since 1976, there has been no evidence of swings; the trend towards depoliticisation has continued unabated.

What are the impacts of these shifts on English language teaching in China? Research into the pedagogical practices of Chinese teachers at the chalkface (e.g. Zheng & Adamson, 2003) shows a complex amalgam of personal beliefs and efforts to realise the pedagogy promoted in official documents. The study of the officially promoted pedagogy shows a link between political orientations and academic, literary approaches to English language teaching, while depoliticisation tends to result in a synthesis of structural and communicative views of language (Adamson, 2004). The trend towards depoliticisation (i.e. the reduction of ideological content), however, raises new socio-political issues. The pioneering work in Shanghai and Guangdong is supported by the availability of high-quality resources (including teachers); other regions of China struggle to keep up. The PEP, which retains a dominant position in curriculum design and textbook production for the less-wealthy regions, has to balance a new set of competing bureaucratic priorities: the state's strong commitment to English language learning and to the use of information technology as a learning tool, and the realities of less-developed parts of the country. This has necessitated a cautious approach to innovation (see Adamson, 2005), as issues of social and educational equality have replaced 'redness' and 'expertise' as key tensions in determining the orientations of the English curriculum.

References

Adamson, B. (2004) *China's English: A History of English in Chinese Education.* Hong Kong: Hong Kong University Press.

Adamson, B. (2005) Developing information technology for English in Chinese secondary schools. In C. Davison (ed.) *Information Technology and Innovation in Language Education* (pp. 81–101). Hong Kong: Hong Kong University Press.

Adamson, B. and Morris, P. (1997) The English curriculum in the People's Republic of China. *Comparative Education Review* 41 (1), 3–26.

Beijing Municipal Education Office Teaching Materials Editorial Team (1974) *English.* Beijing: Beijing People's Education Press.

Chen, H.T. (1981) *Chinese Education since 1949: Academic and Revolutionary Models.* New York: Pergamon.

Dzau, Y.F. (1990) Historical background. In Y.F. Dzau (ed.) *English in China* (pp. 11–40). Hong Kong: API Press.

Lai, A.Y.W.W. (1991) Curriculum dissemination in the People's Republic of China. In C. Marsh and P. Morris (eds) *Curriculum Development in East Asia* (pp. 82–105). UK: Falmer.

Lai, A.Y.W.W. (1994) The Chinese language curriculum in the People's Republic of China from 1978–1986: Curriculum change, diversity and complexity. Unpublished Ph.D thesis, The University of Hong Kong.

Lam, A.S.L. (2005) *Language Education in China: Policy and Experience from 1949.* Hong Kong: Hong Kong University Press.

Leung, Y.M.J. (1989) A study of curriculum innovation in post-1976 China, with special reference to the design and implementation of the senior middle school geography curriculum. Unpublished Ph.D. Thesis, University of Sussex.

Leung, Y.M.J. (1991) Curriculum development in the People's Republic of China. In C. Marsh and P. Morris (eds) *Curriculum Development in East Asia* (pp. 61–81). London: Falmer.

Lewin, K.M., Xu, H., Little, A.W. and Zheng, J. (1994) *Educational Innovation in China.* Harlow: Longman.

Liu, D. (1988) *EFL in Schools in China* (mimeograph). Beijing: People's Education Press.

Löfstedt, J-I. (1980) *Chinese Educational Policy: Changes and Contradictions* 1949–79. Stockholm: Amqvist & Wiksell International.

Löfstedt, J-I. (1984) Educational planning and administration in China. *Comparative Education* 20 (1), 57–72.

Nathan, A.J. (1976) Policy oscillations in the People's Republic of China: A critique. *The China Quarterly* 68, 720–733.

People's Education Press (1963) *Yingyu Jiaoxue Dagang* [English teaching syllabus]. Beijing: People's Education Press.

People's Education Press (1978) *Yingyu Jiaoxue Dagang* [English teaching syllabus]. Beijing: People's Education Press.

People's Education Press (1983) *Yingyu Jiaoxue Dagang* [English teaching syllabus]. Beijing: People's Education Press.

People's Education Press (1989) *Guidelines on the English Syllabus for Compulsory Education in Full-Time Junior Secondary Schools* (mimeograph). Beijing: People's Education Press.

People's Education Press (1993) *Yingyu Jiaoxue Dagang* [English teaching syllabus]. Beijing: People's Education Press.

Qun, Y. and Li, Q. (1991) *Waiyu Jiaoyu Fazhen Zhanlüe Yanjiu* [Research into foreign language education development strategies]. Sichuan: Sichuan Education Press.

Ross, H. (1992) Foreign language education as a barometer of modernization. In R. Hayhoe (ed.) *Education and Modernization: The Chinese Experience* (pp. 239–254). Oxford: Pergamon.

Ruyen, E. (1970) Moderate and radical traits of socialist construction in China: Historical perspective of the Great Cultural Revolution. Seminar paper. Uppsala: University of Uppsala.

Sautman, B. (1991) Politicization, hyperpoliticization, and depoliticization of Chinese education. *Comparative Education Review* 35 (4), 669–689.

Shanghai Secondary and Primary Teaching Materials Editing Team (1973) *English.* Shanghai: Shanghai People's Education Press.

Shen, J. (1994) Educational policy in the People's Republic of China: A political influence perspective. *Journal of Education Policy* 9 (1), 1–13.

Tang, L. (1983) *TEFL in China: Methods and Techniques.* Shanghai: Shanghai Foreign Languages Press.

Zheng, X. and Adamson, B. (2003) The pedagogy of a secondary school teacher of English in the People's Republic of China: Challenging the stereotypes. *RELC Journal* 34 (3), 323–337.

Chapter 4

Language in Tibetan Education: The Case of the Neidiban

GERARD POSTIGLIONE, BEN JIAO, AND MANLAJI

Language and Schooling for Tibetans

Unlike many indigenous ethnic minorities in the developing world, Tibetans have had a highly sophisticated written script for over a thousand years (Chodag, 1988). Originated during the reign of Songsten Gampo in the sixth century, this script was developed over the next fourteen centuries in an area that came to extend as wide as the continental United States (Iredale *et al.*, 2001). Within the contemporary discourse over indicators of Tibetan cultural survival, indigenous language vitality is viewed as central (Bass, 1998; Goldstein, 1989, 1997). As compulsory state schooling has taken hold in Tibetan communities, medium of instruction policy has become a focus of some debate, as it is also in other parts of China's ethnic minority regions (Ma, 2006). This is more relevant to Tibetan secondary schooling, since most primary schooling in the Tibetan Autonomous Region (TAR) is still conducted through Tibetan. Moreover, a significant sector of Tibetan secondary schooling, known as *neidiban* (Tibet Inland schools and classes), is dislocated from the TAR to other parts of China. This sector has constituted between 10% and 25% of all junior secondary school admissions since 1985 and adds more complexity to the issue of language education (Zhu, 2007). What is the result of language policy in the *neidiban*? The *neidiban* reflects the national aim of producing *Min-Han Jiantong* bilinguals with native-speaker competence in their home language and in standard Chinese, Putonghua. However, in the case of Tibetans, *Zang-Han Jiantong* has come to refer not only to more than linguistic competence in two languages, but also to sociopolitical attitudes and sociocultural competence.

The Context of Language and Schooling for China's Ethnic Minorities

Language is a major component of China's policy edifice for its 55 state designated ethnic minority groups. An elaborate set of preferential policies, grounded in the Constitution, aims to guarantee the right of ethnic minority areas, including Tibet, to use indigenous languages in education.[1] Regardless of language policies, parents in Tibet, like those elsewhere, increasingly want their children to learn Chinese so as to better compete in the expanding market economy. Some initially controversial policies for ethnic minorities have become more acceptable as they provide access to mainstream cultural capital (Postiglione, 1999, 2006). In particular, the 20-year-old policy of sending Tibetan children to boarding schools in inland China (Chinese cities outside of TAR, Qinghai, Ningxia, and Xinjiang provinces) after primary school has produced a new breed of young Tibetans with better Chinese language ability, though poorer Tibetan language skills than their counterparts who remain in Tibet for secondary school. They are also more familiar with, and comfortable in, mainstream Chinese culture than are other Tibetans. Over two decades of *neidiban* schooling, virtually all students of these schools have returned to Tibet after graduation. Their long-term impact is significant for the development of language and culture in Tibet, as well as for its economic and social development. The largest number of graduates of the *neidiban* who return to Tibet go on to become school teachers and play a role in the language education of the next generation of students. When set against the *Min-Han Jiantong* policy, we believe that the perspective of "sent out" students about the language education they received in the inland boarding schools can provide insight into the linguistic transformation of Tibetan education and society.

This chapter begins with a brief review of Tibet's language policy in education and a sociological framework concerning language, schooling, and the state. It then briefly describes the main characteristics of the inland boarding schools and poses the question of what the 20-year policy of sending Tibetan children to schools across China has meant for language learning. After a description of the research methodology, a discussion and analysis based on data from interviews with graduates is presented. Data is drawn from oral histories in which graduates were asked a variety of questions about their *neidiban* experience. The data is organized according to students' perceptions of (1) their adaptation to the language environment of *neidiban*, (2) Tibetan language learning experience in *neidiban*, and (3) their capability in Chinese and Tibetan on graduation, and their ability to communicate and work effectively in Tibetan language on their return to Tibet after graduation.

China's Language Policy in Ethnic Minority Regions

The constitution contains an assurance that ethnic minorities within the 148 autonomous areas of the China can use their own languages (Ma, 1985; Mackerras, 2003). Fifty-three of 55 ethnic minority groups have at least one spoken language. Some have had a written script for hundreds of years and others were provided with one by missionary groups or government over the past two centuries (Wang, 1994; Yu, 1995; Zhou, 2000). The implementation of minority languages as a medium of instruction can increase attendance rates and strengthen socialization into national ideologies (Baker, 2001; Qi, 2004; Spack, 2002; Street, 2001). China provides minority groups with bilingual education in order to produce competence in both their ethnic language and *Hanyu* or standard Chinese (Teng, 2000).[2] Twelve minority scripts are used in both primary and secondary school textbooks and nine more are being piloted in the schools (Zheng, 2002). China produces 3500 textbook titles in more than 30 ethnic minority languages (some minority groups have more than one language). Yet, there has been no comprehensive review of the minority language development and use in China's schools (Zheng, 2002).[3]

Although the provision of education for ethnic minorities at all levels has been steadily increasing, the education attainment levels of most minorities are below the national average and this is especially the case for minority women (Lee, 2001; Postiglione, 2001, 2002; Treuba & Zou, 1994). Nevertheless, education policies, especially those focused on ethnic minority languages, have attempted to correct this situation and have met with varying levels of success. Dai *et al.* (1997) and Stites (1999) have studied China's efforts to develop a viable bilingual system of education. Stites notes, "the history is full of mistakes. Nevertheless, the Chinese state has gone to great lengths to accommodate minority languages" (Stites, 1999).

Unlike religion, language is viewed as essential for achieving the goals of China's state schooling (Dai *et al.*, 1997; Fei, 1980, 1989; Gladney, 1996; Hansen, 1999; Harrell, 2001; Heberer, 1989; Lam, 2005). Moreover, as the education gap between ethnic minority areas and Han regions becomes more glaring, attention to language policies and practices has increased. China's constitution protects the right of ethnic minorities to use their language, and the education system has used minority languages as a medium of instruction and as a taught subject, depending on the particular situation. However, as school access problems are solved, there is less emphasis on minority languages in school. This is compounded by the effect of the market economy, which creates a demand for competent Chinese speakers in both the job market and university entrance. Moreover, the policy discourse is shifting to a "let the market decide" mentality about parental school choice (Ma, 2006). For example, many minority parents can now choose a Chinese-medium secondary school over a native-language-medium school, regardless of the student's readiness to learn through the Chinese medium (Fang, 2001; Postiglione, 2006).

The case of Tibetan education is particularly illustrative of the dilemma of ethnic minority languages in education in China (Bass, 1998; Nyima, 1996; Upton, 1999). Upton's fieldwork in the Tibetan prefecture of Abba in Sichuan convinced her that China has done well in certain respects in the way it has handled minority language issues, even though it is perhaps not always as well as most Tibetans seem to want or expect. Few Tibetans advocate not learning any Chinese, whereas an increasing number want to learn Chinese well enough to ensure their day-to-day survival, as well as access to broader occupational opportunities. Moreover, some would like to study as much English in school as do Han Chinese students. Dual track education (Tibetan and Chinese) is generally available in the urbanized areas, but after the primary school Grade 3, there is a stronger shift to Chinese as the medium of instruction, with only language and literature courses taught in the Tibetan language (Wang & Zhou, 2003; Zhu, 2007). However, there are many variations. In the western regions of Qinghai, for example, there are opportunities to learn all courses (science, math, history, etc.) in Tibetan up through senior middle school. In other places, instruction for most courses is in the Chinese language. There have been experiments that use Tibetan as the language of instruction for all the science and mathematics subjects in the TAR. Tibetans who advocate the trial programs want to make Tibetan a language of science and modernity, as well as increase their opportunities to go into higher education since they will learn efficiently and perform better in entrance examinations. Yet, such proponents of Tibetan language education risk being pigeonholed as separatists.

Research Methods and Language at *Neidban*

Language policy in the context of neidiban aims

This research is not about the determination of language policy, but rather about the perceptions of language practices and their results. Despite the fact that all of the graduates return to work in Tibet where Tibetan is the language of over 90% of the population, the language is not emphasized. This is because the *neidiban* was established primarily to bring young Tibetans closer to the national mainstream of China, help modernize Tibet's economy, and fill the void after it became illegal to send children to India for secondary school. Thus, the aim of the *neidiban* is not only to prepare specialized talent for Tibet's development, but also to create a class of Tibetans that can bring Tibet into the national fabric. In this sense, they create cultural middlemen with more potential to access mainstream social capital within the context of a market economy.

Oral history methods

Given the subjects' age and experience, and the research aims, the oral history questions were divided into three segments having to do with a student's prior education and home life prior to selection for *neidiban*, their experiences of living and learning at *neidiban*, and their reintegration into the TAR after graduation. Each interview took approximately 2 hours. The interviews were conducted in workplaces, homes, and restaurants and a number was assigned to each case. The interview environments were non-threatening and subjects were self-assured, especially as graduates of the inland schools, which have a relatively high status in Tibet. That *neidiban* graduates are scattered throughout Tibet made the access difficult. The subjects for this study were drawn from graduates of various locations. Some *neidiban* schools were visited to learn more about the education provided. Subjects were located in three major centers of Tibet: Lhasa, Shigatse, and Nackchu. Sixty subjects were interviewed from each of these three population centers, together totaling 180 subjects. An oral history guideline was constructed with three sections covering education before going to inland, education in inland schools, and life and work after returning to Tibet. The interviews averaged 2 hours each and were conducted in Tibetan in most cases and sometimes in Chinese. Data was recorded and transcribed, then grouped into sets of 10 for summary and analysis according to each interview questions.

Neidiban background

By 1985, *neidiban* were established in provinces and municipalities across China, including Shanghai, Tianjin, Liaoning, Hebei, Henan, Shandong, Jiangsu, Shanxi, Hubei, Chongqing, Anhui, Shanxi, Hunan, Zhejiang, Jiangxi, and Yunnan. Tibetan schools in Beijing, Lanzhou, and Chengdu began to recruit students in 1986. The majority of the Tibetan boarding students attend segregated classes in urban secondary schools. At least 18 of the schools were junior secondary schools, but later, three (Beijing, Chengdu, and Tianjin) came to have junior and senior secondary levels. A gradual conversion to senior secondary schools is underway. In September 1985, 1300 primary school graduates from the seven TAR prefectures were sent to 16 classes or schools in inland cities. From 1985 to 2001, more than 23,560 primary graduates were selected and sent to study in these schools. This figure does not include all TAR students enrolled outside the TAR. For example, 13,000 students were attending 104 schools in 26 provinces in 1994. Of those who graduated from junior secondary school, 75% went on to senior secondary technical schools; most of the remainder progressed to regular senior secondary education. These numbers also include graduates of both *neidiban* junior secondary schools and TAR junior secondary schools who enrolled in short-term *neidi* in-service teacher training. Between 1985 and 1995, nearly 25,000 Tibetan students were sent to study in junior secondary schools in different provinces and municipalities of China. The proportion of primary school graduates from the TAR that are sent to *neidiban* has ranged between 10% and 20% each year with an average of 14% between 1985 and 2000.

Complete Tibet Inland secondary schools are 4-year junior secondary schools, and some offer a further 3 years for senior secondary school. The first year is for review and catching up on anything missed in primary school, as well as for the Chinese language that students need for the rest of their education in the school. In 1985, Tibetan Inland classes were expanded to include 15 inland cities, including Beijing and Jiangsu. The most noted Complete Tibet Inland secondary schools are Beijing Tibet Middle School and Changzhou Tibet Middle School in Jiangsu province, the latter founded in 1987. The former school recruits junior and senior students, while the latter recruited only junior secondary students. Nantong Tibetan School in Jiangsu province was founded in 1995 and accepts both junior and senior secondary students. Chengdu Tibet School in Sichuan province was opened in 1998 for junior and senior secondary students. Chongqing Tibet School opened in 1995 and has both Han Chinese and Tibetan students, at both secondary levels. Inland Tibet schools receiving senior secondary students also include those in Tianjin and Changzhou.

A 1984 regulation states that Tibetan language is to be the teaching medium in junior secondary school, replaced by Chinese language in senior secondary school. Chinese language and literature (*Hanyuwen*) and Tibetan language and literature (*Zangyuwen*) are two main subjects in the curriculum. In fact, Chinese language has now become the main teaching medium in all inland Tibet secondary schools, including junior and senior levels, and this is also the case for secondary schools in urban regions of the TAR. Students are still required to learn a foreign language.

Tibetan and Chinese languages are compulsory curriculum subjects for these students. English language was not originally a compulsory subject but was later made so. Tibetan history and cultural tradition have some minor emphasis in class. A 1988 State Education Committee notice stated that it should be the duty of all levels of schooling in and for Tibet to enable the Tibetan people to inherit and develop Tibetan history and cultural tradition, as well as learn advanced scientific technology and the cultures of other ethnic groups. The notice suggested that educational content, textbooks, and curriculum design for the Tibetan children should not copy indiscriminately the experience of schools in the region where the inland schools are located, but should pursue study and reform according to Tibetan history, culture, production, and economic life. The 1988 notice also demanded that inland Tibet classes (schools) strengthen the instruction of Tibetan language curriculum and content. Nevertheless, most inland Tibet classes (schools) have simply followed the curriculum of other mainstream schools. Consequently, more careful attention to parts of the curriculum concerning Tibetan history, geography, and culture was proposed again in a 1993 Educational Support for Tibet Work Conference.

Discussion and Analysis

Language abilities prior to admission to neidiban

The majority of the students had studied Tibetan in primary schools in TAR. Very few never studied Tibetan before they entered the *neidiban*. The great majority studied Tibetan language for 2–6 years in primary schools. More than two-third (70.93%) attended Tibetan track (*Zang wen ban*, Tibetan as the medium of instruction) primary schools and less than one quarter (23.26%) attended Chinese track (*Han wen ban*, Chinese as the medium of instruction) in primary schools (which means that they studied Tibetan language and literature only as a subject). Only about 1% (1.16%) attended all Chinese schools with no exposure to Tibetan language. The students who attended Tibetan language medium primary schools and the Tibetan track classes in two track schools naturally have better knowledge and facility in the use of Tibetan language. Meanwhile, their Chinese language skills are quite limited since their families and communities are predominantly, if not totally, Tibetan. On the other hand, the students who attended Chinese track classes with Tibetan as a subject tended to have better Chinese than their counterparts in the Tibetan language track classes. There were still others who attended all Chinese schools, which were usually schools run by the military or government owned enterprises (*qiye*) for the children of their staff. Not all students who attended *neidiban* were ethnic Tibetans. A few of those interviewed were of the Han nationality living in Tibet, or those who have one parent (often the father) who is a Han Chinese. Most of them did not learn any Tibetan in primary schools, or learned 1 or 2 years of Tibetan before being recruited into *neidiban* schools.

Students from the rural or nomadic areas, although in the minority, had a higher level of Tibetan language ability since they had had little contact with Chinese language situations. The students from the more urbanized districts such as Rigatse and Shannan generally had higher capability in Tibetan than students from Changdu and Linzhi districts. In short, the better the students were in Tibetan, the poorer they were in Chinese, and vice versa. Around 48% of the students reported that one or both of their parents have some level of basic literacy in Tibetan and Chinese, while 13.96% said that one or both of their parents have only some level of literacy in Tibetan. Less than 2% (1.74%) reported that their parents are literate in Chinese only. A quarter (25.58%) said their parents are illiterate.

A study of the test results in Chinese language taken by the Tibetan students demonstrated the gap. The first cohort of the 100 students selected from Naqu District in 1985 who attended the Tianjin Hongguang Secondary School were selected by the end of their final year (primary Grade 5) of primary school and had the highest total scores of the enrollment exams in Tibetan, as well as Mathematics and Chinese. The students were given a test to check their level of Chinese after they arrived in Tianjin. The test was based on the national standard Chinese language textbooks for Grade 3 of primary schools. The average score for Chinese was 22.5 (out of 100), and only three students had passed the exam, scoring higher than 60 (Tibet Education Research, 1985, as cited in Xia Zhu *et al.*, 1993).

Language education in the junior secondary neidiban education

All junior secondary schools that recruited Tibetan students also offered Tibetan language classes. Due to the different achievement levels of Tibetan students, they were grouped into two language classes, basic and advanced. The Tibetan language textbooks used are those published and used in the TAR. Tibetan language teachers were selected from the TAR on 2-year assignments. The Tibetan language and literature class in junior secondary school was regarded by students as a main subject of study for them and ranged between 5 and 7 hours per week. The subject was examined with the standard examination paper used in the TAR. The objective stated is to enable the students to achieve the same level of Tibetan proficiency as their counterparts inside TAR.

Many interviewees, such as L07, had good Tibetan instruction in junior secondary school, consisting of 7 hours of instructional time, about the same amount as for Chinese language study. L07 reported that Tibetan language study at junior secondary schools was encouraged and was considered an important subject in the school. However, whether students graduated from junior secondary school with a good knowledge of Tibetan language largely depends on the Tibetan teachers' performance and initiatives and whether the study of Tibetan was encouraged in the school curriculum.

Since the data consisted of views from students of different age cohorts who attended the _neidiban_ at different times, it was possible to see a trend in which students from earlier cohorts learned better Tibetan language than those of later cohorts.

> The school emphasized Tibetan language classes. We had a teacher, a special expert teacher for Tibetan, from Tibet we had a few. The student classes were split into fast track and slow track, the latter class more simple, the former with students who all had been in Tibetan medium primary schools do their Tibetan was pretty good. (N36)

It also was the case that the study of Tibetan language was encouraged more at the junior secondary school level than it was at the senior secondary level. Finally, students of the advanced Tibetan language and literature class performed better than those in the basic class, obviously having much to do with their primary school language track experience than the teaching they received at the _neidiban_ schools. Some students stated that, at best, their knowledge of Tibetan language would reflect the standard junior secondary school graduates inside TAR, while others said that their Tibetan has deteriorated since joining the _neidiban_, because all the efforts were put on the study of Chinese and other subjects. As one student put it:

> Our boarding school had Tibetan language. I should say that through junior secondary education we studied it very well. We also studied it well in primary school, but the Chinese teaching was poor – only taught for examinations and at that time it was not taught properly. At primary school, I studied Mathematics and Tibetan especially well. After that I began to study Math in Chinese, Math through Chinese, and also had Tibetan, at junior middle school also studied. After that at Junior secondary school the Tibetan was relatively mixed up. The school planned and emphasized it, with seven classes per week. In the end, our Tibetan and Chinese teaching was about equal. (L07)

The student cohort of 1985–1989 had better Tibetan language classes than those who attended *neidiban* after 1989, ie, more hours of study, better teachers, more after-class activities on Tibetan writing. The students from Rigatse, especially from the cohort recruited in 1985–1989 were able to maintain a fairly good level of Tibetan knowledge. As a result, they were now probably the only group of graduates who were able to teach bilingually. The later cohorts could not do so as well. A principal of a school in Rigatse, who had also taught Tibetan language class in a *neidiban* school, noted

> ... before, in Tibet, when I only knew about studying Tibetan, well, the things we studied were all from the textbook. Now when we were in *neidi*, for the first year or two my Tibetan was alright, at the time of graduation in that last year, the whole class, you can say the whole year's students (regular Tibetan language class of students), at their Tibetan language level all went downhill. This was because over there all of our contact, except with the Tibetan teachers, was with Han ethnic teachers. Normally, at that time, the interaction was in Chinese (*Hanyu*) between us. Except for those of us who came from the city and were accustomed to communication in Chinese (*Hanyu*), the rest of us from the rural areas were not so accustomed and our standard of Tibetan at *neidiban* dropped. (N01)

There was a conscious decision from the educators and the administrators from Rigatse district to emphasize on the learning of Tibetan. In late 1980s, alerted by the deteriorating situation of Tibetan language study, a group of Tibetan educators pleaded with the ninth Panchen Lama to intervene and to urge the schools to restore Tibetan language class. One of the Tibetan educators recalled his meeting with the Panchen Lama, and the actions taken consequently in the schools:

> After the meeting with the Panchen Lama, Tibetan became a core subject and part of the national college entrance examination. After this, we Tibetan teachers emphasized the importance of Tibetan language education to the higher authorities – noting that after graduation we would be facing Tibetans comrades. Therefore, without Tibetan language it would not be a good situation. After it became part of the national college entrance examination, Tibetan students emphasized it more. At the time of the classes of the first three cohorts of 1985, 86, 87 as Tibetan became part of the national college entrance examination, the TAR government education commission sent the Tibetan script for the national examinations to the *neidi* schools.

Language study at senior secondary level

A major setback occurred during the later student cohorts when the ministry of education moved to a more conservative position on the national university entrance examination and no longer included scores of Tibetan and other ethnic minority language examinations in the total scores for university entrance. This immediately had a negative impact on the studying of Tibetan at the senior secondary school level. The majority of the students commented that the schools did not pay enough attention to the Tibetan classes and it was not treated as a core subject (zhuke). For example, less hours of study (2 hours a week) were dedicated to it and Tibetan classes were pushed off to be offered on the weekends. Tibetan students then began to loose the motivation to study Tibetan well. It was not encouraged and they were obsessed with the studies of other courses. More importantly, as one student put it, "Tibetan language classes have to give way to the goal of passing the college entrance examinations (*gaokao*)." Since the score for Tibetan language examination was not included in the *gaokao*, it was natural that the teachers and the students had given very little time and effort to studying it well.

Students with different Tibetan language levels attended different level language classes (one for beginners and one for advanced learners). However, when the students entered into the senior secondary schools, this division no longer existed as all students were mixed together for Tibetan language class. The instruction tended to accommodate those with lower levels of Tibetan. As a result, the students who previously had a stronger command of the Tibetan literacy were unable to receive advanced instruction.

> One had to be examined in Tibetan on the national college entrance examination, but it did not count for anything. ... There were only five subjects, only five subjects were counted, not Tibetan where the score was not counted. (L46)

In short, students of later cohorts had less and less hours of Tibetan classes. Students reported that the schools did not pay enough attention (*bugou zhongshi*) to the Tibetan study.

> It was not a core course. Over there, we wanted to take the national college entrance examination, and Tibetan was not counted in the point score (zangwen zaihao). If one wanted to apply for admission to a very good inland university, Tibetan language was of no use. Sure, going to class was going to class, but after it review, you can almost say that (it was studied) only for a little bit of time. After getting into senior

secondary inland school, the Tibetan and Chinese language classes were mixed, so we restudied what we learned in junior secondary school, after that the curriculum was more limited.... Now Tibetan language learning is basically in junior secondary school only.

Tibetan language teachers

Tibetan language teachers play a major role in encouraging or discouraging the students in their study in Tibetan language and literature subjects. The ones that had very good knowledge taught the textbook knowledge well and organized after-class activities for Tibetan learning. Some of them also taught more general knowledge about Tibetan history, religion, and culture. As these students recount, these teachers and their activities often made a positive impact on students' Tibetan learning.

Our Tibetan teacher at that time was terrific, really good (*tinghao*). His teaching ability was very high. Moreover, he paid a great amount of attention to Tibetan language and literature. The students overwhelmingly liked to take his course. (N58)

At junior secondary school there was not much Tibetan language class. However, the Tibetan teacher was very responsible, requiring the students to keep a Tibetan language diary and every day he corrected them, made the students know how to use spoken Tibetan and write Tibetan compositions, made Tibetan class become a strong topic. (R14)

At that time in the two 1985 class groups, there were many rural students who could speak Tibetan very well, so they all passed. Their first Tibetan teacher at junior middle school, that teacher is now vice mayor of X county. His Tibetan level in Rigatse, is superior and he is famous for it. Therefore, under his tuteledge and guidance, his students' Tibetan was amazing, higher than my class. Because we were all urban kids, so they went through the kind of composition, send that kind of manuscript to Tibet and after that received *gaofei* (a publishing fee). (R30)

When we were in junior middle school Tibetan was emphasized. We had a teacher named Dawa Tseren who accompanied us to the inland boarding school. He had just graduated from the Lhasa Teacher Training College and stayed with us for four years, during which time he was a very responsible teacher. Usually the other Tibetans teachers would only stay for two years and return to Tibet. That was the rule, a Tibetan teacher could teach for two years and then return home. But this teacher Dawa, ... had much cooperation with the other teachers of the school, then after two years, he passed the exam for entrance to the Tibetan Medical University, but he left it and returned to Zhapoxing to continue to teach us.

Usually aside from the lectures, there is a semester of Tibetan knowledge lectures, for example in one week there were two lectures, in one class it would be a history lecture, definitely was Tibetan. (N55)

At that time, we had a Tibetan teacher whose teaching method deeply affected me. Perhaps my teacher from primary school on to university made a deep impression, but this Tibetan teacher left one on me. (L09)

However, teachers who could not adjust to the life in China experienced homesickness, often drank, or simply did not teach well, and had negative impact on students' Tibetan learning.

Many Tibetan teachers were not willing to go to the inland Chinese boarding school to teach, because they all had families. They were required to go for two years. The teachers we did have were recent graduates of about 20 or so years old. Anyway, for whatever reason, may be unwilling, each person had their own reasons. (L04)

R45 enjoyed studying Tibetan the least and was asked why:

Really, I don't know why I did not enjoy studying Tibetan. Actually, how could I explain this, our Tibetan teacher is not. . . . how could I say this. Comparing the quality of the Tibetan teacher with the neidi teachers, I/we had disadvantages. I believe this could probably have a great impact. Because perhaps our teacher, our Tibetan teacher preferred drinking wine. . . . (R45)

Tibetan language teachers from different regions spoke local dialects and in many cases, students coming from other regions could not follow their dialects, resulting in some cases of failure and giving up on studying Tibetan.

The Tibetan teacher at the time came from Xigaze, but there were some students who came from Nagqu in our class. Due to the differences in Tibetan dialects, students from Nagqu did not understand what the lectures were about; they did not have any solution and resolved to read extra-curricular books.

At first, there was a teacher, the Chief Editor for a senior secondary Tibetan textbook, who used to write the lesson out in Tibetan and then explained it in Chinese. This is because students from Nagqu could not fully understand that Tibetan accent of the Houzang 后藏 region used by the teacher. We could understand his/her accent better because it was more or less the same if not similar to ours. Later, this teacher left us and his successors did not really pay much attention to this matter apart from regarding teaching as a job to be completed and that's it. Students did not like to pay attention in class. (L53)

The Tibetan teacher who was assigned to teach us had a very strong regional accent; he spoke his own regional dialect and we spoke the Lhasa dialect. (L07)

Another problem affecting the quality of the Tibetan language classes was teacher turnover rate. This had a compounding effect, especially in cases when the academic level of students was modest.

Sometimes the teachers were changed too frequently, which was very disruptive and also had negative impact on students' learning. (L07)

Within four years, we had a change of teachers about twice or thrice; in fact it was thrice. Can you say that we have really learned something? Maybe a little bit. To be exact, we did not understand it at all and did not know what they were talking about. Actually, Tibetan was something profound if not abstruse; by approaching it only once or twice, what can we really learn anything about it? We children never accessed it at all, but were eager to learn it. Later when we attended senior secondary specialized school, and a teacher was assigned to teach us. To us, he was a senior secondary school teacher, almost like a professor teaching primary one students; in fact, he taught us nothing at all, simply because we did not understand what he said. It was rather naïve and funny. Finally, he stayed for awhile, maybe for about a semester and then he left. Afterwards, the school employed a graduate from a teachers' training school to teach us; he was about 21 or 22 years old. Every day, lessons carried on as usual and we did not learn anything at all. (L53)

Language and identity among neidiban students

When asked what language they used for communication in *neidiban*, some students replied they often talked to each other in Tibetan. As the dialect problem also existed among students from different regions, they chose the dialect of Lhasa, the capital city of Tibetan, as the means of communication.

Question: What language did you use for communication at that time?
Answer: Tibetan most of the time. Most of us are Tibetan. Ours was not a Chinese class. So we used Tibetan for communication (L28).

Question: Then, what language did you use for communication?
Answer: Tibetan most of the time. We preferred using Tibetan (29).

The interview data also show that when *neidiban* students reached senior secondary school, many used Han Chinese for communication among themselves.

At the junior secondary school, most students would use Tibetan. However, when they reached high school, students came from different regions, not just from Qamdo. Therefore, different regions were not the same, the Qamdo dialect was especially different from that of Lhasa, therefore most senior secondary school classmates would generally communicate in Chinese, and we were from Qamdo, Qamado were different, Quado and Nagqu were different from Lhasa, Shannan, Xigaze, those were very different, and could only speak Chinese. (L46)

Many students felt that it is important to maintain their linguistic identity but there was too little time for Tibetan language class. So they asked the school to increase the hours of Tibetan class by not showing up to class and refusing to eat.

A strike broke out at school. Two classes joined the strike simultaneously; first were the boys, and they complained they did not have sufficient Tibetan lessons. We followed them and made proposals to the school authority. Nonetheless, the teachers did not care about us. Nobody did. As our parents and our Tibetan people gave us to you, at least you should be more responsible to us. Besides, we were still Tibetans at that time. How could we claim ourselves as Tibetans if we don't even know our own names in Tibetan? After the boys went on a strike, we girls acted as spokespersons. We put forward our demands to the teachers. All the boys skipped classes and later on, we even decided that if the school did not increase the number of our Tibetan classes, we would fast. It really happened. (L53)

After graduating from neidiban

After returning to Tibet after graduation, *neidiban* students came to realize the difference between themselves and their counterparts who remained in Tibet for their secondary schooling.

> I admit that my Tibetan was comparatively not as fluent as my primary school classmates. (L04)

> Those who returned from neidi were definitely not very fluent in the Tibetan language. (N01)

> Concerning the Tibetan class in general, their proficiency in the Tibetan language was like this. (L17)

> The Tibetan language, there are many neidi graduates who are returning to Tibet nowadays; it would be difficult for them to speak Tibetan. (L03)

> When we arrived there, we used Tibetan at the beginning, then we started to use Chinese, afterwards, we gradually forgot most of our Tibetan, when we return home, we could not speak. When I graduated there [from primary school], my Tibetan ranked first, but when I reached the junior secondary level, my Tibetan was still acceptable, but it was deteriorating when I was studying at *zhongzhuan* (senior secondary specialized education). There were not many Tibetan lessons at *zhongzhuan*, only 3 lessons. Gradually, I seemed to forget it, it was like I wasn't a Tibetan at all. (L11)

Many graduates reported a limited skill in dealing with Tibetan language newspapers.

Question: Do you understand the Tibetan version of the Xizang rebao?
Answer: No. I couldn't understand it. (L02)

Question: Do you read books published in the Tibetan language?
Answer: I can't read it. (L03)

Most of the interviewees said that they had difficulty in writing Tibetan.

> I have published articles, also in Xizang rebao, but not anymore, now I could only recognize alphabets. I could write it, but with many mistakes. People write Chinese in this way. When people write Tibetan, there are prefixes and suffixes. However, I often omit them. I have

forgotten most of my Tibetan. I wrote a poem at that time about my mother. It was so touching to think of it now. Unfortunately, I could not write anything like that now. (L06)

Most *neidiban* graduates were assigned to work in urban areas and did not need Tibetan in their work. Documents were usually prepared in Chinese.

When we are working in the organization now, most of the written work are in Chinese, yes, my writings in Tibetan are therefore not fluent. (L1)

However, the graduates working in the villages and township often found that they needed to use Tibetan at work but found themselves handicapped in Tibetan language skills. These groups of the students said that the curriculum for Tibetan study at *neidiban* was insufficient. This was particularly the case for those who become school teachers.

However, concerning the way we teach, the teaching method, we now have lots of materials, but materials in Tibetan are not as sufficient as those in Chinese. In my case, I teach Tibetan, and as like any other language, I need to read reference materials about language. (L21) (Teaching in a primary school in Lhasa)

Sometimes, students ask me something about Tibetan during the Tibetan class and I cannot answer them; I have to ponder it after class before I could come up with the answer, but it is different for Chinese. When they ask me a Chinese word, I could reply to them immediately. When I answer them, I could also explain the meaning to them; Therefore, I believe *neidi* graduates are generally weaker in Tibetan. (N01) (Teacher in Nakchu district)

There were exceptions. Some graduates had very good knowledge of Tibetan language. These usually had attended Tibetan-track classes in primary school, were self-motivated or motivated by their Tibetan language teachers, siblings, or classmates, and had to use Tibetan as working language. These people generally had good Tibetan language skills and were also self-learned during their work. In short, exposure at the workplace mattered.

Because I attended the Tibetan track at primary school, I feel my Tibetan is good; because I am a part-time deputy secretary, as well as the deputy chairperson of the Chinese Central Government, when I have official government meetings, so I need to speak in Tibetan, and when I read reports or other documents, I need to use it. If you work in the organization, maybe you have not thought about this, the present education is like that, when you graduate from the university, you need to first work for the rural community, if you couldn't read the documents, then you could hardly handle most of the duties. Yes, I had never attended Tibetan classes at the junior secondary level, not even at *zhongzhuan*, after I have begun working in the planning commission; I was working with the statistics, but the agricultural reports and charts all used Tibetan, therefore I had exposure to the Tibetan language. (L13)

I studied in the Han language track in Tibet before going to *neidi*, but my Tibetan was rather good. I often visit the common people in the rural areas in order to promote the party policies, so there were all kinds of meetings and conferences held in the rural areas that were conducted in Tibetan. There, they use Tibetan, not Chinese. For me, I could explain and read Tibetan without great difficulties. (L14)

Although a large sector of *neidiban* graduates become schoolteachers, their lack of good Tibetan language skill affects their recruitment and work, especially in rural and nomadic areas. Many schools in Tibet would not employ *neidi* graduates because their Tibetan was generally not fluent, and they could only teach Chinese and Mathematics, but nothing else. On the contrary, local Tibetan teachers could teach Tibetan and Mathematics or Chinese and Mathematics, they could teach more subjects.

I have some friends working at a primary school as school teachers. People without connection could hardly be employed; the school would not prefer *neidi* graduates whose Tibetan is really poor. The English classes are well-organized in *neidi* now, but they should emphasize more on Tibetan. I think graduates like us could not work in such an organization. There is a need to be trained to know how to read Tibetan documents and hold meetings with the villagers. You could not just be able to read in Chinese. You must at least be able to read the Tibetan documents. Many *neidi* graduates could not even read documents in Tibetan. (L13)

Tibetan teachers need to improve themselves and enrich their knowledge, because education is very important. As a Tibetan, one should know more about his/her own history. Besides, you have to face a class of farmers or herdsmen. If you can't speak good Tibetan, well my experience last year in helping the poor in the rural areas made me realize that I am not up to the standard of fluency to communicate effectively with them; I have the difficulty in explaining clearly certain policies to the people as someone from our organization asked me to do so. (L45)

A primary school principal was interviewed about his views on the performance of the *neidiban* graduates who were now teaching in his school. This principal emphasized the problem that the graduates were unable to teach the Tibetan language subject. In TAR, like elsewhere in China, teachers at the primary schools are required to be able to teach both the language class and the mathematics class. In the case of the TAR, the primary school teachers are expected to be able to teach the subjects of Tibetan and Chinese, as well as mathematics. But many *neidiban* graduates were not able to teach Tibetan. Moreover, the *neidiban* graduates' Chinese language skills were not necessarily as good as many people believed they would be. In short, they were not doing well in teaching because they lacked proper language ability. Therefore, this principal strongly suggested that the *neidiban* teacher training programs should address the problems by training students who are able to work in rural areas where the dominant language is Tibetan.

The situation here is that students are mainly fluent in Tibetan, they all speak Tibetan, that's to say, it is not realistic to teach the class in Hanyu. If you teach in Hanyu, the students will definitely not understand it. But on the contrary, the teachers who graduated form the neidiban are not good enough to teach in Tibetan either. For quite a while, Tibetan has been the main medium of instruction in teaching; apart from the teaching of the subject Hanyu, every other subject was taught in Tibetan, like Mathematics. As far as the teaching in Tibetan is concerned, like the training of teachers, the emphasis should be put on the improvement of their ability in handling Tibetan well; for example, I have been to many Tibetan classes in *neidi*, such as in Shanxi and Zhejiang; Tibetan has already been prescribed as a course, but it depends on whether you regard it as important or not, it gives me this impression. The point is, Tibetan is excluded as a subject from all examinations in *neidi*. In this way, students did not have the pressure to take Tibetan seriously. It doesn't matter; the whole situation is like this: everybody uses Hanyu. This is not acceptable. We have to make sure the language of the ethnic minority survives to the next generation, but once in *neidi*, the situation changes completely to favor the momentum of the *neidi* mentality, therefore upon the return to Tibet, they are still deficient in every aspect of language.

Actually, the *neidiban* is really good. It helps to promote the development of the local ethnic minorities, but the problem is a matter of integration. It seems that one tends to forget the language which he/she uses originally while learning a new one. (Document N City, interview with a primary school principal).

Almost all of the interviewees said that they wanted to learn Tibetan reading and writing, but it was difficult as adult learners with job and family responsibilities to balance. Most of the interviewees said that they regretted not being able to study Tibetan well and felt ashamed for the fact that they were illiterate in reading and writing, and consequently knew very little about Tibetan culture and history.

Conclusion

From the perspective of most of the students attending the *neidiban*, the study of Tibetan language was regarded as one of the major subjects for them at the junior secondary school level. However, the greater emphasis on the study of Chinese and other subject matters outweighed the study of Tibetan. After the 4 years of junior secondary schools, less and less attention was given to the study of Tibetan. It was considered as a minor area. A major setback occurred when the Tibetan examination score was no longer taken into account in the total scores for national university entrance examinations. There was also a great pressure to learn Chinese well, which culminated in measures taken to make the school environment monolingual in Chinese. The situation was further complicated by the fact that the students had different level of Tibetan language skills (and regional dialects) before they were recruited to the *neidiban*. Because of this, as a common practice, many opted to speak in Chinese among themselves, particularly when they moved up from junior to senior secondary schools. However, there is also some indication that when the students from different dialect areas spoke together, they tended to use the Lhasa dialect at junior secondary schools.

The overall result of language teaching in the inland schools has been a loss or deterioration in Tibetan language skills among the *neidiban* graduates. After returning to Tibet, not all of them need to use Tibetan as a working language, but those who are working in the countryside and those who are teaching face the challenge of not being able to work or teach effectively. This situation is highlighted by the fact that there is a great need for bilingual teachers in TAR, and the *neidiban* graduates seemed not be able to fulfill this need. According to Zhou (2003), 16% of the TAR population is in urban area. Many urban Tibetan residents are either bilingual or have achieved bi-literacy in Tibetan and Chinese. The other 84% of population are rural or nomadic, and hence usually are only speakers of Tibetan. By 1999, more than 95% of the primary schools in the TAR were using Tibetan as the medium of instruction. However, only 13% of secondary school students and 5% of senior secondary school students were attending classes that use Tibetan as the medium of instruction.

It is also assumed that the language plays a role in shaping their attitude toward their home culture, along with other things such as the ideological study, Han teachers' view toward minority culture, and their understanding of the social development. It seems that the distance of the *neidiban* graduates' experience from their home culture is in part caused by the loss of language skills in reading and writing in Tibetan. This situation is reinforced by not having close contact with family and community during the many years away from Tibet and the years it takes to reintegrate back into the home culture.

In short, the *neidiban* graduates realize the importance of Tibetan language in their work environment and in their understanding of their native culture. Most regret not learning Tibetan well and wish to improve the language skills. While the *neidiban* does attempt to reflect the national aim of producing *Min-Han Jiantong* bilinguals with native-speaker competence in their home language and in standard Chinese, Putonghua, the reality is hardly so. In the case of Tibetans from the TAR in the *neidiban*, *Zang-Han Jiantong*, linguistic competence in two languages, has been subjugated to other national aims.

Notes

1. Implementation of these measures has been complicated by the "Tibet question" but also by the post-1950 boundaries that put most of the Tibetan population outside of the Tibetan Autonomous Region (TAR).
2. In fact, bilingualism has become embraced by the Han majority as a tool for foreign language competence, particularly English. A system has emerged in which English as well as standard Chinese are used as media of instruction.
3. With the exception of the Huis and Manchus who generally use the Chinese language.

References

Baker, C. (2001) *Foundations of Bilingual Education and Bilingualism* (3rd edn). Clevedon, England; Buffalo, NY: Multilingual Matters.

Bass, C. (1998) *Education in Tibet: Policy and Practice Since 1950*. London: Zed Books.

Chodag, T. (1988) *Tibet: The Land and People*. Beijing: New World Press.

Dai, Q., Teng, X., Guan, X. and Dong, Y. (1997) *Zhongguo shaoshu minzu shuangyu jiaoyu gailun [Introduction to Bilingual Education for China's Minorities]*. Shenyang: Liaoning Nationalities Press.

Fang, J., Wang, K. and Linda, X. (2001) *Dangdai zhongguo shaoshu Minzu Shuangyu jiaoxue lilun yu shijian [China's Contemporary Ethnic Minority Bilingual Education Theory and Practice]*. Xian: Shaanxi Jiaoyu chubanshe.

Fei, X. (1980) Ethnic identification in China. In *Social Science in China* (Vol. 1, pp. 97–107). Beijing: Chinese Academy of Social Sciences Press.

Fei, X. (1989) Zhonghua minzu de duoyuan yiti geju [Plurality and unity in the configuration of the Chinese nationality]. *Beijing daxue xuebao* 4, 1–19.

Gladney, D. (1996) *Muslim Chinese, Ethnic Nationalism in the People's Republic of China*. Cambridge, MA: Harvard Univ. Press.

Goldstein, M.C. (1989) *A History of Modern Tibet, 1913–1951: The Demise of the Lamaist State*. Berkeley, CA: Univ. of California Press.

Goldstein, M.C. (1997) *The Snow Lion and the Dragon: China, Tibet, and the Dalai Lama*. Los Angeles, CA: Univ. of California Press.

Hansen, M.H. (1999) *Lessons in Being Chinese: Minority Education and Ethnic Idenntity in Southwest China*. Seattle, WA: Univ. of Washington Press.

Harrell, S. (2001) *Ways of Being Ethnic in Southwest China*. Seattle, WA: Univ. of Washington Press.

Heberer, T. (1989) *China and Its National Minorities: Autonomy or Assimilation*. Armonk, NY: M.E. Sharpe.

Iredale, R. *et al.* (2001) *Contemporary Minority Migration, Education and Ethnicity*. Cheltenham, UK: Edward Elgar Press.

Lam, A. (2005) *Language Education in China*. Hong Kong: Hong Kong Univ. Press.

Lee, M.J.B. (2001) *Ethnicity, Education and Empowerment: How Minority Students in Southwest China Construct Identities*. Aldershot: Ashgate Press.

Ma, Rong (2006) A new perspective in guiding ethnic relations in the 21st century —'De-politicization' of Ethnicity. Unpublished manuscript, Beijing University Department of Sociology.

Ma, Yin (1985) *Questions and Answers About China's Nationalities*. Beijing: World Press.

Mackerras, Colin (2003) *Ethnicity in Asia*. New York: Routledge Curzon.

Nyima, P. (Nima, B.) (1997) The way out for Tibetan education. *Chinese Education and Society* 30 (4), 7–20.

Postiglione, Gerard A. (ed.) (1999) *China's National Minority Education: Culture, Schooling, and Development*. New York: Falmer Press.

Postiglione, Gerard A. (ed.) (2001) Bilingual education in China. Special issue. *Chinese Education and Society* 34 (2).

Postiglione, Gerard A. (ed.) (2002) Strengthening Ethnic Minority Education: Research from an Asian Development Bank Technical Assistance. Special issue. *Chinese Education and Society* 35 (3).

Postiglione, Gerard A. (ed.) (2006) *China's Educational Inequality*. New York: M.E. Sharpe.

Qi, Guozhong (2004) A Report on the First Year and a Half of the Bilingual Education Experimental Class at Narisi Primary School, Dongxiang County. *China Education Forum* 5 (1). University of Hong Kong Wah Ching Centre for Research on Education in China. On WWW at http://www.hku.hk/chinaed/newsletter/2004_1.PDF, pp. 3–8.

Spack, Ruth (2002) *America's Second Tongue: American Indian Education and the Ownership of English, 1960–1900.* Lincoln, NE: Univ. of Nebraska Press.

Stites, Regie (1999) Writing cultural boundaries: National minority language policy, literacy planning, and bilingual education. In Gerard Postiglione (ed.) *China's National Minority Education.* New York: Falmer Press.

Street, Brian (ed.) (2001) *Literacy and Development: Ethnographic Perspectives.* London/New York: Routledge.

Teng, Xing (2000) *Webhua bianqian yu shuangyu jiaoyu [Cultural Change and Bilingual Education].* Beijing: Jiaoyu kexue chubanshe.

Trueba, Henry and Zou, Yali (1994) *Power in Education: The Case of Miao University Students and its Significance for American Culture.* Washington, DC: Falmer Press.

Upton, Janet (1999) The development of modern school based language education in the PRC. In Gerard A. Postiglione (ed.) (1999) *China's National Minority Education: Culture, Schooling, and Development.* New York: Falmer Press.

Wang, Chengzhi and Zhou, Quanhou (2003) Minority education in China: From state preferential policies to dislocated Tibetan schools. *Educational Studies* 29 (1), 85–104.

Wang, Yuanxin (1994) *Zhongguo minzu yuyanxue lungang [The Study of Minority Languages in China: A Critical Introduction].* Beijing: Central University of Nationalities Press.

Yu, Huibang (1995) *Shuangyu yanjiu [Research on Bilingualism].* Chengdu: Sichuan Univ. Press.

Zheng, Xinrong (2002) *Woguo yiwu jiaoyu jieduan shaoshu minzu wenzi jiaocai jianshe diaocha yanjiu [Research on China's Ethnic Minority Language Teaching Materials Development for the Compulsory Education Years of Schooling].* Beijing: Beijing Normal University manuscript; report to the Ford Foundation, Beijing.

Zhou, Qingsheng (2000) *Yuyan yu renlei [Language and Mankind].* Beijing: Central Univ. Nationalities Press.

Zhou, Wei (2003) *Xizang de yuyan he shehui [Tibetan Language and Society].* Beijing: China's Tibetology.

Zhu, Zhiyong (2007) *State Schooling and Ethnic Identity: The Politics of a Tibetan Neidi Secondary School in China.* Lanham, MD: Lexington Press.

Part 2

Varieties in Bilingual Education

Chapter 5

Typology of Bilingualism and Bilingual Education in Chinese Minority Nationality Regions

QINGXIA DAI AND YANYAN CHENG*

Introduction

Bilingual education for Chinese minority nationalities is an organic and important part of Chinese national education. It is of vital importance not only to the improvement of literacy and civilization on the part of minority nationalities to meet the needs of social development, but also to the unity and cooperation of different nationalities. The central government and local governments at all levels therefore attach great importance to bilingual education for minority nationalities.

Bilingual education for minority nationalities in China refers mainly to the teaching and learning of both minority languages and Mandarin Chinese. China is a multinationality country with the Han nationality as the majority. The Han nationality, residing all over the country, has the largest population and is relatively more developed in economy than are minority nationalities. Over a long period of time, the Han nationality and minority nationalities have been mutually dependent and in close communication and have gradually formed close and friendly ties. The minority nationalities, from their own experience of development, have come to recognize that it is impossible to keep up with modern science and technology without first grasping Mandarin Chinese. This very national situation determines the necessity and significance of acquisition of Mandarin Chinese for minority nationalities and forms the foundation of bilingual educational system in national education.

* Translated by Guangyou Jiang (an associate professor in the School of Foreign Languages of Chongqing Institute of Technology, now working for his doctor's degree in Linguistics at Central University for Nationalities in Beijing)

Historical Background

Bilingualism has a long history in China. He (1998: 62) argues that in the distant past (roughly 2600–1600 BC), China was already a pluralistic country dominated by the Huaxia nationality (Huaxia is the ancient name of the Han nationality). Separation, migration, and fusion due to wars and disputes among states and nationalities led to the distributional pattern of either mixed settlement with different nationalities or compact settlements of individual nationalities within small geographic locations. All these provided the preconditions for concurrent use of different languages. As time went by, political and economical ties among different nationalities were steadily strengthened and exchanges among them by way of trade, marriage, and mixed settlement were gradually advanced. As a result, the phenomenon of bilingualism became widespread. It was not uncommon to find that some upper-classmen of minority nationalities took up the study of Mandarin Chinese and gained a good command of both their native tongue and Mandarin Chinese. For example, to subjugate other states and assimilate their people, the rulers of the Xia dynasty (2070–1600 BC) set up an official organization and assigned officials who were exclusively responsible for language translation. When people of other nationalities moved into the land of Xia, communication was facilitated by these officials. They were understood by means of interpretation and translation. This historical fact shows that at that time bilingualism came into existence as a result of both natural conditions (regional contact, for example) and official compulsion. In *the Spring and Autumn Period* (770–476 BC), it was recorded that many Yue people were also able to speak the language of Chu in addition to their own native Yue language (Yue and Chu were separate ancient states in *the Spring and Autumn Period*).

In the Han dynasty (206 BC–AD 220), the Huaxia nationality, having assimilated and mixed with many minority nationalities, was then called the Han nationality and Mandarin Chinese became the lingua franca for many nationalities. At the same time, some minority nationalities in the northeast and northwest, such as South Xiongnu, Wuhuan, Xianbei, Di, Jie and Qiang, moved into the Central Plains (comprising the middle and lower reaches of the Yellow River) in the name of allegiance and submission and settled there, living together with the Han nationality. As a consequence, the people of these nationalities gradually mastered Mandarin Chinese. According to the records of *Annals of the Northern Qi Dynasty* (550–577), "although languages were different, they all could understand Mandarin Chinese. This was because of mixed settlement." After the Kingdom of Wei (220–265) and the Jin dynasty (265–420), Xianbei, a minority nationality that settled in the Central Plains, united ancient northern China and most northern nationalities came under its jurisdiction. These nationalities gradually grasped the language of Xianbei and thus formed the type of bilingualism of one minority nationality understanding the language of another minority nationality (Wang, 1990: 290).

From the Qin dynasty (221–206 BC) to the Han dynasty (206 BC–AD 220), the Han people in the Central Plains were sent to the south in large numbers. They settled and intermarried with minority nationalities there. For example, in the third century BC, tens of thousands of soldiers led by Chu Zhuangqiao, a famous general, marched into Dian (now Yunnan Province) and intermarried with the local minority nationality, the Bai nationality. In the Western Han dynasty (206 BC–AD 24), soldiers from northwest Bashu (now Sichuan Province and Chongqing Municipality) and inlanders who moved there to reclaim wasteland were finally assimilated into the Bai nationality. Consequently, there appeared a lot of bilingual Bai people who could speak both their own language and Mandarin Chinese. From the Song dynasty (960–1279) throughout to the Ming dynasty (1368–1644) and the Qing dynasty (1644–1911), the Han nationality and the Tibetan nationality migrated into each other's areas and lived in mixed settlement. Owing to this, there appeared widespread language contact and bilingual speakers of Mandarin Chinese, and Tibetan increased sharply.

As for the minority nationalities in Xinjiang (now the Xinjiang Uygur Autonomous Region), as early as the Western Han dynasty (206 BC–AD 24) many upper-classmen began to learn Mandarin Chinese. In the Tang dynasty (618–907) and the Northern Song dynasty (960–1127), at Loulan and Gaochang districts of Xinjiang, public schools (managed by government) and free schools (managed by privates and free of tuition fee) were set up to teach and popularize Confucian classics. Also, at Gaochang and Beiting districts, there were official organizations devoted to translation of Buddhist scriptures written in Mandarin Chinese. In the areas of the Zhuang nationality, private schools were set up in the Western Han dynasty (206 BC–AD 24); public schools were set up in the Sui dynasty (581–618); prefecture schools, county schools, and academies of classical learning were set up in the Tang dynasty (618–907). These educational and academic organizations later prospered greatly in the Qing dynasty (1644–1911). One thing in common in the Zhuang areas was that the language of Zhuang was first taught in these organizations, and later Mandarin Chinese. A lot of bilingual speakers of Zhuang and Mandarin Chinese were trained (Dai, 1992: 95). To facilitate communication among different nationalities, the government of the Ming dynasty (1368–1644) specially founded an official establishment to deal with translation of minority languages and neighboring foreign languages, and this tradition continued until the end of the Qing dynasty (1644–1911). This establishment was divided into eight sections, responsible respectively for the translation of Mongolian, Nüzhen, Tibetan, Sanskrit, Huihui, Dai, Uygur, and Burmese. In the Qing dynasty (1644–1911), a Manchu-Tibetan-Mongolian-Uygur-Mandarin Chinese contrastive vocabulary book was compiled and it included 18,671 entries.

In the era of the Republic of China (1912–1949), a series of educational policies were officially adopted. The imperial examination system[1] was abolished. Public schools were set up. The training of practical subjects of science and engineering was advocated. What is more, Mandarin Chinese as a course was required at schools of all levels. For example, in public Mongolian–Tibetan training schools in Tibetan areas, Mandarin Chinese, Mongolian, and Tibetan were required courses (Su, 1999). The government of Yunnan Province enacted a guideline of educational policy concerning borderland education. According to this guideline, primary schools and adult training schools were set up, in which Mandarin Chinese was taught, focusing mainly on the teaching of Mandarin Chinese characters. This guideline was actively carried out as an educational policy and was further supported financially by the central government of the Republic of China. Up to 1935, 337 primary schools were founded in 25 districts of Yunnan Province. With the development of education of Yunnan Province, bilingual education developed to some degree. However, because Mandarin Chinese was obligatory in these schools, a great number of pupils from minority nationality areas had to drop out due to the fact that they were not able to understand Mandarin Chinese. Besides, owing to ethnic separation, poverty, and insufficiency of financial and human resources, borderland education of Yunnan Province was actually in a very difficult situation (Cang, 1998).

From the developmental history of bilingualism up to 1949 in China, we conclude that political, economical, and cultural exchanges together with mixed settlement and intermarriage among different nationalities were the chief contributing factors of bilingualism and bilingual education. In addition, the wide spreading of religion and Confucianism facilitated to a certain degree the development of bilingualism and bilingual education under the historical conditions.

Types of Bilingualism in Chinese Minority Nationality Regions

China has 56 nationalities speaking over 80 languages and using over 30 writing systems. Most nationalities have their own native languages except for a few cases such as Hui and Manchu nationalities who have adopted

Mandarin Chinese as their mother tongue. Of course, there have always been individuals from other minority groups who have chosen to turn to speaking Mandarin Chinese as their first language. Languages spoken in China fall into five language families and about 30 of the languages are also spoken in other countries. The size of geographical distribution and population of each language varies greatly. Even within each language, there exist differences in various degrees. Some nationalities use different writing systems. For example, the Dai nationality uses four writing systems. Some nationalities use the same writing system. For example, the Han nationality, the Hui nationality, and the Manchu nationality all use the Mandarin Chinese writing system. Bilingualism in Chinese minority nationality regions reflects the features of pluralism and complexity, which are determined by various factors, such as the unique characteristics of each minority language, the settlement pattern of wide scattering of compact communities, and the historical background of relations among different nationalities. The most typical type of bilingualism is undoubtedly the use of minority languages and Mandarin Chinese. However, many other types can also be found. The following sections present a typology of bilingualism in minority regions, which is based on the research findings of a national project of social sciences in 1996, which was directed by Qingxia Dai (cf. Dai, *et al.*, 2000: 165–172).

Minority languages–Mandarin Chinese

This is the dominant type of bilingualism in China. Many people of minority nationalities have a good command of both their own language and Mandarin Chinese. According to statistics, these people amount to about 18,060,000, accounting for 37.7% of the total population of minority nationalities. From 1986 to 1988, the project group organized by Chinese Academy of Social Sciences and the State Ethnic Affairs Commission of the PRC made a survey of the status quo of language use in Chinese minority nationality regions. On the basis of this survey, the group concluded that concurrent use of both minority languages and Mandarin Chinese among minority nationalities roughly falls into the following five subtypes, with the degrees of assimilation by Mandarin Chinese ranging from "the most assimilated" to "the least assimilated."

The overwhelming majority of a certain nationality have converted to Mandarin Chinese speakers, while a tiny minority of them still use their own language besides Mandarin Chinese. This subtype includes the She nationality, the Gelao nationality, the Tujia nationality, and the Hezhen nationality. According to statistics, for the She nationality, less than 1% of the total population still use their own language besides Mandarin Chinese. For Gelao, Tujia, and Hezhen, the percentage is 2%, 3%, and 15%, respectively.

Over 80% of the total population use Mandarin Chinese together with their own language, while the remaining 20% use their own language only. This subtype includes the Qiang nationality, the Gin nationality, the Yugur nationality, the Bonan nationality, and the Xibe nationality.

About 50%–80% of the total population use Mandarin Chinese together with their own language, while the remaining 20%–50% use their own language only. This subtype includes the nationalities of Salar, Daur, Li, Dongxiang, Mulam, Bouyei, Bai, Ewenki, Zhuang, Pumi, Maonan, and Jino.

The people using Mandarin Chinese together with their own language account for 20%–50% of the total population, while the rest 50%–80% use their own language. This subtype includes the nationalities of Yao, Mongolian, Naxi, Korean, Achang, Dai, Yi, Nu, De'ang, Shui, Hani, Dong, Lahu, Jingpo, Miao, Blang, and Va.

Only a tiny minority of people use Mandarin Chinese together with their own language, while the vast majority use their own language only. This subtype includes the nationalities of Lisu, Derung, Tibetan, Lhoba, Monba, Uygur, Kazak, Kirgiz, Tajik, Uzbek, Tatar, and Russian.

Other Types

Minority languages–minority languages

Some minority nationalities use other minority languages together with their own mother tongue. These nonnative languages are typically widely used languages in particular regions. For example, the majority of the people of the Ewenki nationality living in the Mongolian Autonomous Region use Mongolian together with their own language and about one-third of them use Daur as well as their own language. In the Guangxi Zhuang Autonomous Region, 55% of the Yao nationality people who use Bunu also speak Zhuang. Of course, many of these people can also speak Mandarin Chinese, and in this case, they are also included in the above-listed types.

Mandarin Chinese–minority languages

Some people of the Han nationality who live in minority nationality regions can speak a particular minority language. For example, in the Xinjiang Uygur Autonomous Region, some Han people also use Uygur or Kazak. In the Ewenki Autonomous Banner of the Inner Mongolia

Autonomous Region, 60,000 Han people living there can also speak Mongolian.

Bilingualism Within a Nationality

Some nationalities have more than one native language. For example, many Jingpo people speak Jingpo, Zaiwa, and Langsu equally well. This type differs from the "minority languages–minority languages" type in that the former involves a single nationality with different mother tongues, while the latter concerns more than one nationality with their respective native language. Again, many people of this type can also speak Mandarin Chinese, and thus can be grouped into the "minority languages–Mandarin Chinese" type as well.

Categorization by fluency

High fluency of both languages. Some nationalities, for example, the nationalities of Bai, Qiang, Mulam, and Yao, have a high fluency of both their native language and Mandarin Chinese.

High fluency of native language and low fluency of nonnative language. Most of the minority nationality people who can use Mandarin Chinese usually have a high fluency of their native language and a low fluency of Mandarin Chinese. It is the case with those Han people who can speak a particular minority language.

High fluency of nonnative language and low fluency of native language. Many Lisu children in Lanping County of Yunnan Province have a higher fluency of Mandarin Chinese than of their native language. In Xinjiang, some Tatar bilingual speakers can speak Uygur more fluently than their native tongue.

Categorization by language dominance

Native language dominance. The frequency of use of either language varies according to social situations. One example is the Kazak people who can speak Uygur. They use Uygur only when they communicate with Uygur people or people of other nationalities who can also speak Uygur. In other situations, they use their native language. According to statistics of the same survey from 1986 to 1988, 19 nationalities belong to this type in China.

Nonnative language dominance. In some situations, the nonnative language is more widely used. Uzbek people seldom use their native language. Instead, they mainly use Uygur even in their daily life. According to statistics of 1986, 7 nationalities belong to this type in China.

Native language and nonnative language dominance. This refers to the situation where bilingual or multilingual speakers attach equal importance to the languages they use. This phenomenon mainly exists in the areas where two or more minority nationalities live mixed with each other and their population size and economical situation are almost identical. For instance, Ewenki people in Helongjiang Province use their native language, Mandarin Chinese and Ewenki alternately. According to statistics of 1986, 19 nationalities belong to this type in China.

Categorization by acquisition channels

Informal acquisition. Bilingualism comes into being as a result of close language contact. In the process of language contact, people gradually pick up a nonnative language. This is especially true with the nationalities in areas of mixed and scattering settlement of different nationalities.

Formal acquisition. Bilingualism comes into being as a result of systematic school education. For example, college students of the Han nationality learning minority languages in the Central University for Nationalities or minority nationality students learning Mandarin Chinese at school are bilingual or even multilingual speakers. This is the major type of bilingual education in China.

Informal and formal acquisition. Bilingualism comes into being as a result of both language contact and systematic school education. For example, people of some minority nationality who live in the urban areas or some people of the Han nationality who live in the multinationality areas gradually become bilingual or multilingual speakers through language contact as well as school education.

Bi- or Unidirectional Bilingualism

Bidirectional. Two nationalities mutually use each other's native language. For example, in Qiongzhong Li-Miao Autonomous County of central Hainan Province, Miao people use Li together with their native language and a significant portion of Li people use Miao besides their native language.

Unidirectional. People of one nationality use their own native language and the native language of another nationality, but the latter does not use the native language of the former. One typical instance is De'ang people in the Dehong Autonomous Prefecture, who also use Dai besides their own native language. However, Dai people never use De'ang.

Bilingualism or Biliteracy

Bilingualism of only spoken languages. This refers only to spoken bilingualism. In the vast pastoral areas, the majority of the semiagricultural and semipastoral banners and some Mongolian compact communities of the Inner Mongolia Autonomous Region, a small percentage of Mongolians can speak Mandarin Chinese. However, because only Mongolian is taught at schools in these areas, these people cannot use the writing system of Mandarin Chinese.

Bilingualism in both spoken and written forms. Most bilingual speakers in Chinese minority nationality regions can speak and write in Mandarin Chinese besides their own native language.

Bilingualism plus a Foreign Language

Some Chinese minority nationalities live along Chinese borderlines. People of these nationalities are usually bilingual speakers of a foreign language and their mother tongue. For example, many Jingpo people also speak Burmese.

Models and Approaches of Bilingual Education

In the decade after the founding of the People's Republic of China, there was no systematic bilingual education. During the 10 years of the "Cultural Revolution" (1966–1976), monolingual education was forced to be popularized—only Mandarin Chinese was taught at schools of minority nationality regions as a national obligation, which greatly hindered the development of education for minority nationalities. It was not until the 1980s that Chinese bilingual education took a turn for the better. Looking back on the bilingual education in the past half century, we have the following typology summarizing the experience of bilingual education for reference.

Models

In Chinese minority regions, models of bilingual education have been developed according to the local conditions and could be classified into the following seven categories:

(1) *Regional models*—the model of the Yanbian Korean Autonomous Prefecture, the model used in the Inner Mongolia Autonomous Region, the model in the Tibet Autonomous Region, the model of the Xinjiang Uygur Autonomous Region, and the southwest model (Yan, 1985).

(2) *Syllabus models*—these models are established on the basis of monolingual syllabus, transitional bilingual syllabus, and long-term bilingual syllabus (Zhang, 1987).

(3) *Models by dominant language in the classroom*—the model of minority language dominance and the model of Mandarin Chinese dominance. For the former, Mandarin Chinese is of secondary position in bilingual education. This typically applies to minority nationalities whose languages have a large native speaker population and a wide geographical distribution. For the latter model, Mandarin Chinese is the first language in bilingual education, while a minority language is of secondary position. This generally applies to the regions of mixed settlement where mainly the majority language is used for communication.

(4) *Models by school type*—preschool, primary school, and high school. In some places, bilingual education begins at preschool level. But generally, bilingual education begins in primary schools. In borderland areas of compact settlement, especially in remote borderland pastoral areas, bilingual education begins in high schools (Dai *et al.*, 1997).

(5) *Models by sequences*—simultaneous model in which two languages are taught at the same time, sequential model in which one language is taught first and then the other, and insertion model in which one language is taught in the middle of the teaching of another. A typical instance of the simultaneous model is the bilingual education at Zhaojue County of Sichuan Province—some schools use Yi as classroom language while Mandarin Chinese is simultaneously taught as a course, and others use Mandarin Chinese as classroom language while Yi is simultaneously taught as a course.

(6) *Models by textbooks used*—Mandarin Chinese model and minority language model. The former uses Mandarin Chinese textbooks, while the latter uses minority language textbooks.

(7) *Models by the medium of instruction and literacy*—the model of bilingualism with monoliteracy, the model of bilingualism with biliteracy, the model of multilingualism with monoliteracy, the model of multilingualism with biliteracy, and the model of multilingualism with multiliteracy. For the first model, a certain minority language is used to explain Mandarin Chinese but only Mandarin Chinese literacy is developed in the classroom. For instance, in some Lisu primary schools at Nujiang County of Yunnan Province, from preschool to year three, Lisu is used only as a "helping language" for students to learn Mandarin Chinese more easily. In these schools, only Mandarin Chinese writing system is used while the writing system of Lisu "never goes into classroom" (Hu & Yang, 1995). Many Zhuang primary schools at Wenshan

of Yunnan Province adopt the second model in which the minority home language and Mandarin Chinese are used, including both spoken and writing systems. For the third model, the local language, the minority language pupils speak, and Mandarin Chinese are simultaneously used as media of instruction, but only Mandarin Chinese literacy is developed in formal education. For example, in some Yao primary schools at Dahua of Guangxi, Yao, Zhuang, and Mandarin Chinese are simultaneously used as media of instruction, but only the Mandarin Chinese writing system is taught. The fourth model is the same as the third with one difference in that for the former two writing systems are developed at the same time in the classroom. For example, in some Ewenki primary schools, Ewenki, Mongolian, and Mandarin Chinese are simultaneously used but only the Mandarin Chinese writing system and Mongolian literacy are promoted. As for the last model, in some primary schools in the Qinghai Henan Mongolia Autonomous County, three languages—Tibetan, Mongolian, and Mandarin Chinese—are used and taught simultaneously, aiming at trilingualism and triliteracy.

Current approaches

Bilingual education for Chinese minority nationalities in different areas generally has the following aspects in common. From the perspective of recipients, bilingual education mainly refers to primary and high school bilingual education (and preschool bilingual education in a few areas). That is, bilingual education begins even when children's native linguistic competence has yet to be well-developed. In terms of content, bilingual education typically centers upon the teaching and learning of Mandarin Chinese, including pronunciation, spelling, grammar, and texts. Sometimes another nonnative minority language is also included, especially in areas with two or more minority languages commonly and widely used. From the perspective of teaching aims, bilingual education focuses mainly upon the training of language skills, such as listening, speaking, reading, writing, and translation. In the classroom, usually the teacher is the center of activities and students follow by listening to the teacher. The whole teaching process is generally textbook-centered, classroom-centered, and linguistic knowledge-centered. Teachers usually adopt such teaching methods as translation, contrast, and the structural–functional approach.

In recent years, in order to explore applicable and effective ways to promote bilingual education, experiments have been conducted in many places. For example (Dai *et al.*, 1997: 271–292), in Yanbian Korean Autonomous Prefecture, an experiment aiming at improving pupils' spoken

Mandarin Chinese as well as reading and writing in Mandarin Chinese was carried out in primary schools. In this experiment, Korean pupils began to learn Mandarin Chinese when they started their schooling. Mandarin Chinese *pinyin* and transcription rather than Mandarin Chinese characters were taught first. After pupils had a good command of Mandarin Chinese *pinyin* and transcription, they were taught Mandarin Chinese characters and on that basis, speaking, reading, and writing were gradually introduced. The experiment proved to be a success and the result has been popularized. Now, in many Korean primary schools, the traditional curriculum of Mandarin Chinese originally designed for 6 years is accomplished when the third year concludes. Korean pupils' level of Mandarin Chinese in speaking, reading, and writing in general has obviously been improved more rapidly than that before the experiment.

Another experiment which has been regarded as a success is from the Guangxi Zhuang Autonomous Region (Dai *et al.*, 1997: 271–292). Before the experiment, only Mandarin Chinese was taught in primary schools. The experiment started in 1980, aiming at popularizing both the language of Zhuang and Mandarin Chinese. In this experiment, the language of Zhuang was used as the primary language of instruction all through primary school and Mandarin Chinese was taught only as an obligatory language course when the fourth year began. When primary school education ended, pupils were expected to have a good command of the language of Zhuang and 2500 Mandarin Chinese characters in sentence-making as well. The experiment proved to have brought the role of the native language in language-learning into full play. Furthermore, it helped Zhuang people to recover their sense of linguistic identity.

In other areas of minority nationalities, for example, the Inner Mongolian Autonomous Region, the western Hunan Province where the Miao nationality resides, the Xinjiang Uygur Autonomous Region, and Yunnan Province, etc., similar experiments were also conducted. Some are still under way. Whether successful or not, these experiments have helped to accumulate rich experience and insights for the future development of Chinese bilingual education.

Issues and Solutions

Bilingual education is a systematic project which must be viewed holistically. The activities of bilingual education consist of overall curriculum designing, text-book compiling, classroom teaching, and assessment. Each activity should be organically and logically related to the other activities.

To promote bilingual education, an integrated and scientific bilingual educational system should be set up.

At present, there are two bilingual educational systems for minority nationality regions in China. In relatively remote, monolingual areas or areas of compact settlement of one nationality, the minority language is the primary classroom language in bilingual education, while Mandarin Chinese is secondary, but compulsory. In areas of mixed settlement of different nationalities, Mandarin Chinese is the primary medium of classroom instruction and the minority language is secondary, also compulsory. These systems are based on the Constitution and the Law of Compulsory Education of the People's Republic of China. Local educational authorities are expected to follow the general principles of bilingual education according to the local as well as national situations of China. Of course, language equality and nationality equality can also find expressions in these systems.

Undoubtedly, there is always room for improvement due to the complexity of minority bilingual education and because of the challenges posed by the national project of popularizing 9-year compulsory education and by the trend of internationalization of education. We shall present three main issues and make suggestions to address them in the following sections.

Principle of voluntary selection and participation

As a prerequisite, any bilingual educational system should be suited to the characteristics of a pluralistic society. When a bilingual educational system is needed, various concrete situations related to different nationalities should be taken into consideration. Emotions and wishes of different nationalities should be respected. The basic principle of voluntary selection and participation should be followed.

One basic fact is that different nationalities have different attitudes toward bilingual education. Some nationalities are active and enthusiastic, while other nationalities are relatively passive and reluctant. This difference is caused by various factors, such as the extent of economic development, cultural difference, geographical and mental distance, and even the sense of ethnic identity. Under this condition, any tall order and enforced programs would not work.

For example, in many northern areas of compact settlement of minority nationalities, minority language education has a long history. Mandarin Chinese education was added relatively recently. As a result, their bilingual educational system is relatively developed and mature. Now, in these areas, the minority language is the primary classroom language and

Mandarin Chinese is taught at the same time. However, in southern China, minority language education and bilingual education has a relatively short history. Many nationalities have no writing systems for their native languages. Consequently, their bilingual educational system is relatively new. Now, in theses areas, Mandarin Chinese is the primary classroom language and the minority language is simultaneously taught. For the latter case, there is still much to be desired.

What's more, the internal structure of the teaching process should be adjusted according to practical situations and the needs of minority nationalities. For example, in the Liangshan Yi Autonomous Prefecture of Sichuan Province, two bilingual educational models are adopted in primary schools according to the local conditions of different places. In one model, the ratio of Yi to Mandarin Chinese in the first school year is 9:5, and 8:6 in the second. In the other, the ratio is 5:9 and 6:8, respectively. When the first model is smoothly under way, the second model is gradually introduced to replace the first one. In a primary school where the first model is successfully adopted, the total hours of Yi will be gradually reduced and the total hours of Mandarin Chinese will be increased accordingly (Deng, 1998: 43).

It is worth noting that the present bilingual educational policies in most minority nationality regions in China were made after repeated practice and experiments. For instance, in Dehong Prefecture of Yunnan Province, monolingual education of Mandarin Chinese was once carried out. Then the model of "combining the minority language with Mandarin Chinese with the minority language as the priority language from primary school to college" was adopted. Now, in this prefecture, a more pragmatic model has been adopted. According to this model, in primary schools, the minority language is taught first and then Mandarin Chinese and the minority language are simultaneously taught with Mandarin Chinese being the priority language. In high schools and teacher-training schools that are specially set up for nationalities, a minority language, typically a native language, is added as a course. In other conventional high schools and colleges, Mandarin Chinese is taught and used as the only language of instruction except for those students majoring in minority languages and literature.

Mediating mother tongue and mainstream language

At the early stage of bilingual education after the founding of the PRC in 1949, monolingual education of either the minority language or Mandarin Chinese was adopted. This practice led to low education quality, because it did not help students to overcome language barriers and greatly influenced students' cognitive development and acquisition of knowledge. Another consequence was that students eventually became illiterates again because they quite easily forgot what they learnt at school.

In recent years, a new model of bilingual education has been widely adopted. According to this model, bilingual education starts with native language learning and then moves to learning in Mandarin Chinese, mainly through training of Mandarin Chinese conversation. This model attaches equal importance to both languages and steadily moves to meet the requirement of the national curriculum. This model differs from the traditional way of treating minority language only as a "walking stick" to help students to learn Mandarin Chinese without paying due attention to minority language. The first step is native language learning when children begin their schooling. After students have a good command of their native language, Mandarin Chinese learning will then be on the agenda. This is in accordance with not only the law of language acquisition and language use but also the principles of cognitive development. The age of 6 to 7 is widely acclaimed as the critical age of native language learning. The vocabulary acquired at this age accounts for about one-third of the total vocabulary in one's whole life (Chen, 1987). Furthermore, native language environment will make a pupil more confident, more interested, more motivated, and thus more successful in his or her learning. In addition, native language learning also plays a key role in literacy education. In terms of social functions, native language learning will help a nationality to improve its level of civilization, strengthen its self-esteem and confidence, and maintain its own culture. In a word, native language learning occupies a decisive position in bilingual education. Decades of years of practice of bilingual education in China demonstrate that where native language learning is properly emphasized, bilingual education is more successful.

Sustainable development

Before the founding of the PRC in 1949, minority language teachers and bilingual teachers were in serious shortage. Up to the 1980s, there was a sharp rise in numbers, but qualified bilingual teachers were still in short supply. The situation still holds. What is more, the structure of bilingual teaching force is unreasonable in two aspects. On the one hand, there is a lack of young and mid-aged teachers. On the other, senior teachers usually have a lower degree in education; some are clearly unqualified. According to a national survey in 1984, 30% of the teachers in minority primary and secondary schools were not qualified for their posts. For example, in Xinjiang, the percentage of unqualified teachers was 26%, 61%, and 46% in senior high schools, junior high schools, and primary schools, respectively. The percentage of teachers with the right qualifications was only 18.5%, 13.5%, and 41%, respectively (Nurtiyip, 1986). The shortage of qualified teachers, coupled with other factors (such as insufficient financial resources and biased conceptions to be briefly mentioned next), leads to the so-called "three low percentages" (low percentages of school entrance, class attendance, and due graduation) and "three poverties" (teachers with poor qualifications, poor teaching quality, and poor teaching methods).

To develop bilingual education, we must strengthen the construction of bilingual faculty. First, in-service teachers should be further trained in order to renew their knowledge structure. Second, talents who are well trained in bilingualism and willing to be devoted to bilingual education should be encouraged to take up the career of bilingual education. Third, measures should be taken to solve the difficulties facing bilingual teachers, including pay, welfare, housing, and promotion.

As a prerequisite, we need to deal with a narrow and harmful view held by many people that bilingual education is of secondary importance and bilingual teacher training is unnecessary. The concomitant consequence of this view is that few people are willing to take up the job of bilingual education and in-service teachers cannot get equal opportunities in pay rise and promotion. Many teachers are frustrated and in some places there is a lack of fresh applicants for a career in bilingual education (Shu Jiexun, 1985). Put simply, it is unlikely to have sound and sustainable development of bilingual education without first addressing the problem of bilingual human resources.

An additional issue is the shortage of bilingual textbooks. For a long time, bilingual textbooks were in fact translated versions of Mandarin Chinese textbooks. They failed to meet the needs of bilingual education because they were not suited to practical situations of minority nationalities. To develop bilingual education, team efforts should be made for the compiling of bilingual textbooks. Textbook compiling should be based on the national syllabus, of course. The basic principle is that textbooks should meet the national requirements of elementary education. However, translated versions of Mandarin Chinese textbooks only reflect the logic of progression for the children of mainstream culture: from the easy to the difficult, from the simple to the profound, and from the concrete to the abstract. They may not address the principles of language learning and cognitive development for the minority children who have developed a different set of background knowledge and thus follow a different route of logical thinking. We would therefore argue that the efforts of an interdisciplinary team formed by ethnologists, linguists, psychologists, educationists, interculturalists, etc., are necessary for the development of cognitively and culturally legitimate textbooks.

Conclusion

Over a long time, there have existed three major issues concerning bilingual education. First, bilingual education was considered only as the implementation of national policy. Second, minority languages were taken only as transitional languages in bilingual education to help the learning of Mandarin Chinese. Third, there was the long-held fear that Mandarin Chinese would gradually replace minority languages (Dai *et al.*, 2000: 183).

With the development of society and economy and the popularization of Mandarin Chinese in minority nationality regions, the value of minority languages is increasingly under questioning. Those who are less good at the majority language find themselves disempowered in various social situations. This phenomenon to a certain extent causes the decline of native language enthusiasm and native language level, especially among young people. In some places, language decline appears. In this process, negative attitudes to minority languages begin to dominate. Some people even mistakenly hold the view that minority languages are being assimilated into Mandarin Chinese and are on the verge of extinction. Others think that minority languages are of no position and there will, sooner or later, be a sudden transition or change from minority languages to Mandarin Chinese. This tendency may appear in a changing society where people attach more importance to economical interest than to the overall balanced development of society and therefore more importance to the "common language" (Mandarin Chinese) than to the minority languages.

On the other hand, with the development of the whole of China, communication and cooperation among different nationalities and exchanges between different nationalities and the world are speeding up. More and more people in minority nationality regions feel an urgent need for bilingual education. They have come to recognize that a good command of bilingualism is needed not only for personal communication but also for learning advanced science and technology. They want to learn modern knowledge. They want to break away from regionalism and go out to contact other nationalities and the outside world.

We have to face these challenges. First of all, we need to be aware, and make the society aware, that bilingual education is by no means a simple matter of language learning. It is an effective way to maintain linguistic identity and develop education for minority nationalities. Second, bilingual education is related closely to national equality and unity. Third, bilingual education is of vital importance to national policies of language, culture, education, politics, and economy. And lastly, it is an important part of internationalization of education, a marked feature of the 21st century.

Theory and practice developed in recent years suggest that research into bilingual education has developed into a new branch of study both at home and abroad in the sense that it has become multidisciplinary and covers many dimensions of social science research. In recent decades, many educators and scholars in China have been researching bilingualism and bilingual education from perspectives of various disciplines, trying to construct systematic theories and concepts concerning bilingualism and bilingual education. The research findings of linguistics, pedagogy, psychology, ethnology, sociopolitical sciences, and even mathematics are being utilized to promote the research of bilingualism and bilingual education. In particular, experimental projects in bilingual education have been providing valuable materials for the theoretical research of bilingual education.

In short, the research of bilingualism and bilingual education is extremely complex and multidimensional. It requires the joint efforts of theorists and practitioners of differing disciplines for its development. We wish to conclude the chapter by quoting Yan's (Yan Xuequn, 1986) philosophical statement that the research "must follow the principles of integrity, relatedness, comprehensiveness, coherence, and synchrony" and "it must be viewed in different ways, statically and dynamically, qualitatively and quantitatively, in depth and in breadth, macroscopically and microscopically."

Note

1. The imperial examination system refers to the nationwide official examination in ancient China started in the Sui dynasty (581–618) and ended in the late Qing dynasty (1644–1911), i.e. in 1905. It was designed to recruit officials through examinations. This system covered a long history (about 1300 years) and has always been a topic of controversy in Chinese academic circle.

References

Cang, Ming (1998) Minguo Yunnan biandi minzu jiaoyu gaikuang [An overview of minority education in border areas in Yunnan during the Republic era]. *Minzu Jiaoyu Yanjiu* [*Ethnic Education Studies*] 35, 72–77.
Chen, Tao (1987) Dui Guizhou minzu jiaoyu tizhi gaige de tantao [An inquiry of the reformation of ethnic educational system in Guizhou province]. *Minzu Jiaoyu* [*Education for Nationalities*] 4, 16–18.
Dai, Qingxia (1992) *Hanyu yu shaoshuminzu yuyan guanxi gailun* [*An Outline of the Relationships between Mandarin Chinese and Minority Nationality Languages*]. Beijing: zhongyang minzu daxue chubanshe [The Central University for Nationalities Press].

Dai, Qingxia *et al.* (1997) *Zhongguo shaoshuminzu shuangyu jiaoyu gailun* [*An Outline of Bilingual Education for Chinese Minority Nationalities*]. Shenyang: Liaoning minzu chubanshe [Liaoning Nationalities Press].

Dai, Qingxia *et al.* (2000) *Zhongguo shaoshuminzu yuyan wenzi yingyong yanjiu* [*Applied Studies of Chinese Minority Nationality Languages and Orthographies*]. Kunming: Yunnan minzu chubanshe [Yunnan Nationalities Press].

Deng, Chenglun (1998) *Yi-han shuangyu jiaoxue yanjiu yu shijian* [*Research and Practice in Yi-Mandarin Chinese Bilingual Education*]. Cheng Du: Shi Chuan minzu chubanshe [Shi Chuan Nationalities Press].

He, Junfang (1998) *Zhongguo shaoshuminzu shuangyu yanjiu* [*Studies of Bilingualism in Chinese Minority Nationality Regions*]. Beijing: zhongyang minzu daxue chubanshe [The Central University for Nationalities Press].

Hu, Gui and Yang, Chunmao (1995) Lisu-han shuangyu jiaoyu yanjiu [A study of Lisu-Mandarin Chinese bilingual education]. In *Yunnan shaoshuminzu shuangyujiaoxue yanjiu* [*Studies of Bilingual Education for Minority Nationalities in Yunnan Province*]. Kunming: Yunnan minzu chubanshe [Yunnan Nationalities Press].

Nurtiyip (1986) Xinjiang minzu jiaoyu de huigu yu zhanwang [Retrospects and prospects of ethnic education in Xinjiang]. *Minzu Jiaoyu* [*Education for Nationalities*] 4, 6–8.

Shu, Jiexun (1985) Tan shaoshuminzu ganxunban de hanyu jiaoxue [On Mandarin Chinese teaching in the minority nationality cadre-training course]. *Zhongyang minzuxueyuan xuebao* [*Journal of the Central University for Nationalities*] 57, 35–37.

Su, Faxiang (1999) Minguo shiqi zangqu jiaoyu gaishu [A brief introduction to Tibetan education in the Republic of China (1912–1949)]. *Minzu Jiaoyu Yanjiu* [*Ethnic Education Studies*] 41, 17–21.

Wang, Huiyin (1990) Woguo weijin nanbeichao shiqi beifang shuangyu xianxiang shuolue [An Introduction to Bilingualism in the Northern Areas of the Kingdom of Wei, the Dynasty of Jin and the Northern and Southern Dynasties]. *In yuyanguanxi yu yuyangongzuo* [*Language Relationships and Language Work*]. Tianjin: Tianjin guji chubanshe [Tianjin Ancient Literature Press].

Yan, Xuequn (1985) *Zhongguo duibi yuyanxue qianshuo* [*An Introduction to Contrastive Linguistics in China*]. Wuhan: huazhong gongxueyuan chubanshe [Central China University of Technology Press].

Yan, Xuequn (1986) Shuangyu jiaoxue yu yanjiu yao zai gaige shang xia liqi (Exertions must be made in bilingual teaching and research reform). *Zhongnan minzuxueyuan xuebao* (*Journal of the South-Central College for Nationalities*), 3, 1–5.

Zhang, Wei (1987) Qiantan shuangyu jiaoyu leixing [A brief introduction to the typology of bilingual education]. *Guizhou minzuyanjiu* [*Ethnic Studies in Guizhou*] 3, 42–44.

Chapter 6

The Juggernaut of Chinese–English Bilingual Education

GUANGWEI HU

A scenario of an information technology class

Teacher: Boys and girls, we are going to give some presentation on our study results, then we shall choose the best group. Are you ready? Ok, please look at the rules.

[*Teacher shows students a table with three budgets for assembling a computer and three aspects of a presentation that will be evaluated.*]

First, let A give their presentation. He represents the investigation group of the computer of ¥6000.

Student A: Please look at our report. [*Student A presents the group work.*] Ask some questions about it.

Student D: Can CPU be made in China now?

Student A: Yes, the first CPU is LongXin.

. . .

I wish the report and reply can help you learn more. Thank you!

Teacher: Thank A. What he said is wonderful. The second one is the investigation group of the computer of ¥8000. B, please.

A summary of a geography class

(1) Show the [English] video of earthquakes.
(2) Ask student to describe [mainly in English] the earthquakes.
(3) Show the [bilingual] Richter Scale of earthquake.
(4) Show the [English] video and help student to understand why did those earthquakes happen?
(5) Let students tell us the reason of earthquakes [either in English or in Chinese].

(6) Show the [all-English] picture of the distribution of the volcanoes and the earthquakes, and show them the location of our city Tianjin.
(7) Ask them are there any major earthquakes happened in China, and let them known some of the major ones [in English].
(8) Let's them discuss [either in English or in Chinese] and find out some way to avoid being hurted, when earthquakes happened.

The two excerpts above give glimpses into what is happening and what non-language subject teachers are expected to do in many classrooms in Mainland China (hereafter China). Both excerpts are taken verbatim from articles authored by practitioners to describe and analyze how they used English as an instructional language. The first one records the opening part of an information technology class in which Junior Secondary 2 students presented their group reports on a project assignment requiring each group to come up with the best plan for assembling a computer on a specified budget (He, 2004: 28). The second excerpt is a summary of the major instructional activities carried out in a Senior Secondary 1 geography class (Zhao, 2002: 61). Both excerpts are intended by their authors to illustrate how English was used successfully as a medium of instruction for a non-language school subject. Content-based English language teaching (ELT), or the use of English as an instructional medium (Brinton *et al.*, 1989), is widely known in China as bilingual education/instruction. This type of bilingual education is distinct from the traditional notion of bilingual education in China, namely the education of ethnic minorities in Chinese and their indigenous languages (Feng, 2005; Ye, 2003; W.J. Zhang, 2002; Zheng, 2004). In this chapter, bilingual education is used, in line with terminological practice in China, to refer to the use of English in teaching a non-language school subject, rather than language education that involves a majority and a minority language.

Although a small number of schools in socioeconomically advantaged areas were exploring the use of English as an instructional medium in the 1990s, large-scale government-supported experimentation with Chinese–English bilingual education started in Shanghai only in 2001 (Lin, 2001; Shen, 2004; Y.P. Zhang, 2003). Within a space of 5 years, this form of bilingual education has gained tremendous publicity and momentum and is sweeping across a country that has until recently taken great pride in its culture and indigenous languages dating back over 5000 years. As Feng (2005: 529–530) observes, "from kindergartens to tertiary institutions, bilingual education has become part of the everyday vocabulary not only of educationists but also of ordinary people." Introduced as a reform initiative to improve the quality of ELT, bilingual education has been controversial from the beginning (Liu, 2002; Nian *et al.*, 2002; Zheng, 2004). Advocates hail it as the vanguard of educational reform, a key component of quality education, and a vital means for China to interface with the rest of the world (Qian, 2003; Sun, 2002; Wen, 2001; Zheng *et al.*, 2006). Opponents, however, argue that there exist a myriad of constraints that undermine, compromise, and frustrate the optimistically envisioned goals for bilingual education (Lu, 2002; X.J. Wang, 2003; Xie & Wang, 2002). Furthermore, they are concerned with the possible negative educational and cultural consequences that may follow from promotion of mass bilingual education (Hou, 2000; Li, 2006; K.Q. Xu, 2004; Ye, 2002; Zhai, 2003; P. Zhang, 2002). Although the intense debate engendered by the reform initiative is ongoing, bilingual programs are mushrooming across China. Apparently, it is an understatement to refer to the drive for bilingual education as a "bandwagon"; it is more appropriate to describe it as a "juggernaut," in the sense of the word as used by Giddens (1990) in his critique of modernity.

This chapter presents a critical analysis of Chinese–English bilingual education in the Chinese context. It is divided into four major sections. The first section provides a brief overview of the background against which bilingual education has been promoted as a major reform initiative to improve the provision and quality of ELT in the basic education sector of the Chinese education system. The section then describes the extent to which bilingual education is staking out its territory in the educational landscape, looks at various instructional models currently in use, and discusses the commonly perceived constraints on bilingual education in China. This is followed by a close look at bilingual programs developed and implemented by two schools in Shanghai. The third section examines the driving forces behind the bilingual education craze, focusing on the modernization discourse, the academic discourse, and the self-interests of stakeholders. The final section draws on Bourdieu's (1986, 1991) sociological theory to critique the educational, economic, and sociocultural consequences of Chinese–English bilingual education in China.

Bilingual Education in China: Background, Scale, Models, and Constraints

The historical background

Shortly after the decade-long Cultural Revolution was brought to an end upon the death of Mao Zedong in 1976, the post-Mao Chinese leadership adopted the twin policies of reform and opening up and launched a national modernization program (Ross, 1993). The new leadership was convinced that China would need a large pool of English-proficient personnel to ensure its access to worldwide scientific and technological advances in its modernization drive. This conviction led to a persistent top-down endeavor to expand the provision, and improve the quality, of ELT in the last 30 years (Adamson & Morris, 1997; Hu, 2002). Despite a constant lack of ELT resources, the grade level at which formal English instruction is provided has been lowered successively from Junior Secondary 1 to the upper primary grades to Primary 3 nationwide and Primary 1 in socioeconomically advantaged areas (Hu, 2005b). By 2004, there were about 80 million junior and senior secondary students and 50 million primary students learning English in the school system (Hu, 2005a). Along with the expansion of English provision, efforts have also been made to raise the quality of English instruction through a range of reforms carried out in areas of curriculum development, syllabus design, textbook production, teacher training, and pedagogy (Adamson & Morris, 1997; Hu, 2002). These efforts have led to considerable improvement in the English proficiency of students progressing through the education system (Gill, 2004; Hu, 2005a).

The rising standard of English instruction has, however, fallen short of expectations, and since the late 1980s there have been mounting criticisms of the quality of English provision. At a debriefing by English-language educators, Li Lanqing, then Deputy Prime Minister in charge of education, characterized foreign language teaching in China as "costly and ineffective" (cited in K.Q. Xu, 2004: 87) and called for more effective pedagogical approaches. Li's comment fuelled public criticisms of the school system's failure to turn out students with good English proficiency (Wen, 2001). There were frequent complaints that after studying English for years, fresh university graduates could not even carry out simple communication in the language, and they were said to have ended up with a "deaf and mute" English (Du, 2002; H.D. Jiang, 2002; Lin, 2001; Sun, 2002). It was partly in response to these criticisms that experimentation with Chinese–English bilingual education started in the socioeconomically advantaged areas and caught much public attention (Liu, 2002; Y.P. Zhang, 2003). The content-based ELT programs offered in these places were not a language teaching novelty in China, as claimed by many advocates. In the second half of the 19th century, both Chinese and foreign languages were used as instructional mediums in institutions of foreign languages and military-technical schools set up during the Self-Strengthening Movement and in missionary schools spreading across China (Fu, 1986; Ross, 1993; F.J. Zhang, 2003). In later years, those schools were viewed as tools of Western colonization, enslavement, and spiritual contamination, and the use of a foreign language as an instructional medium did not survive the founding of the People's Republic in 1949. It is ironic that half a century later, with a conceptual twist,

English-medium instruction began to be actively explored as an effective ELT approach to facilitate China's modernization.

The 1990s saw only isolated efforts to offer bilingual instruction in a few large urban centers. Several early programs were reportedly successful. These included a bilingual science program developed by Peizheng Middle School in Guangzhou in 1993 (Wu, 1997), a similar one run by the secondary school affiliated to East China Normal University in Shanghai (Li *et al.*, 2003), a bilingual elective science program initiated at Shanghai Secondary School in 1992 (Lin, 2001), a primary-level program offered by the 21st Century Experimental School in Beijing (Zhu, 2000), and the China–Canada Collaborative English Immersion Program developed by a team of university-based Chinese and Canadian language educators in 1997 and implemented at selected kindergartens and primary schools in Xi'an (Qiang & Zhao, 2000). These programs shared a number of features. First, virtually all the schools involved were prestigious, well-resourced schools known for their competent teaching staff and high-caliber students. Second, nearly all the schools had long-established connections with domestic tertiary institutions or overseas educational institutions. Third, most of the programs were developed in partnership with overseas-based organizations or individuals. The overseas partners provided strong support in the form of teacher training, program design, and learning materials. Some programs were even staffed by native English speakers. Although the successful stories of these programs contributed to a rising interest in bilingual education, the "prairie fire" of bilingual education would not have blazed so rapidly and with such ferocity without the active involvement of the Shanghai municipal government.

The scramble for bilingual education

Shanghai was one of the several socioeconomically advantaged regions for which curricular autonomy was allowed by the central government in the late 1980s. It was entrusted with, among other things, the task of pioneering reform in ELT (Hu, 2005a). In response, the Shanghai Education Commission started a two-phase curricular reform project (Hu, 2002). In the first phase (1988–1998), curricular time for ELT was drastically raised, the grade at which ELT started was lowered from Primary 5 to Primary 1, and the *Oxford English* series was introduced to replace the existing textbooks. At the close of the first phase, however, the Education Commission felt that those curricular changes were not sufficient to "develop world-class foreign language teaching programs" which would be "a prerequisite for turning the municipality into a world-class international metropolis" (cited in Hu, 2002: 33). The Education Commission turned its attention to the experimental programs of bilingual instruction being undertaken by a few schools in the city, was impressed by their results, and decided to encourage experimentation with bilingual instruction in its action plan for phase-2 curricular reform (Hu, 2002). This initiative led to the expansion of bilingual programs into eight schools in 2000 (Su, 2003c).

The Education Commission stepped up its effort to expand bilingual programs in 2001, when a ministerial directive required that, within 3 years, 5–10% of undergraduate courses in institutions of higher learning must be taught in English (Ministry of Education, 2001). Taking the directive as the central government's support for bilingual education, the Education Commission required all its district educational departments to work out plans for experimentation with bilingual education. As a result, nearly 100 kindergartens, primary schools, and secondary schools set up bilingual programs in the autumn of 2001 (Lin, 2001). The media were mobilized to report on the experimental efforts at the schools. Subsequently, experimental bilingual programs snowballed to involve about 30,000 students in 2002 (Su, 2003a), 45,000 in 260 schools in 2003 (Su, 2003c), and 55,000 in 2004 (M. Xu, 2004). Recently, the Education Commission announced its plan to increase the number of bilingual teachers from 2,000 to about 10,000, of bilingual schools from 260 to 500, and of students attending bilingual programs from 55,000 to 500,000 by 2010 (Shen, 2004).

Local governments in other parts of China were not content to watch Shanghai's "great leap forward" for bilingual education. Provincial departments of education in Guangdong, Liaoning, and Shandong at once staged "100 bilingual education schools" projects (Song & Yan, 2004). Other provinces and cities scrambled to set up their own bilingual programs (Li *et al.*, 2004). In the process, numerous public and private kindergartens and schools that totally lacked the means of providing even an apology for a watered-down version of bilingual education joined the stampede and declared themselves bilingual overnight (Gui, 2004; Liu, 2002; Nian *et al.*, 2002; Xie & Wang, 2002). Today, bilingual programs can be found almost anywhere, for all school subjects, and at all levels of education. Some schools have even turned Chinese language and Chinese history into bilingual courses (Xie & Wang, 2002; F.J. Zhang, 2003). No one knows how many students are receiving "bilingual education" across the country. And there is no sign that the enthusiasm for bilingual education will abate.

Models of bilingual education

As local governments fear that they may fall behind in the bilingual education scramble, few bother to establish any quality control over the mushrooming bilingual programs and many take a *laissez-faire* stance toward the issue of what models of bilingual education to adopt. The result is a wide range of bilingual education models that vary in program goals, the proportions of time allocated to the two languages on the curriculum and in the classroom, the school subjects chosen for bilingual instruction, the grade levels at which bilingual programs are run, and so on (Su, 2003a). Beneath these variations, however, a few general considerations are discernable in the literature on bilingual education. These considerations concern the relative difficulty, complexity, and potential consequences for teachers to teach, and students to learn, a subject bilingually. The typical progression followed by most schools is from easy to difficult, from simple to complex, and from low- to high-stakes subjects. This general progression is reflected in several trends.

Firstly, most schools offer bilingual programs to students at lower- rather than upper-grade levels (Zhu, 2003). This is particularly true of secondary schools. For example, few schools run bilingual programs for students at Junior or Senior Secondary 3 who are faced with promotion or college entrance examinations. This is a telling pattern: it says a great deal about the schools' confidence in the quality of their bilingual programs despite public claims to the contrary. Secondly, most schools seem to take into account the nature of curricular content when deciding which subjects go bilingual. Thus, it is electives rather than core subjects that are typically chosen for bilingual instruction (Pi, 2004; P. Zhang, 2002). Similarly, activity courses (e.g. physical education, music, and arts) are more likely to be conducted bilingually than those that require more use of language (e.g. social studies, economics, and world history). It is also more likely for sciences than the humanities to be taught bilingually (Shen, 2004; Su, 2003a; P. Zhang, 2002). Furthermore, few schools develop bilingual programs for curricular subjects that are tested in promotion or other high-stakes examinations (P. Zhang, 2002). Thirdly, there are incremental increases in, or expected progressive expansions of, the use, scope, and functions of English in classroom instruction. This gives rise to four different patterns of language use across the bilingual programs. Type A is characterized by the use of Chinese for teaching subject content, with the use of English being restricted to classroom management and, sometimes, to translation of selected concepts, formulae, and definitions (Yang, 2005). In the case of Type B, Chinese is still the dominant medium of instruction, though English is used more frequently than in Type A to provide supplementary explanation, description, exemplification, etc. (B.H. Wang, 2003). Type C is a reversal of Type B in that English is more frequently used as an instructional language, with Chinese being used for explication of difficult and complex content (Chi & Zhao, 2004; Qiang & Zhao, 2000). Finally, Type

D is characterized by almost exclusive use of English for instruction (B.H Wang, 2003). Language use patterns in most bilingual programs fall into the categories of Types A and B. Types C and D are found only in bilingual programs offered by a small number of well-resourced elite schools.

There is considerable terminological confusion with respect to the labels used to designate bilingual programs distinguished by the four types of language use pattern. Types A and B programs are often referred to as "maintenance" programs, and Types C and D programs as "transitional" ones (B.H. Wang, 2003). However, Types B and C programs sometimes are also labeled "partial immersion," while Type D programs are called "(total) immersion" (Jin & Zhuang, 2002). Clearly, the labels are borrowed from bilingual programs in North America. The wholesale borrowing of these terms reflects either a very superficial understanding of the nature of various bilingual education programs in North America or a disregard for fundamental political, ideological, economic, and sociocultural differences between the North American and Chinese contexts of language education (see Brinton *et al.*, 1989; Cummins, 1998; Grinberg & Saavedra, 2000; Lyons, 1990; McGroarty, 1992).

Constraints on bilingual education in China

The majority of bilingual programs are fraught with intractable difficulties. In fact, both advocates and opponents recognize the many constraints on bilingual education in China. The two groups, however, differ in one crucial respect: advocates are optimistic that there are ways to address the constraints, whereas opponents contend that these constraints are incapacitating and extremely difficult, if not impossible, to overcome or alleviate. A survey of the literature reveals the most often mentioned constraints as follows.

The most extensively discussed constraint is an acute shortage of bilingual teachers (Gui, 2004; Luo & Liu, 2006; Zhang & Liu, 2005). Because the Chinese teacher education system did not run bilingual teacher education programs until very recently (Du, 2002), most teachers staffing bilingual programs have been trained to be either subject teachers or teachers of English as a foreign language (Jin & Zhuang, 2002; W.J. Zhang, 2002). Thus, they lack systematic training either in subject content or in English, let alone pedagogy of bilingual education. Typically, the teachers do not have the oral or academic language competence to teach non-language subjects bilingually. Opponents of bilingual education argue that teachers' lack of proficiency in English defeats the purposes of bilingual education and seriously compromises the quality of instruction (Jiao, 2004). Advocates, however, advance the counterargument that qualified bilingual teachers can only "emerge in the process of bilingual instruction" (Shen, 2004: 2). They also advocate various solutions, many of which are measures of expediency, to cope with teacher shortages: (1) having a subject teacher team up with an English-language teacher in lesson preparation and classroom instruction, (2) sending subject teachers with relatively good English proficiency to intensive English courses run at home or abroad, (3) providing crash subject courses for English-language teachers who are reasonably good at non-language subjects, (4) "luring" returnees trained in English-speaking countries, (5) recruiting native English speakers from abroad and expatriates living in the country (e.g. overseas students studying in Chinese universities or family members of expatriates working in China), and (5) setting up and expanding bilingual education programs in teacher training institutions (Du, 2002; H.D. Jiang, 2002; Jin & Zhuang, 2002; Li, 2004; Zhu, 2003). Clearly, some of these measures can create more problems than they can solve, while others either take time to implement or entail heavy spending, something that only the small number of prestigious resource-rich schools can afford to do.

Another major constraint has to do with learning materials (Liu, 2002; Shen & Feng, 2005; W.J. Zhang, 2002). Due to a shotgun approach to bilingual education and because of the great diversity of the bilingual programs in operation, appropriate instructional materials are in dire shortage, though domestic and overseas publishers have recently quickened their pace to fill the market niche (Kexue Shibao, 2003; Su, 2003b). The learning materials used for bilingual instruction come from various sources. Well-resourced elite schools typically purchase textbooks published overseas for students in English-speaking countries (Lin, 2001). Many of them are also provided with free textbooks by overseas-based organizations or alumni/alumnae (Pi, 2004; Wu, 1997). Other schools either adopt the few available translated versions of the existing textbook series or ask their teachers to develop their own learning materials (L. Jiang, 2002; Lin, 2001; Y.P. Zhang, 2003). In the latter case, teachers adopt strategies ranging from translating parts of current textbooks written in Chinese to culling materials from textbooks published overseas to putting together materials gleaned from various sources, for example, the Internet (Wu, 1997). There are various problems with learning materials thus sourced (Gui, 2004). Textbooks published overseas cost more than most schools and students can afford, and they often mismatch the Chinese context with respect to curricular requirements, ideological underpinnings, political orientations, and sociocultural content (Li *et al.*, 2003; P. Zhang, 2002). Textbooks translated from those published originally in Chinese are more often than not plagued by the problem of "inauthentic" English (Li, 2004; P. Zhang, 2002). Teacher-developed materials tend to lack systematicity and are not subject to any quality control (Li *et al.*, 2003). Advocates of bilingual education concede these problems but are optimistic that the situation will improve (B.H. Wang, 2003; Zhu, 2003).

A third major constraint is that China lacks a sociolinguistic environment for Chinese–English bilingual education (W.J. Zhang, 2002; Zhu, 2003). Opponents point out that English is neither a working language nor a second language in China and there is hardly any need for using English for sociocultural purposes (Jiao, 2004). Advocates agree that the sociolinguistic context of China is not conducive to English learning but counterargue that it is precisely because of the lack of social use of English that schools should provide a bilingual environment to enable students to develop high English proficiency (H.D. Jiang, 2002). They suggest that to make up for the lack of a favorable sociolinguistic environment, schools should spare no means to create an "English" environment. Thus, schools should be filled with English songs, set an English Day, organize English carnivals, hold English contests, conduct flag-raising and oath-taking ceremonies in English, show English movies, broadcast English radio/TV programs, and paint every wall with English (W.J. Zhang, 2002; Z.F. Zhang, 2003; Zheng *et al.*, 2006; Zhao, 2002). Some schools have indeed done so (L. Jiang, 2002; Xinwen Chenbao, 2003; Y.P. Zhang, 2003). Obviously, to create and maintain such English-rich environments requires financial resources and has important sociocultural implications which are totally ignored by the advocates.

Another constraint concerns students' lack of a threshold proficiency in English to benefit from bilingual education (Gui, 2004). Ye (2002) likens secondary students' English proficiency to chicken wings that cannot propel them up into the bilingual education sky. Strangely, Li *et al.* (2003) suggest that the problem can be solved by raising students' proficiency through the teaching of English as a school subject. One cannot but wonder: if the English-subject course can achieve this, why should bilingual education be promoted in the first place? Other constraints and issues raised in the literature include (1) the lack of a coherent curricular structure to coordinate bilingual programs offered at different levels of education (W.J. Zhang, 2002), (2) misunderstandings of the nature, objectives, and means of bilingual education (Y.P. Zhang, 2003; Zhang & Liu, 2005; Zheng, 2004), (3) the absence of curriculum standards to guide program development (Liu, 2002), and (4) the lack of an evaluative mechanism to enforce quality control. On top of all these issues, there is the question of whether Chinese–English bilingual education is legal in China (Li, 2006; Xie & Wang, 2002).

Strictly speaking, bilingual education, especially the immersion types, violates the National Language Law enacted in 2001 and the Compulsory Education Law enacted in 1986, both of which stipulate the Chinese language as the medium of instruction in educational settings. Some advocates (e.g. Huang, 2005) are aware of the illegality of Chinese–English bilingual education and are calling for amendments to the relevant laws.

Bilingual Education Programs at Two Schools

By way of fleshing out the general discussion above, this section describes in some detail the bilingual education programs developed and implemented at two schools in Shanghai, the locomotive of bilingual education in China. The description is based on two case studies reported in Pi (2004).

School A was a senior secondary school. As a "municipal key school" with a strong contingent of well-trained teachers and excellent facilities, it had won numerous national and municipal awards for its quality education and was a research site for the municipality's English Curricular Reform Project. The school had a long tradition of giving priority to its ELT. It had an English school newspaper, an English radio program, an English TV station, an English club, and an "English-Speaking Corner." Pushed forward by the school leadership, School A's first bilingual education program came into being in 2001. This program was a collaborative effort between School A and Texas Instruments, a US international company specializing in classroom technology. The latter supplied the learning materials and equipment for the program and provided language training to the Chinese teachers staffing the program. However, Chinese-language textbooks were also used for complex and difficult topics that would require technically sophisticated explanation. While initially the program involved only one school subject, later it was extended to cover four subjects: mathematics, physics, chemistry, and environmental protection. Each subject on the program was allocated 2–3 hours of classroom instruction per week and was offered as an elective only to students at Senior Secondary 1. Every year, about 100 applicants with good listening and speaking competence in English were selected for the program. Each elective was team-taught by a Chinese subject teacher and an expatriate language teacher. If the Chinese teacher had good English competence, he/she cotaught the subject with the expatriate teacher in the first half of the first semester, with the latter being responsible for "clearing the language barriers" for the students. The Chinese teacher then taught the course solo for the remaining time. In the case of a Chinese subject teacher with a less than satisfactory command of English, the two cotaught every lesson throughout the school year.

School A had a second bilingual program, put in place 6 months after the program described above. Again, this program started as a collaborative effort between the school and a US nonprofit organization, Junior Achievement. The program was an elective economics course offered to Senior Secondary 1 students who survived screening tests of English and computer skills. Junior Achievement provided free textbooks, computer software, and volunteer "teachers and tutors," most of whom were Junior Achievement members in Shanghai. School A assigned three collaborating teachers to the program and invited expatriate members of the Shanghai Entrepreneurs Association to give seminars to the students on a monthly basis.

School A also had independently developed bilingual courses: an elective titled "Fun Mathematics" for selected Senior Secondary 2 students and an elective in "History/Chinese Culture" for Senior Secondary 1 students. Both courses were taught with learning materials developed or compiled by teachers at School A. Like the teachers assigned to the other two programs, the teachers responsible for these courses were young teachers who had a relatively strong command of English. Despite their reasonably good English proficiency, they reported considerable difficulty teaching in English. To overcome the difficulty, the school leadership encouraged teachers from the English Department to help the subject teachers practice and improve their oral English. In addition, because of the school's connection with a normal university, teachers of the bilingual courses were able to attend the university's oral English courses for free. In 2002, the school sent its first batch of six teachers to overseas institutions for language training.

How well did School A's bilingual education programs fare? Questionnaire and interview data collected from the teachers staffing the bilingual programs revealed highly divided opinions. Some teachers were full of praise for the bilingual programs, claiming that they had contributed to students' greater motivation to learn English, improved English proficiency, increased English vocabulary, better study skills, and development in other respects. Other teachers, however, were less positive and commented that bilingual instruction had compelled them to reduce curricular content and had had a negative effect on their students' subject learning. One teacher complained that students lacked the specialized vocabulary to study content subjects in English, the reading ability to understand learning materials in English, and the oral proficiency to communicate in English. Another teacher commented that teacher–student interaction in English left much to be desired, with the result that students suffered in subject learning and experienced little significant improvement in English. The teachers also pointed out that although the various training courses they had attended helped them improve their oral English proficiency, the training had been far from enough and had done little to prepare them to teach content subjects bilingually. Finally, the principal acknowledged the lack of financial resources as a major constraint on expanding bilingual education in the school. Because of financial difficulties, he had to defer the plan of giving financial incentives to his bilingual teachers.

School B was an ordinary junior secondary school. In terms of school facilities and staff quality, School B could not hold a candle to School A. The school was pressurized to provide bilingual education because of a new policy adopted by the district department of education in 2001. According to the policy, provision of bilingual education would constitute a major criterion for evaluation of schools. The principal understood what the new policy would entail for his school and persuaded other members of the school leadership to support his plan to offer bilingual courses. Subsequently, he called a staff meeting and exhorted every staff member to work hard and "push the school up to a higher rung" by offering bilingual courses. Two school subjects were then chosen for experimentation with bilingual instruction in the autumn of 2001: music for students in the preparatory classes and at Junior Secondary 2; integrated science for students in the preparatory classes and at Junior Secondary 1.

As it was an initial attempt to offer bilingual instruction, School B did not make any requirement about the extent to which Chinese and English should be used as instructional mediums. The teachers were only asked to use English "at their discretion." The music course was offered only to classes with relatively good English proficiency, whereas the science course was open to all students in the preparatory classes and at Junior Secondary 1. The learning materials for the music course were prepared by the teacher herself, and the *Oxford English* Series (Shanghai edition) was selected for use with the science course. Classroom observations and an interview with the music teacher revealed that English was not used in all lessons but on a sporadic basis. As a matter of fact, only in lessons open to observation was English used as an instructional medium. In one such lesson, the teacher used simple English for classroom management and gave the English names of some musical instruments but switched to Chinese to impart knowledge about symphonies, the topic of the lesson. According to the teacher, bilingual education in the music course was realized mainly through teaching classic English songs (with the lyrics provided in both English and Chinese) and using English to organize instruction. An interview with the science teacher indicated that he taught mainly in

Chinese. These two were the only teachers involved in bilingual education in School B, and neither of them had received any formal in-service training in English or bilingual instruction.

Both the music teacher and the science teacher were less positive about bilingual education than some of their counterparts at School A. Although she felt that bilingual education was conducive to her own professional development, the music teacher reported that some students were very weak in English and could not understand her lessons. The science teacher, who taught 15 hours a week, complained that bilingual instruction required more time for lesson preparation and was worried about the effect of this added workload on his professional development. Explaining why he used a minimum of English in his instruction, he said that he had to choose between spending a large portion of class time preteaching English technical terms and finishing the required curricular content.

It is clear from the above description that School B was not equipped adequately to offer bilingual instruction. School B is not an isolated example; numerous schools in other places do not fare any better than School B in their attempts to offer bilingual education (Lin, 2003). If all but a small number of elite schools lack the resources for bilingual education, why have schools been turning "bilingual" in droves?

Driving Forces Behind the Bilingual Education Craze

Several driving forces have been behind "the great leap forward" for bilingual education. They are an entrenched modernization discourse that links national development to English proficiency, an academic discourse that embraces bilingual education unreflectively, and the vested interests of stakeholders and major players in the field.

The modernization discourse

As mentioned earlier, the modernization discourse giving great prominence to mastery of English emerged in the late 1970s under the post-Mao leadership headed by Deng Xiaoping. The linkage of English to China's modernization was initially formulated by Deng and can be summarized as follows: (1) China must modernize itself to survive in the modern world; (2) advanced science and technology held the key to China's modernization; (3) the scientific knowledge base needed for China's modernization was constituted by advances worldwide; (4) English was the international medium of scientific and technological information; and (5) consequently, to have a large pool of English-proficient personnel would be vital to

China's modernization drive (Hu, 2005a). This formulation of the relationship between English and China's modernization drive has since become a truism and has been extended to give English an ever greater role, concomitant with the growing momentum and quickening pace of the modernization endeavor in the last 30 years.

The all-encompassing discourse of modernization has been the very _raison d'être_ for the public advocacy of bilingual education in China. It has been used to justify bilingual education with specific reference to China's increasing economic, educational, and cultural contact with other parts of the world (H.D. Jiang, 2002); the globalization of economic and educational undertakings (Feng, 2002; Li _et al._, 2003); the ever growing importance of English as the leading international language (Zhu, 2003); the emergence of knowledge-based economies (Wen, 2001; W.J. Zhang, 2002); developed countries' adoption of bilingual education (Yu & Han, 2003; Y.P. Zhang, 2003); the need for China to "interface with the world" (Zhou, 2004) and to gain access to the "Information Highway" (Qiang & Zhao, 2000); the need for China to have multitalented human resources to remain competitive in the 21st century (Huang, 2005; Shen & Feng, 2005); China's accession to the World Trade Organization and the ensuing challenges it must face (Sun, 2002; Wang & Wang, 2003); Beijing's successful bid for the 2008 Olympics (Zhao, 2002); and Shanghai's effort to become an international metropolis (Zhu, 2003). To illustrate the importance of English proficiency, H.D. Jiang (2003) gives an example which is repeatedly cited by other advocates of bilingual education. According to him, India exported US$4.6 billion worth of software products in 1999, in contrast to the US$50 million worth of software products sold by China. Jiang claims that China did not lose out to India because of its software technology but because of Indians' better English proficiency. The moral of the story, to advocates of bilingual education, is that every Chinese child must learn English, and learn it well, so that China can catch up in terms of development with countries where English is widely spoken. Thus, the importance of English for China is blown out of proportion.

The modernization discourse stressing the crucial role of English proficiency in national development does not bear close scrutiny. It reflects an outdated, lopsided view and blurs the distinction between language and development, elevating English from an international language for development to the language of development (Hu, 2005b). In actuality, no evidence exists for a correlation between national development and proficiency in English. It is not difficult to find countries (e.g. India) that possess greater English proficiency than China but are economically less vibrant and developmentally far behind China. Dor (2004: 102) presents convincing evidence that "the very process of economic globalization has by now detached itself from the dynamics of Englishization and has adopted a much more sophisticated, multilingual strategy." China itself provides the best support for Dor's thesis. Despite intensive domestic criticisms of its education system's failure to turn out citizens with good English proficiency, China has seen an average annual growth rate of more than 9% in the last quarter century, its GDP increased by 20 folds from 1980 to 2000, and in 2001 it had 370,000 foreign-invested businesses (Cai, 2001). Nearly 400 of the world's top 500 multinational corporations had streamed into China by 2002, and for 7 years in succession China had attracted the most foreign investment among the developing countries (Lin, 2002). All these would not have happened if China, as the modernization discourse claims, had depended vitally on English for its development.

The academic discourse

If the modernization discourse has foisted an exaggerated importance of English on China, the prevalent academic discourse has misinformed the public with its biases, misconceptions, and misinterpretations of research on bilingual education at home and abroad. As a result, it has dismissed, in a mistaken and irresponsible manner, doubts about bilingual education as a viable and effective alternative to raise the effectiveness of English instruction. A close scrutiny of the academic discourse on bilingual education reveals a number of problems. Due to space constraints, only three will be discussed here.

To begin with, the academic discourse paints a rosy picture of bilingual education in other parts of the world, especially in the developed countries. Advocates of bilingual education (e.g. Chi & Zhao, 2004; H.D. Jiang, 2003; Qiang & Zhao, 2000; Sun, 2002; Yu & Han, 2003) frequently cite Canada, the United States, Australia, Japan, Singapore, Hong Kong, and other developed countries or regions as examples of successful bilingual education without ever discussing the many controversies and problems surrounding bilingual education policies and practices in these places (see Gopinathan, 1998; Grinberg & Saavedra, 2000; Gu & Dong, 2005; Lyons, 1990; Secada, 1990). For example, many of them have hailed Canadian French Immersion and Singapore's bilingual education practices as resounding successes and presented them as models for China to emulate, but few have mentioned, even in passing, such problems as the high dropout rates found in Canadian immersion programs (Cummins, 1998) and Chinese Singaporeans' accelerating shift to English in all domains of language use at the expense of their mother tongue (Gopinathan, 1998), a consequence feared by many opponents of bilingual education in China. The academic discourse is also guilty of only reporting and, in many cases, misinterpreting those findings from research conducted outside China that favor bilingual education. For instance, citing early research done in Canada and the United States (e.g. Peal & Lambert, 1962) that indicates *potential* positive effects of bilingualism on children's cognitive development, many academics (e.g. H.D. Jiang, 2003; Qiang & Zhao, 2000; Wen, 2001; Zhu, 2003) claim that extensive research has shown that bilingual or multilingual children *have* greater cognitive flexibility, better competence in making judgments, a stronger capacity for divergent thinking, better learning skills, greater linguistic sensitivity, stronger comprehension, better cross-cultural understanding, and so forth. These academics present as factual information potential benefits that may be reaped under optimal conditions and perhaps when a high-threshold level of bilingualism is attained (Cummins, 1979). It is also very common for academics to cite reports that suggest effectiveness of bilingual education programs but totally ignore those that indicate otherwise (e.g. Rossell & Baker, 1996). Furthermore, although research findings in favor of bilingual education are frequently adduced to dismiss concerns about potential negative effects on academic achievement of instruction through a second/foreign language, it is seldom made clear that much of the cited research did not make comparisons between language-minority students on bilingual programs and mainstream students instructed in their first language but compared language-minority students on language programs varying in terms of the use of their mother tongue as an instructional medium (see Greene, 1998; Willig, 1985).

Another and related problem with the academic discourse concerns various misconceptions of bilingual education. A few examples would suffice to illustrate this problem. First, quite a few advocates (e.g. H.D. Jiang, 2002; B.H. Wang, 2003) embrace the discredited "time on task" claim. According to this claim, the more and the earlier children are exposed to a second or foreign language as a medium of instruction, the more successful their language learning experience would be. Research, however, has shown that it is not just the quantity but, more importantly, the quality of exposure that matters (see Cummins, 1999). Second, some supporters of bilingual education fail to distinguish theoretical hypotheses from empirical findings or base their arguments for bilingual education on controversial or discredited theoretical speculations, such as the Critical Age Hypothesis, the Acquisition-Learning Hypothesis, and the distinction between integrative and instrumental motivation (Deng & Jiang, 2001; Qiang & Zhao, 2000; Wen, 2001; W.J. Zhang, 2002; L. Zhao, 2004). Third, some researchers aggrandize the benefits of bilingual competence. Qian (2003: 53), for example, claims that bilingual education "gives one an extra pair of eyes and ears, one more mouth, and even an additional brain" and that it plays a key role in developing "modern global citizens with a perfect character." Fourth, quite a number of advocates claim that bilingual education will not affect Chinese children's first language development on the grounds that they live in a Chinese-dominant environment and study Chinese as a subject at school (Shen, 2004; Zhu, 2003). These people are clearly unaware that what is at stake is advanced first-language literacy, especially academic language competence, which takes systematic instruction and use in academic contexts to develop (Cummins, 1999). As a final example, some advocates cite successful stories of bilingual programs in the United States to justify bilingual education in China, without realizing that such programs have been developed mainly to raise language-minority students' academic achievement through provision of instruction in their dominant language (Lyons, 1990; Swain, 1978). While many US bilingual programs have been developed to foster academic achievement by reducing language barriers faced by minority students with limited English proficiency, bilingual programs in China are creating language barriers for students by making them study in a language in which they have only limited proficiency.

Last but not least, the academic discourse is long on claims and short on empirical research in China (Gu & Dong, 2005; Zheng, 2004). In his survey of articles on Chinese–English bilingual instruction published in Chinese academic journals between 1994 and 2003, Zheng (2004) noted that the majority of reports on bilingual education practices actually gave no clear or detailed description of what was happening in classrooms. Most of these reports followed the same pattern: a description of students' positive responses to the researcher-cum-practitioner's initiative to adopt bilingual instruction, a narrative of the latter's painstaking effort to prepare and teach in English, and a selective presentation of anecdotal evidence suggesting students' impressive progress in English. Worse still, most of the small number of evaluation studies on the effects of bilingual education conducted in China and given much hype in the academic discourse were egregiously flawed in design, were aimed ostensibly at finding favorable results, and overinterpreted or misinterpreted research findings. For instance, in an evaluation of the kindergarten-level implementation of the China–Canada Collaborative English Immersion Program, L. Zhao (2004) reports that the research team asked a kindergarten immersion group, a junior secondary group, and a senior secondary group to respond to two statements: (1) "I like learning English" and (2) "I think that my English is good." L. Zhao presents the preponderance of affirmative responses by the kindergarten group (95% in both cases) as evidence of the effectiveness of the immersion program. The author also makes much of questionable anecdotal evidence—for example, parents frequently reported that their kindergarteners spoke English even in their dreams; a little girl in dispute with a little boy was observed to challenge her opponent to debate in English, and not to be outdone, the boy accepted the challenge. Rather than interpreting the observed incident as showing how good the two children were at English, as L. Zhao does, it seems more plausible to suggest that they chose to debate in English for any reason but their "good" English proficiency, because it is questionable that they could argue more effectively in English—a language they had been exposed to for only 2–3 hours a day for less than 2 years—than in their mother tongue.

In another evaluation study on the same program, Qiang and Zhao (2000) report that after a weekly 15 hours of immersion in English for a year, the primary students acquired an active vocabulary of 400 words and a passive vocabulary of 600 words. The researchers go on to claim that the students were able to "think in English." Furthermore, they report that most experimental groups ranked top at their grades in Chinese and mathematics; that children in the experimental groups were found to be livelier, more open-minded, more creative, more responsive, more intelligent, more confident, more active, and fonder of thinking than their control counterparts; and that an experimental kindergarten group was even found to be significantly taller and heavier than its control group. It really stretches one's imagination to see the connection between bilingual education and physical development. Equally "amazing" results have been found by a large-scale evaluation project conducted in Shanghai that involved hundreds of schools. The project is reported to find that *all* students receiving bilingual instruction outperformed *all* students receiving no such instruction in *all* school subjects and on *both* written and oral tests of English and Chinese (Xinwen Chenbao, 2003). As unreliable and exaggerated as they are, such research results are widely publicized and eagerly used as evidence to support policy initiatives.

The academic discourse is not free of interests. In fact, many contributions to the academic discourse have come from stakeholders and key players with vested interests in the provision of bilingual education. It is to these vested interests that the following section turns.

Vested interests

Bourdieu's (1986, 1991) concepts of *field*, *capital*, and *distinction* offer a sociological vocabulary for analyzing, and a useful framework for interpreting, the various vested interests in bilingual education. In Bourdieu's theory of social practice, "field" (used interchangeably with "market") refers to a structured social space in which individuals or institutions act. This structured multidimensional space is "constructed on the basis of principles of differentiation or distribution constituted by the set of properties active in the social universe under consideration" (1991: 229). The properties current in a field are material and immaterial resources, or various forms of *capital*, that "govern its functioning in a durable way, determining the chances of success for practices" (1986: 242). Thus, individuals or groups are "distributed . . . according to the overall volume of the capital they possess and . . . the relative weight of the different kinds of capital in the total set of their assets" (1991: 231). For this reason, a field is also an arena of struggles in which the occupants seek to preserve or change the status quo, that is, the current distribution of capital. The composition and volume of capital, "like trumps in a game of cards, are powers which define the chances of profit in a given field" (1991: 230).

According to Bourdieu, there are four major forms of capital. *Economic capital* is comprised of material goods and resources that can be quantified and thus have numerical values in the form of money. It can be accumulated, bequeathed, and invested. *Cultural capital* consists of knowledge, competencies, and other cultural resources that individuals come to possess. The acquisition and accumulation of cultural capital require socialization and inculcation as well as investment of time and economic capital. Cultural capital "derives a scarcity value" and "yields profits of distinction for its owner" (1986: 245). *Social capital* "is the aggregate of the actual or potential resources which are linked to possession of a durable network of more or less institutionalized relationships of mutual acquaintance and recognition—or in other words, to membership in a group—which provides each of its members with the backing of the collectivity-owned capital, a 'credential' which entitles them to credit" (1986: 248–249). An important property of these forms of capital is their mutual convertibility. Thus, cultural capital in the form of academic qualifications can be cashed in for economic capital yielded by lucrative employment or social capital that a powerful position affords. For the various forms of capital to be current and deployed to procure profits, they must be acknowledged by players in the field as having convertible value and symbolic power in the form of prestige, status, and reputation. In other words, they need to be recognized as *symbolic capital*, "the form assumed by these different kinds of capital when they are perceived and recognized as legitimate" (1991: 230). As *distinction* derives from capital that is recognized as legitimate, symbolic capital is "another name for distinction" (1991: 238). Holders of distinction, or symbolic capital, "are able to impose it as the only legitimate one in the formal markets (the fashionable, educational, political and administrative markets)" (1991: 56–57) and thus secure "a profit of distinction" (1991: 55).

In light of Bourdieu's theory, it is not difficult to see that bilingual education in China is a field of struggles in which different stakeholders and players compete to maximize their various forms of capital and to redefine their relative positions in the economic, educational, and sociocultural markets. It can be argued that major promoters of bilingual education, such as local governments in Shanghai, Guangzhou, and Shenzhen, have been driven by a desire for a maximal profit of distinction and to maintain their positions as centers of power. These large urban centers were able to occupy their leading positions because of their economic power. However, a large crop of cities have been quickly catching up in the last few decades as a result of the central government's reform and "Open Door" policies. To distinguish themselves from the upstarts and to take the lion's share of the available capital (i.e. capital as conceptualized by Bourdieu), these older power centers are determined to join the rank of *international* metropolises rather than remain merely *domestic* centers, knowing that capital accrues to the most powerful (Bourdieu, 1991). An obvious strategy for them to retain their powerful positions is to exploit their existing advantages. One such advantage has been their much greater resources for ELT. Thus, as current holders of distinction, they have imposed English proficiency as a legitimate and prestigious form of symbolic capital. This strategy is clearly reflected in the Shanghai Education Commission's action plan for the 21st century: "To develop world-class foreign language teaching programs in Shanghai is a prerequisite for turning the municipality into a world-class international metropolis" (cited in Hu, 2002: 33). The upstarts, however, have refused to be mere onlookers.

The same psychology of distinction also underlies the strong enthusiasm for bilingual education showed by district educational departments and prestigious schools. Thus, the principal of a highly prestigious school in Shanghai gloated about his school's high-quality bilingual program on the one hand and insinuated at the low quality of startup programs elsewhere (Lin, 2001). Other schools struggle to set up bilingual programs because their interests are at stake. The principal of School B mentioned earlier knew that his school would remain on the periphery of the field if it did not take action to offer bilingual programs. Similar vested interests sent universities vying to offer bilingual courses after the Director of the Higher Education Department under the Ministry of Education announced that the number of bilingual courses offered would be taken into account in the assessment of universities (Zheng, 2004). This led to 48 bilingual courses at Fudan

University, 164 at Zhejiang University, and 216 at Wuhan University (Huang, 2004; Wang, 2006; Zheng, 2004).

Many teachers welcome bilingual education because it brings with it opportunity for them to procure more economic, cultural, and symbolic capital at a much faster speed than they normally can hope for. These are typically junior teachers who have not established themselves and have to slog their way slowly and patiently up the professional and social hierarchy. Thanks to their possession of greater English proficiency than most of their more senior colleagues, bilingual education offers them a much sought-after opportunity to appreciate in value, to excel in the eyes of their superiors and colleagues, to be recognized, and to be better remunerated. All these are possible because to encourage teachers to teach bilingually, most schools offer various incentives: honorific rewards, promotions, salary increases, bonuses, subsidies, favorable formulae for workload calculation, sponsored training at home or abroad, grants for bilingual education research, and many other rewards (Li, 2006; Shen & Feng, 2005; Xu & Zhang, 2003; P. Zhang, 2002; Zheng *et al.*, 2006).

Parents and older students support bilingual education because English proficiency has become a most valorized form of cultural capital. It is a passport to a host of economic, social, educational, and professional opportunities and resources (Hu, 2005b; Li, 2006). For example, promotions for professionals depend crucially on passing a national English test. "Failing in this test," Y.J. Jiang (2003: 4) bemoans, "even a Nobel Prize winner will be rejected for promotion to professor, senior researcher, chief physician, or even class-I teacher in a school." Consequently, parents, especially those from a middle-class background, want their children to learn English well for an improved future (Lin, 2003). They are willing to pay higher school fees or donate generously in order to get their children into bilingual schools (Feng, 2005). Two incidents show how the signboard of bilingual education can work wonders for schools because of parents' eagerness to give their children a head start in English learning. A kindergarten in Beijing was on the brink of closure because of its small enrolment (Liu, 2002). To get out of the difficult situation, the kindergarten declared itself a bilingual education kindergarten and did some publicity work. Immediately parents queued to enroll their children in the kindergarten. In the second incident, 1000 parents were queuing up in the sun outside a little-known primary school in a small town for places in an "experimental bilingual education class" (Lin, 2003). Some of them had rushed there the night before from large cities like Guangzhou and Shenzhen.

Finally, many other individuals, organizations, and businesses have self-interests in bilingual education because it is a gold mine. Indeed, English proficiency has become a very expensive commodity in China. According to Y.P. Zhang (2003), there are 3000 English language tuition centers in Shanghai alone. In a tuition center that has an enrolment of more than 2300, a 48-hour course charges ¥7300 (more than US$900). Another tuition center charges ¥9980 for a 6-month course. These are hefty amounts in a country whose GDP per capita was only slightly above US$1000 in 2005. The New Oriental School in Beijing, the largest private English-teaching school in China, had an annual income of US$25 million in 2001 (Y.J. Jiang, 2003). In the craze for English, publishers also make big money. According to a report quoted in Niu and Wolff (2003: 30), "of the 37 billion yuan annual book sales, ESL [English as a second language] takes up as much as 25% of market share." The drive for bilingual education has also created a highly profitable market for reprinting textbooks published overseas (Kexue Shibao, 2003). Given the huge economic profits, it is little wonder that various bilingual education services have been springing up everywhere (Lin, 2001; Nian *et al.*, 2002).

Consequences of Bilingual Education for China

Because of the driving forces discussed above, there is no sign that the bilingual education craze will dissipate or even abate in the foreseeable future. The runaway expansion of bilingual programs requires serious consideration of the consequences of bilingual education for China. What educational, economic, and sociocultural consequences has it already produced? What potential consequences may it give rise to? This final section is an attempt to answer these questions.

Educational consequences

Bilingual education has been promoted ostensibly to make English learning more effective and to greatly raise students' English proficiency. Has this objective been attained by the extant bilingual programs? At first sight, the few available formal evaluations suggest that this would be the case. At the National Seminar on Bilingual Education held in 2003, the Deputy Director of Shanghai's Commission on Bilingual Education reported several statistics from a large-scale evaluation study: around 40% of primary school leavers from bilingual education programs attained an English proficiency level equal to, or higher than, that reached by Junior Secondary 2 students in 1997, and about 30% of Junior Secondary 2 students studying on bilingual education programs were found to be equally or more proficient in English than Senior Secondary 1 students in 1997 (Shen, 2004). A quantitative study of bilingual instruction by

H.D. Jiang (2002) made comparisons between primary school leavers from bilingual programs and junior secondary students without receiving bilingual education and reported findings in favor of bilingual education. Qiao (2003) reported another study which compared the effects of all-English, all-Chinese, and mixed-mediums instruction at the university level. The reported results of the study were also in favor of all-English and mixed-mediums instruction.

A close scrutiny of the studies raises doubts about the validity of their findings and suggests that the effectiveness of the costly bilingual education efforts fell far short of the claims. The studies suffered many of the problems plaguing evaluation research on bilingual education discussed in Greene (1998), Swain (1978), and Willig (1985). These include (1) the use of largely discrete-point grammar and vocabulary tests as criterion variables which did not measure students' ability to use English for communicative purposes; (2) a lack of information about the reliability and validity of criterion measures; (3) a lack of control for various confounding variables; (4) the use of intact groups/schools which did not yield equivalent experimental and comparison groups/schools, with the former often being formed by students who were intellectually stronger and had greater English proficiency in the first place; (5) inappropriate use of statistical procedures; and (6) misinterpretation of results. The Shanghai study, for example, compared student achievement in 2003 to that in 1997. Such comparisons do not make any sense. For one thing, the general level of English proficiency has been rising in the last decade, and therefore higher English proficiency in 2003 could not be attributed unambiguously to bilingual education. For another, primary school leavers and students at Junior Secondary 2 in 2003 had studied English at school for 5 and 6 years, respectively, whereas students at Junior Secondary 2 and Senior Secondary 1 in 1997 had studied English as a subject for 4 and 6 years respectively. This is because the latter cohorts started English instruction at Primary 5, whereas the former cohorts did so at Primary 1 and Primary 3 respectively. When the length of instruction is taken into account, it can be argued that the statistics from the Shanghai study indicated that the majority of students receiving bilingual education did worse than the junior and senior secondary students in 1997. Considering the quality of the bilingual programs, such results are expected.

Then what are the chances for the goal of mass Chinese–English bilingualism to be achieved in the foreseeable future? A rational answer would be in the negative, given the poor English proficiency of most "bilingual" teachers (see the two excerpts at the beginning of this chapter), the actual extent of English use in the classroom, the dubious quality of bilingual learning materials, the lack of curricular standards, the general lack of professional training in bilingual education among teachers, the lack of a threshold English proficiency in students to benefit from bilingual instruction, and so on. Research (e.g. Swain & Johnson, 1997) suggests that only under favorable conditions can the potential benefits of bilingual education be reaped and a full additive bilingualism be achieved. Cummins (1998), a strong supporter of bilingual education, has pointed out that students from French immersion programs—programs widely considered in China to be models of highly successful bilingual education—lag behind native speakers of the immersion language in spoken and written competence, especially in the grammar of the target language. If this is the case in Canada, it is more likely that Chinese students will develop only half-baked bilingualism, given China's limited resources for bilingual education.

It is also important to consider how bilingual education, a synonym for quality education in China, may affect students' academic achievement in the long run. Although there is no report of systematic longitudinal research conducted to examine the effect on academic attainment of learning nonlanguage subjects in English, there are already some indications that the use of English as a medium of instruction may very well affect students' academic achievement negatively. The large-scale evaluation study mentioned earlier admits that bilingual instruction may "injure subject learning" and calls for strategies to prevent this from happening (Shen, 2004). Many teachers have also complained that they have to reduce or simplify curricular content to accommodate bilingual instruction because their students lack the academic language competence to understand complex topics and engage in higher-order thinking in English (Pi, 2004; Ye, 2002). Jin and Zhuang (2002) report that in one school after half a semester of bilingual instruction in mathematics, the teachers had to reteach major topics in Chinese because the students had performed poorly in assessment. Such examples suggest that bilingual education is carried out at the expense of curricular content. As Liu (2002) observes, while bilingual education has been pushed forward as a way of correcting the evils of "costly and ineffective" approaches to ELT, it has made the teaching of other school subjects costly and ineffective. In light of Hong Kong's unsuccessful English immersion education, Gu and Dong (2005) draw attention to potential problems that may result from a mass shift in the medium of instruction and call for great caution in promoting bilingual education in Mainland China.

There are other real and potential consequences of great concern. Safty (1992) argues that in evaluating bilingual education programs, it is important to examine wider educational issues such as school integration, teacher employment, and staff morale. There is every possibility that "the great leap forward" for bilingual education will bring along, if it has not already done so, unwelcome consequences in these respects. To solve the problems of bilingual teacher shortages, many local governments and schools have redefined what it takes to be a qualified teacher. As Feng (2005: 540) points out, "qualified educators from preschool up to tertiary levels now need to be bilinguals who can teach their subjects in a foreign language, particularly English." In some schools, teachers are classified according to their ability to teach bilingually: those who are "qualified," those who are "sub-qualified," and those who are "probationers" (Shen, 2004). While such policies create golden opportunities for the minority of teachers who possess the much sought-after English proficiency, they can pose serious threats to the majority who do not have such capital. The latter's prowess is threatened with depreciation because they cannot display it in English. Thus, they face losing their symbolic capital in the form of professional recognition and reputation (Bourdieu, 1986, 1991). Marginalization and dislocation loom real. All this can have a demoralizing effect on teachers who cannot hope to teach bilingually and cause resentment for those who occupy privileged and envied positions afforded by bilingual education. "Divergence of interest and conflict within the group," Safty (1992: 27) notes, "will result if a segment is perceived as having acquired prestige and social mobility not previously available or accessible to the rest."

Economic and sociocultural consequences

Massive promotion of bilingual education in China also has huge economic and financial consequences for the central government and local governments at various levels. It entails tremendous governmental spending because of its requirements for teacher training, teacher employment, instructional facilities, and learning materials development (X.Y. Zhao, 2004). Su (2003c) reports that between 2000 and 2003, Shanghai alone sent nearly 2000 teachers to English-speaking countries for training and recruited about 1600 expatriate teachers for its primary and secondary bilingual programs. In addition, 400 teachers were sent to universities in Shanghai for training. This translated to governmental expenditure of millions of dollars. Bilingual education also means more expenditure on the part of schools. For example, Zhejiang University spent more than ¥1 million in 2002 in setting up bilingual courses (Huang, 2004). Schools serious about bilingual education have to expend their often limited financial resources on school-based training for their bilingual education teachers, on wage hikes, bonuses, and/or subsidies for their bilingual education teachers, on recruiting new staff for their bilingual programs, and on equipment and other facilities needed to create an "English environment" conducive to bilingual education (Lin, 2003). Even some advocates admit that bilingual education is expensive and suggest that it should be implemented on a restricted scale (Su, 2003b; Sun, 2002; Zhang & Liu, 2005). It is difficult to justify the huge spending on bilingual education, whose effectiveness in China has yet to be proved, when numerous schools in the vast rural areas of the country are poorly equipped for basic education and when the great majority of children in these underdeveloped areas do not go beyond a nine-year compulsory education (Hu, 2005a).

Even more disconcerting are some of the sociocultural consequences following from the drive for bilingual education. Even before bilingual education was officially promoted, English proficiency was already a commodity of strong exchange value (Bourdieu, 1986) and a gatekeeper of economic, cultural, and social opportunities (Cai, 2005; Feng, 2002). The bilingual education craze has further consolidated its symbolic capital status, that is, as a most valorized form of cultural capital. Mastery of English has come to be regarded as a defining characteristic of talents in the 21st century (Huang, 2005; Shen & Feng, 2005), an essential part of "a perfect character" (Qian, 2003), and a sign of distinction. It is now a widespread belief that "everything is low but English is high" (Xu, 2004). This belief is well illustrated by a news report of a group of children standing under the Oriental Pear, the television tower in Shanghai, and shouting in unison "No English, no future!" (Y.J. Jiang, 2003: 3). Hu (2005b) provides a further example of how English has been perceived as synonymous with competitiveness and quality as well as how the demand for English has often been created artificially.

It is all too obvious that English has become the language of social and economic prestige and has the power to confer greater possibilities on those who can command it. On the face of it, the explosive growth of bilingual education seems to offer opportunity for a large segment of the Chinese society to acquire the scarce symbolic capital of English proficiency. However, this opportunity exists only in theory. Researchers (e.g. Valdés, 1997; Walsh, 1995; Yau, 1988) notice that it is generally students of higher socioeconomic levels who benefit most from successful bilingual education programs in the United States, Canada, and Hong Kong. Expectedly, there are also indications that bilingual education in China is becoming a service to the elite (Gill, 2004; P. Zhang, 2002). This is happening because, as Bourdieu (1986, 1991) points out, the education system serves as a principal institution for the accumulation, production, and distribution of cultural capital and for the reproduction of social inequality. Thus, at the school level, a minority of elite schools can take advantage of their much greater volume of various types of capital—greater financial resources, excellent infrastructure, wider social networks, well-trained staff, and high-caliber students—to offer bilingual programs of a quality that the majority of schools with limited capital cannot hope to emulate. At the personal level, students from higher socioeconomic backgrounds can benefit more from bilingual programs than those from lower socioeconomic backgrounds because of the much greater resources their families can invest in creating conditions of success for them (Feng, 2005). Thus, bilingual education not only perpetuates the existing unequal and hierarchical distribution of power and access to cultural and symbolic capital but is creating new forms of inequality and further differentiating the Chinese society vertically as well (Hu, 2005a).

To conclude, Giddens' (1990: 139) characterization of modernity as a juggernaut is an equally apt description of Chinese–English bilingual education in China:

The juggernaut crushes those who resist it, and while it sometimes seems to have a steady path, there are times when it veers away erratically in directions we cannot foresee. The ride is by no means wholly unpleasant or unrewarding; it can often be exhilarating and charged with hopeful anticipation. But . . . [the riders] shall never be able to control completely either the path or the pace of the journey. In turn, [all those involved] shall never be able to feel entirely secure, because the terrain across which it runs is fraught with risks of high consequence.

References

Adamson, B. and Morris, P. (1997) The English curriculum in the People's Republic of China. *Comparative Education Review* 41, 3–26.
Bourdieu, P. (1986) The forms of capital (R. Nice, Trans.). In J.G. Richardson (ed.) *Handbook of Theory and Research for the Sociology of Education* (pp. 241–258). New York: Greenwood Press.
Bourdieu, P. (1991) *Language and Symbolic Power* (G. Raymond and M. Adamson, Trans.). Cambridge, MA: Harvard University Press.
Brinton, D.M., Snow, M.A. and Wesche, M.B. (1989) *Content-based Second Language Instruction*. New York: Newbury House.
Cai, J.G. (2005) Daxue yingyu jiaoxue ruogan wenti sikao [Some thoughts on college English teaching]. *Waiyu Jiaoxue yu Yanjiu* 37(2), 83–91.
Cai, X.M. (2001) Zhongri jingji chaju zai suoxiao [The economic gap between China and Japan is narrowing]. *Lianhe Zaobao*, 27 June.
Chi, Y.P. and Zhao, W. (2004) Woguo xiaoxue jinrushi jiaoxue shiyan zongshu [A review of English immersion experiments in Chinese elementary schools]. *Bijiao Jiaoyu Yanjiu* (7), 13–18.
Cummins, J. (1979) Linguistic interdependence and the educational development of bilingual children. *Review of Educational Research* 49, 222–251.

Cummins, J. (1998) *Immersion Education for the Millennium: What Have We Learned from 30 Years of Research on Second Language Immersion?* On WWW at http://www.iteachilearn.com/cummins/immersion2000.html.

Cummins, J. (1999) Alternative paradigms in bilingual education research: Does theory have a place? *Educational Researcher* 28(7), 26–32, 41.

Deng, L. and Jiang, H.Y. (2001) Youer shuangyu jiaoyu wenti tantao [A discussion of issues in pre-school bilingual education]. *Xueqian Jiaoyu Yanjiu* (1), 40–41.

Dor, D. (2004) From Englishization to imposed multilingualism: Globalization, the Internet, and the political economy of the linguistic code. *Public Culture* 16,97–118.

Du, X.H. (2002) Chutan shuangyu jiaoyu jiqi shizi peiyang de tujing [Bilingual education and means of bilingual teacher education]. *Zhongguo Gaojiao Yanjiu* (1), 90–91.

Feng, A.W. (2005) Bilingualism for the minor or the major? An evaluative analysis of parallel conceptions in China. *The International Journal of Bilingual Education and Bilingualism* 8, 529–551.

Feng, Z.J. (2002) Shuangyu jiaoyu yu zonghe yingyu jiaoxue shiyan [A bilingual education experiment on the integrated English program]. *Tianjin Shifan Daxue Xuebao* 3(4), 54–58.

Fu, K. (1986) *Zhongguo Waiyu Jiaoyushi* [The history of foreign language education in China]. Shanghai: Shanghai Waiyu Jiaoyu Chubanshe.

Giddens, A. (1990) *Consequences of Modernity*. Cambridge: Polity Press.

Gill, C. (2004) *China Offers an English Future for Some*. Available at http://education.guardian.co.uk/tefl/story/0,5500,1332331,00.html.

Gopinathan, S. (1998) Language policy changes 1979–1997: Politics and pedagogy. In S. Gopinathan, A. Pakir, W.K. Ho and V. Saravanan (eds) *Language, Society and Education in Singapore* (pp. 19–44). Singapore: Academic Press.

Grinberg, J. and Saavedra, E.R. (2000) The constitution of bilingual/ESL education as a disciplinary practice: Genealogical explorations. *Review of Educational Research* 70, 419–441.

Greene, J.P. (1998) A meta-analysis of the effects of bilingual education. Available at http://ourworld.compuserve.com/homepages/JWCRAWFORD/greene.htm.

Gu, Y.Q. and Dong, L.Z. (2005) Xianggang shuangyu jiaoxue changshi de jingyan ji qishi [Lessons from Kong Kong's experiment with English-medium instruction]. *Xiandai Waiyu* 28(1), 43–52.

Gui, S.C. (2004) Wode shuangyu jiaoyu [My bilingual education]. *Waiguoyu* (1),47–51.

He, L. (2004) Wode yijie shuangyu jiaoxueke ji pingxi [A bilingual class of mine and analysis]. *Xinxi Jishu Jiaoyu* 5(4), 27–30.

Hou, G.X. (2000) Yingdang guli zhuanyeke jiaoshi yong yingyu jiangke ma? [Should subject teachers be encouraged to teach in English?]. *Fujian Waiyu* (3),33–35.

Hu, G.W. (2002) Recent important developments in secondary English-language teaching in the People's Republic of China. *Language, Culture and Curriculum* 15, 30–49.

Hu, G.W. (2005a) English language education in China: Policies, progress, and problems. *Language Policy* 4, 5–24.

Hu, G. W. (2005b) Reforms of basic English-language education in China: An overview. *International Journal of Educational Reform* 14, 140–165.

Huang, A.Y. (2005) Shuangyu jiaoxue lilun tantao [Theoretical exploration of bilingual education]. *Jiaoyu Tansuo* (4), 61–62.

Huang, W. (2004) Shuangyu jiaoxue: Yu shidai lianwang [Bilingual education: In step with the modern era]. *Zhongguo Jiaoyubao,* 5 March.

Jiang, H.D. (2002) Xiaoxue shuangyu jiaoxue zhengti gaige shiyan yanjiu [An empirical study of bilingual instruction at the primary level]. *Shandong Jiaoyu Keyan* (3), 15–17.

Jiang, H.D. (2003) Lun jichu jiaoyu jieduan de shuangyu jiaoyu [On bilingual education at the basic education stage]. *Tianjin Shifan Daxue Xuebao* 4(1), 52–56.

Jiang, L. (2002) Wei guojihua dadushi peiyang youxiu de jianshezhe [Turning out talented builders for Shanghai, an international metropolis]. *Xiandai Jiaoyubao,* 27 November.

Jiang, Y.J. (2003) English as a Chinese language. *English Today* 19(2), 3–8.

Jiao, X.J. (2004) Guanyu kaizhan shuangyu jiaoxue de sange wenti [Three problems in bilingual education]. *Jiaoshi Bolan* (7), 24–25.

Jin, K. and Zhuang, Y.X. (2002) Shuangyu jiaoxue zheng liaoyuan [Bilingual education is spreading like a prairie fire]. *Jiefang Ribao,* 4 March.

Kexue Shibao (2003) Shuangyu jiaoxue: Tuikai youyishan chuban zhimen [Bilingual education pushing open another door for publishers]. *Kexue Shibao,* 17 July.

Li, X.H., Long, Q., Cai, B. and Hou, L.S. (2003) Zhiyue woguo shuangyu jiaoxue fazhan de keguan pingjin ji duice [Constraints on the development of bilingual education in China and solutions]. *Nanjing Xiaozhuang Xueyuan Xuebao* 19(2), 66–69.

Li, X.H., Long, Q. and Qu, K.L. (2004) Woguo zhongxue shuangyu jiaoxue de fazhan xianzhuang ji yingxiang yinsu [The current state of secondary-level bilingual education and factors affecting its development]. *Jiaoxue yu Guanli* (2), 35–38.

Li, X.L. (2006) Nankai daxue jiaoshou huyu zhizhi shuangyu jiaoxue [Nankai professor calls for an end to bilingual education]. *Zhongguo Qingnianbao,* 22 February.

Li, X.T. (2004) Xinjiapo shuangyu jiaoyu dui woguo gaoxiao shuangyu jiaoxue de qishi [What bilingual education in Singapore has to offer for bilingual teaching in Chinese universities]. *Xiandai Jiaoyu Kexue* (2),111–114.

Lin, D. (2002) Jinnian waishang touzi Zhongguo gaofengnian [A peak year for foreign investment in China]. *Lianhe Zaobao,* 12 April.

Lin, J. (2003) Shuangyu jiaoxue: Jianle zhima diaole xigua? [Bilingual education: Penny wise and pound foolish?]. *Zhongguo Qingnianbao,* 8 October.

Lin, W. (2001) Shuangyu jiaoxue Shanghai qibu [Bilingual education has taken off in Shanghai]. *Zhongguo Qingnianbao,* 24 September.

Liu, H.R. (2002) Shuangyu jiaoxue wuru qitu? [Bilingual education: Going astray?]. *Jingji Daobao,* 4 September.

Lu, X.Y. (2002) Zhiyi shuangyu jiaoxue [Doubts about bilingual education]. *Wenhuibao,* 29 April.

Luo, W. and Liu, W.Y. (2006) Shizi duanque cheng shuangyu jiaoyu pingjing [Teacher shortages: The bottleneck of bilingual education]. *Zhongguo Qingnianbao,* 9 January.

Lyons, J.J. (1990) The past and future directions of federal bilingual-education policy. *Annals of the American Academy of Political and Social Science* 508,66–80.

McGroarty, M. (1992). The societal context of bilingual education. *Educational Researcher* 21(2), 7–9, 24.

Ministry of Education (2001) *Guanyu Jiaqiang Gaodeng Yuanxiao Benke Jiaoxue Gongzuo Tigao Jiaoxue Zhiliang de Ruogan Yijian* [Guidelines for improving the quality of undergraduate programs]. Beijing: Ministry of Education.

Nian, G.Z., You, Z., Lu, Y., Ou, B., Xue, Y. and Wu, M. (2002) Shuangyu jiaoxue de shiyufei [Bilingual education: Pros and cons]. *Zhongguo Jiaoyu Zixunbao*, 24 April.

Niu, Q. and Wolff, M. (2003) The Chinglish syndrome: Do recent developments endanger the language policy of China? *English Today* 19(4), 30–35.

Peal, E. and Lambert, W. (1962) The relation of bilingualism to intelligence. *Psychological Monographs* 76, 1–23.

Pi, W.B. (2004) Zhongxue shuangyu jiaoxue de shijian yu sikao [Bilingual education in secondary schools and reflections]. Unpublished master's thesis, East China Normal University.

Qian, Y.W. (2003) Fenceng duoyuan di shenhua shuangyu jiaoxue shiyan [Promote experimentation with bilingual education at multiple levels and in plural ways]. *Shanghai Jiaoyu Keyan* (7), 53–57.

Qiang, H.Y. and Zhao, L. (2000) Jianada dier yuyan jinrushi jiaoxue moshi jiqi zai woguo shuangyu rencai zaoqi peiyang yanjiu de changshi [Canadian L2 immersion education and its application to early bilingual education and research in China]. *Jiaoyu Daokan* (2/3), 19–22.

Qiao, J.Y. (2003) Daxue yingyu ketang jiaoxue meijieyu duibi shiyan yanjiu [A comparative study of mediums of instruction in university English classes]. *Waiyu Jiaoxue yu Yanjiu* 35, 372–377.

Ross, H.A. (1993) *China Learns English: Language Teaching and Social Change in the People's Republic*. New Haven, CT: Yale University Press.

Rossell, C. and Baker, K. (1996) The educational effectiveness of bilingual education. *Research in the Teaching of English* 30, 7–74.

Safty, A. (1992) Effectiveness and French immersion: A socio-political analysis. *Canadian Journal of Education* 17, 23–32.

Secada, W.G. (1990) Research, politics, and bilingual education. *Annals of the American Academy of Political and Social Science* 508, 81–106.

Shen, P. and Feng, Y.P. (2005) Tuijin shuangyu jiaoxue de tansuo yu shijian [Exploring and implementing bilingual instruction]. *Zhongguo Daxue Jiaoxue* (2), 24–25, 31.

Shen, Z.Y. (2004) Yiyi zai shijian mubiao zai chengxiao [Significance and objectives of bilingual education]. *Zhongguo Jiaoyubao*, 13 May.

Song, Y.Q. and Yan, H.C. (2004) Kaizhan shuangyu jiaoxue de kexingxing ji wenti tantao [A discussion of the feasibility of bilingual instruction and related issues]. *Jilin Gongcheng Jishu Shifan Xueyuan Xuebao* 20(11), 20–22.

Su, J. (2003a) Shanghai wenbu tuijin shuangyu jiaoxue shiyan [Bilingual education in Shanghai is making steady progress]. *Wenhuibao*, 7 January.

Su, J. (2003b) Shuangyu jiaoxue ying bianshijian biantigao [Improve bilingual education through experimentation]. *Wenhuibao*, 21 April.

Su, J. (2003c) Shanghai tuozhan shuangyu jiaoxue shiyan [Shanghai expands experimentation with bilingual education]. *Wenhuibao*, 21 October.

Sun, E.Y. (2002) Shuangyu jiaoxue tanxi [An analysis of bilingual teaching]. *Liaoningsheng Jiaotong Gaodeng Zhuanke Xuexiao Xuebao* 4(4), 51–53.

Swain, M. (1978) School reform through bilingual education: Problems and some solutions in evaluating programs. *Comparative Education Review* 22, 420–433.

Swain, M. and Johnson, R.K. (1997) Immersion education: A category within bilingual education. In R.K. Johnson and M. Swain (eds) *Immersion Education: International Perspectives* (pp. 1–16). Cambridge: Cambridge University Press.

Valdés, G. (1997) Dual-language immersion programs: A cautionary note concerning the education of language-minority students. *Harvard Educational Review* 67, 391–429.

Walsh, C.E. (1995) Critical reflections for teachers: Bilingual education and critical pedagogy. In J. Fredrickson (ed.) *Reclaiming Our Voices: Bilingual Education, Critical Pedagogy and Praxis* (pp. 79–88). Ontario: California Association for Bilingual Education.

Wang, B.H. (2003) Shunying shidai chaoliu yingzao nongyu de shuangyu xuexi fenwei [Follow the trend and create a favorable climate for bilingual education]. *Kecheng, Jiaocai, Jiaofa* 25(6), 49–51.

Wang, H.H. and Wang, S.T. (2003) Shuangyu jiaoxue yu gonggong yingyu jiaoxue de jiekou wenti [Problems in the interface between bilingual and EFL instruction]. *Waiyujie* (1), 26–31.

Wang, L.F. (2006) Shuangyu jiaoxue yu shuangyu jiaoyu [Bilingual instruction and bilingual education]. *Jingjishi* (1), 113–114.

Wang, X.J. (2003) Youeryuan kaizhan shuangyu jiaoxue xu shenzhong [Hold your horses: Bilingual education at kindergartens]. *Jiaoyu Xinxibao*, 11 October.

Wen, J.F. (2001) Zaoqi shuangyu jiaoyu dui peiyang xiandai rencai de zhongyaoxing [The important role of early bilingual education in providing human capital in the modern era]. *Guangzhou Daxue Xuebao* 15(6), 9–11.

Willig, A.C. (1985) A meta-analysis of selected studies on the effectiveness of bilingual education. *Review of Educational Research* 55, 269–317.

Wu, Q. (1997) Huaxueke shishi shuangyu jiaoxue de changshi [An experimental effort to teach chemistry bilingually]. *Huaxue Jiaoyu* (5), 20–22.

Xie, F. and Wang, X.T. (2002) Shuangyu jiaoxue gai hequ hechong [Bilingual education: What course to follow]. *Xiandai Jiaoyubao*, 19 July.

Xinwen Chenbao (2003) Nide haizi xue shuangyu lema [Are your children receiving bilingual education?]. *Xinwen Chenbao*, 28 October.

Xu, K.Q. (2004) Shuangyu jiaoxuere zhong ying guanzhu Zhonghua minzu wenhua yishi wenti [Loss of Chinese culture deserves attention in the bilingual education craze]. *Waiyu Jiaoxue* 25(3), 86–89.

Xu, L. and Zhang, C.M. (2003) Shuangyu jiaoxue chutan [A preliminary discussion of bilingual instruction]. *Zhongguo Chengren Jiaoyu* (7), 71.

Xu, M. (2004) 5.5 wan xuesheng jieshou shuangyu jiaoyu [55,000 students are receiving bilingual education]. *Jiefang Ribao*, 28 April.

Yang, L. (2005) Wo shi ruhe jinxing shuangyu jiaoxue de [How I teach bilingual lessons] *Shengwuxue Jiaoyu* 30(12), 65–66.

Yau, M.S. (1988) Bilingual education and social class: Some speculative observations in the Hong Kong context. *Comparative Education* 24, 217–227.

Ye, B.Z. (2002) Bierang shuangyu jiaoxue zoushang xielu [Stop bilingual instruction from going astray]. *Zhongguo Jiaoyu Zixunbao*, 17 April.

Ye, X. (2003) Shuangyu jiaoxue de shizhi ji zai xiandai Zhonguo de liangzhong xianxiang [The nature of bilingual education and its two forms in contemporary China]. *Shandong Waiyu Jiaoxue* (3), 111–112.

Yu, M.L. and Han, J.X. (2003) Wotaihua yituoshi kecheng jiaoxue jiqi qishi [Content-based instruction in Ottawa and its implications]. *Waiyu Jiaoxue yu Yanjiu* 35(6), 465–468.

Zhai, F. (2003) Yuyanxue zhuanjia zhiyi shuangyu jiaoxue [Linguists raise doubts about bilingual education]. *Zhongguo Jiaoyubao*, 23 January.

Zhang, F.J. (2003) Wo xiang zhongxiaoxue yuwen shuangyu jiaoxue polengshui [Against bilingual instruction in the Chinese language arts classroom]. *Jichu Jiaoyu Waiyu Jiaoxue Yanjiu* (5), 18–20.

Zhang, L.B. and Liu, X.H. (2005) Shuangyu jiaoxue: Gongshi, fenqi ji wuqu [Bilingual education: Consensuses, controversies, and misconceptions]. *Xiandai Jiaoyu Kexue* (6), 73–76.

Zhang, P. (2002) Shuangyu jiaoxue: Redian wenti de lengsikao [Bilingual education: Problems and considerations]. *Dongbei Shida Xuebao* (3), 121–127.

Zhang, W.J. (2002) Shuangyu jiaoxue de xingzhi tiaojian ji xiangguan wenti [The nature and conditions of bilingual education and some related problems]. *Yuyan Jiaoxue yu Yanjiu* (4), 20–26.

Zhang, Y.P. (2003) Shuangyu jiaoxue de yiyi he celue sikao [The significance and strategies of bilingual education]. *Leshan Shifan Xueyuan Xuebao* 18(6), 38–40.

Zhang, Z.F. (2003) Shuangyu jiaoxue de yuanze moshi ji celue [Principles, models, and strategies of bilingual education]. *Zhongxiaoxue Jiaoxue Yanjiu* (2), 15–16.

Zhao, J. (2002) Dili xueke jinxing shuangyu jiaoxue de shexiang yu shijian [Research and practice: Bilingual instruction in geography]. *Tianjin Shifan Daxue Xuebao* 3(4), 59–62.

Zhao, L. (2004) Woguo youeryuan yingyu jinrushi jiaoxue yanjiu baogao [The development of English immersion for young children in China]. *Bijiao Jiaoyu Yanjiu* (7), 19–22.

Zhao, X.Y. (2004) Shuangyu bingbu gudu de shiyan [Bilingual education: Not a lonely experiment]. *Zhongguo Jiaoyubao*, 5 January.

Zheng, H.B. (2004). Zhongguo shuangyu jiaoxue yanjiu lunwen tongji yu pingxi [Statistics and analysis of research papers on bilingual instruction in China]. *Ningbo Gaodeng Zhuanke Xuexiao Xuebao* 16(4), 95–98.

Zheng, S.L., Tian, Z.H. and Li, Y.J. (2006) Goujian xiaoxue shuangyu jiaoxue kecheng tixi de yanjiu yu shijian [Researching and developing a curricular framework for bilingual education at the primary level]. *Jiaoyu Lilun yu Shijian* 26(2), 62–64.

Zhou, R.F. (2004) Shuangyu jiaoxue zhi wojian [My view of bilingual instruction]. *Panzhihua Xueyuan Xuebao* 21(5), 59–60.

Zhu, M. (2000) Yingyu jiaoxue yu xuesheng fazhan: Dui woxiao shuangyu jiaoxue de sikao [ELT and students' development: Reflections on bilingual education at my school]. *Zhongguo Jiaoyubao*, 21 December.

Zhu, P. (2003) Lun Shanghai zhongxiaoxue shuangyu jiaoxue shiyan [On experimentation with bilingual education in Shanghai's primary and secondary schools]. *Kecheng, Jiaocai, Jiaofa* (6), 52–58.

Chapter 7
Research and Practice of Tibetan–Chinese Bilingual Education

MINGGANG WAN AND SHANXIN ZHANG

Introduction

Bilingualism is a common social and linguistic phenomenon. Most countries and most people in the world are bilingual or multilingual. Bilingual teaching, an educational response to the social and linguistic needs for bilingualism of a society, is not only an important cross-cultural and educational means but also, more importantly, a special educational form set against the educational background of minorities. Tibetan–Chinese bilingual education does not only refer to the long-term bilingual teaching activities in primary and middle schools in Tibet and regions of Zang nationality in other provinces, but also a manifestation of the societal aspiration for bilingualism. This chapter, starting with Tibetan–Chinese bilingual teaching, aims to summarize and reflect on bilingual education in minority regions and models used in Zang nationality regions.

An Overview of Tibetan–Chinese Bilingual Education

Recently bilingual education in minority education has not only achieved much in theoretical study but also constantly brought forth new ideas and attempts in practical aspects. These attempts mainly focus on such major issues as bilingual education approaches in general and models for Tibetan–Chinese bilingual teaching in particular. Many also explore fundamental aims for bilingual education in minority regions.

General approach to Tibetan–Chinese bilingual teaching

A teaching model should reflect general theories in bilingual education and teaching principles and pedagogy. It should specify teaching processes and objectives followed by teaching procedures to achieve these aims. This means that a model is an integrated system of teaching methods, teaching means, and teaching organizational forms viewed from teaching practice. A teaching model has a more complicated implication in bilingual teaching. As far as the theoretical basis is concerned, different disciplines and teaching philosophies are involved in developing a bilingual teaching model. As for the teaching objectives, they need to be formulated according to the learning process of two languages. Teaching procedures are also complicated. They are not only dependent on teaching strategies but also influenced by long-term plans and other contextual factors such as different linguistic environments, sociocultural factors, and types of bilingualism in minority regions (Wang, 1994).

People of Zang nationality of China are mainly distributed in Tibet, Qinghai, Gansu, Sichuan, and Yunan. As far as living conditions are concerned, the regions where Zang nationality resides can be divided into large compact communities, small compact communities in mixed communities, and mixed communities. The so-called compact communities of minorities refer to the regions where people of a certain minority group live together with people of other ethnic groups; thus in such a community, people of Han nationality are not excluded and sometimes they are even in the majority. In these regions, large and small compact communities of the Han nationality and communities of minorities are coexistent(Fei, 1989).

Since there are different living and distributing features in regions of Zang nationality, the models used in bilingual teaching are different as well. In Tibet with large compact communities of Zang nationality, content subject teaching is often conducted in the Tibetan language while Chinese only plays a subordinate role. In the Gannan Tibetan Autonomous Prefecture in Gansu with smaller compact communities, an "alternative priority" approach is adopted. In this approach, two alternative models of bilingual teaching are used depending on the specific context of a bilingual program: one uses Tibetan as the main instruction language for all content subject teaching with Chinese language only as a content subject, and the other uses Chinese as the instruction language for content subjects with Tibetan as a separate content subject. The former model is named the "Tibetan plus Chinese" model while the latter "Chinese plus Tibetan" (Han, 1991).

Influence of the attitude of the bilingual speaker of Zang nationality

In order to gain an insight into the attitude toward bilingualism held by bilingual speakers of Zang nationality, an investigation was carried out in Zang minority regions in 1996 (Wan & Wang, 1997). The investigation revealed that most bilingual speakers are emotionally attached to their native language and have a strong desire to maintain it. While holding this attitude toward their native language, they rationally accept the social and economic significance of Chinese. They firmly reject the idea to replace Tibetan with Chinese (Wan & Wang, 1997; more details will be presented later). Through influential Zang policy makers, teachers, parents, administrative officials, students, and so on, this attitude has exerted an impact on the development of bilingual teaching models and thus on the effectiveness of bilingual education. Of various teaching models adopted after 1980s, while the "Tibetan plus Chinese" model is well established, the model with Chinese as the main medium of instruction for teaching content subjects with Tibetan only as a school subject (the "Chinese plus Tibetan" model) has also taken shape in cities and towns where mixed communities of Zang and Han nationalities reside. Zang bilingual speakers in these places are gradually embracing this bilingual teaching model, affectively as well as rationally.

Models in Tibet

Bilingual education has been a special issue in Tibet since its peaceful liberation in 1951. The search for a Tibetan model has undergone the following stages. Before the "Cultural Revolution" in 1966, a bilingual educational system with Tibetan characteristics was initially shaped for primary and secondary schools, which helped cultivate a batch of bilingual personnel for the region. Many Tibetan–Chinese teachers contributed a great deal to developing teaching methodology and textbook compiling. But during the 10-year "Cultural Revolution," bilingual education in its infancy was seriously damaged. During those years, issues surrounding the selection of instruction languages were never handled appropriately, which had a negative effect on minority educational quality and the implementation of national language policy. In 1980s, while making efforts to restore quality bilingual teaching in primary schools, the Tibet Autonomous Region began to explore new bilingual teaching models for secondary schools. Since 1987, in accordance with "Provisions on learning, using and developing Tibetan language in Tibet Autonomous Region," most primary schools have also adopted bilingual teaching with Tibetan as the primary medium of instruction. As for secondary schools, four experimental programs were carried out in four schools, namely the Lhasa Secondary, the Lhasa No. 1 Secondary, the Rikeze Secondary, and the Sannan No. 2 Secondary.

As a result of these efforts, a proposal was made to implement a bilingual teaching model with Tibetan as the primary medium for teaching school subjects (Danzeng, 1996). This proposal takes into consideration the social reality and societal aspiration for future development of Tibet. According to this proposal, in primary and secondary schools, the bilingual teaching model focusing on Tibetan is put into practice. However, in colleges and universities, the bilingual teaching model focusing on Tibetan is adopted only for students in normal universities or teachers colleges. For students in all other colleges, the bilingual teaching model focusing on Chinese is brought into effect. As for the "Tibetan plus Chinese'" model adopted in primary and secondary schools, while both Tibetan and Chinese are offered as language courses in primary schools, all the school subjects are taught in students' mother tongue at the primary-school level. At the secondary school, this model is still used predominantly, first as a default model to address problems arising from transition to using Chinese as the medium of instruction from mother tongue instruction, and second as a means to enhance the teaching quality at the primary education level in order to achieve "two basic objectives" of making 9-year compulsory education easily accessible to all and of eradicating illiteracy. On the other hand, with improvement of students' academic level and native language proficiency, effective measures are taken to regulate teaching content and teaching approaches and to adjust school curriculums so as to enhance the use of Mandarin Chinese in teaching school subjects and foreign language teaching. Consequently, school leavers are able to engage in higher-level learning of all subjects not only in Tibetan but also in Chinese. Meanwhile they will be equipped with basic skills to learn knowledge in a foreign language. This bilingual teaching model using Tibetan as the main medium of instruction is an important achievement in the exploration of elementary education in Tibet and meets the linguistic and cultural needs of Tibetans living the large compact communities of Zang nationality. The model is an important reflection of basic principles of educational psychology and pedagogy for minority education.

"Alternative priority" approach in the Gannan Tibetan Autonomous Prefecture

The Gannan Tibetan Autonomous Prefecture, one of the 10 Tibetan autonomous prefectures in China, is located in the southwestern part of Gansu, the northeastern edge of Qinghai–Tibet Plateau and the upriver of Yangtze and Huanghe River. It has a common border with Gansu, Qinghai, and Sichuan. Its total area is 45,000 km². Hezuo City is its prefecture capital surrounded by 8 counties and cities (Hezuo, Xiahe, Luqu, Maqu, Zhouqu, Tiebu, Zhuoni, and Lintan), 107 towns, and 4 community offices. Its total population is 659,800 made up of 25 ethnic groups such as Zang,

Han, Hui, Menggu, Tu, Sala, Baoan, and Dongxiang, among which 48% are of Zang nationality. The general topographical configuration of Gannan is complex and diversified, high in the west and low in the east. There are three natural zones: alp grasslands, alp forests, and low hills, with an altitude of 1172–4920 m and an average temperature of 1.7°C. With a rainfall of 400–800 mm, it is also one of the regions with most abundant water source.

By the end of 2002, there are 708 schools of various types, among which 640 are primary schools, 37 independent junior high schools (including 29 9-year schools), 19 full-scale secondary schools, 5 vocational schools, 3 teacher training colleges, and 4 polytechnics. Among them, 229 primary and secondary schools (211 primary schools and 18 middle schools), 105 boarding schools, and 11 kindergartens have engaged themselves in the Tibetan–Chinese bilingual education. The number of primary and secondary school students in school in 2002 broke a record by reaching 103,516, an increase of 20,495 compared with the number in 1998. Among 103,516 students, 49,446 students are of Zang nationality accounting for 47.7% of the total. The teaching staff is 6153, among which 2924 are of Zang nationality accounting for 47.5% of the total. This prefecture is a typical "small compact community."

If the "Tibetan plus Chinese" model adopted in Tibet, as described before, is representative for "large Tibetan compact communities," then we can say that the "alternative priority" approach in Gannan is typical of "small Tibetan compact communities." Bilingual teaching in Gannan has not been put on a normal footing until 1980s. The prefecture commission and government have intermittently issued documents such as "Suggestions on restoring and establishing Tibetan courses in Gannan Tibetan Autonomous Prefecture," "Operational ordinance for primary and middle schools in Gannan Tibetan Autonomous Prefecture," and "Resolutions for further developing Tibetan education in Gannan Tibetan Autonomous Prefecture." These documents are intended to ensure reform and improvement of Tibetan education. After over 10 years' efforts, an "alternative priority" bilingual teaching approach that suits the Gannan context has been developed: bilingual teaching with Tibetan as the main language of instruction, the "Tibetan plus Chinese" model, or bilingual teaching with Chinese as the main instruction language, the "Chinese plus Tibetan" model (Yang, 1996). In pasturing and agricultural-pasturing areas where people generally use Tibetan as the means for communication, teaching is conducted mainly in Tibetan and students use the "textbooks co-compiled by and for five provinces and regions"; in Tibetan–Chinese mixed areas where all ethnic groups have a knowledge of Chinese, teaching is conducted in Chinese with Tibetan only as a school subject. Except for the textbook for Tibetan language that is "co-compiled by and for five provinces and regions," other textbooks are those that follow the national curriculum. Both models prove effective in practice in their own context.

Rationale, Aims, and Operational Strategies of the Tibetan Model

Rationale behind the "Tibetan plus Chinese" model in Tibet

This model ensures that in the teaching of primary and secondary schools in Tibet, all the subjects are taught in the students' mother tongue, with Chinese as a second language plus a foreign language course. We can rationalize this model from two major perspectives.

Theoretically, Tibetan language can undoubtedly be used to impart or learn modern scientific knowledge including the most sophisticated sciences owing to its comprehensive linguistic functions. In view of the anthropological theory, bilingual education is not only a form of teaching and learning but also a special channel for transmitting, preserving, and developing minority cultures. Viewed from the theories of minority psychology, it is emphasized that the native language is the foundation to ensure that learning is taking place. The core of the theoretical basis of this model lies in the idea that Tibetan education is understood through a micro-education perspective of integrating minority traditional education into contemporary education. In teaching practice, ethnic minority identities are brought to the fore in constructing bilingual teaching framework. In curriculum planning, preserving traditional culture and imparting modern scientific knowledge are integrated to construct a multiplex curriculum system. Therefore, minority education becomes unified in content and form. Meanwhile, through learning and using the common language, Chinese, minority people could engage better in communication with other nationalities and promote national harmony in China.

From the affective point of view, we need to understand what attitudes Zang bilingual speakers hold toward the two languages and its uses in social situations. Wan and Wang (1997) conducted a survey that aims to address this question. In their study, 119 adult subjects were asked three types of questions as shown in Tables 7.1–7.3.

Data collected from this survey on the bilingual speakers' attitude toward these two languages and their uses clearly show that, despite some discrepancies, they hold firm views about their own linguistic identity and positive attitude toward bilingual education on the whole.

Table 7.1 Tibetan bilingual speakers' attitude toward native language

No.	Questions	Responses % (number)		
1	Why do you use native language?	It is convenient 25.2 (30)	Have used it since young 21 (25)	Hold deep feelings 53.8 (64)
2	If your child cannot speak Tibetan, how will you feel?	It is his fault 73.1 (87)	It doesn't matter 6.7 (8)	He will benefit more 20.2 (24)
3	What is the major ethnic feature of Zang nationality?	Religion 22.7 (27)	Language 51.1 (62)	Clothes and customs 25.2 (30)
4	Should a person of Han working in Tibetan regions study Tibetan?	Yes 77.3 (92)		Indifferent 22.7 (27)

Table 7.2 Tibetan bilingual speakers' attitude toward Chinese

No.	Questions	Responses % (number)		
1	Why do you learn and use Chinese?	It is convenient 58 (69)	Chinese is national language 37.8 (45)	Hold deep feelings 4.2 (5)
2	Do you support your child to speak Chinese at home?	Yes 67.2 (80)		No 32.8 (39)
3	If Tibetan is completely abolished and only Chinese is allowed in teaching, how will you feel?	It is hurting 89.1 (106)		It is good to students 10.9 (13)

Table 7.3 Tibetan bilingual speakers' attitude toward language choice in social situations

No.	Questions	Responses % (number)		
1	What is the language you most like to use in your family?	Tibetan 62.7 (80)	Chinese 10.1 (12)	Both 22.7 (27)
2	Which language do you prefer to use outside the family?	Tibetan 40.3 (48)	Chinese 10.1 (12)	Both 49.6 (59)
3	How do you feel in a conversation in which you are using Tibetan while the other, a bilingual Tibetan is using Chinese?	Uncomfortable 58 (69)	Comfortable	Indifferent 42 (50)
4	What is your view towards mixed languages of Tibetan–Chinese and to persons speaking that mixture of languages?	Disapprove 61.3 (73)	Approve 14.3 (17)	Indifferent 24.4 (29)

Aims and methodology

The general teaching objective is to advance Tibetan bilingual education from a traditional form to a modern system that meets the challenge of the contemporary world. The emphasis of bilingual education today is put on facilitation of the students' command of their own minority language and culture and the acquisition of modern scientific knowledge. This is to enable them to attain the aim of *"Min-Han Jian Tong"* [mastering both Tibetan and Mandarin Chinese] in both oracy and literacy, and to develop themselves into modern talents with minority identity.

In terms of teaching procedures, as mentioned before, both Tibetan and Chinese are offered in primary schools as language course, but Tibetan is used as the language of instruction for all other content subjects. In secondary schools, bilingual teaching is gradually achieved through combining Tibetan and Chinese in teaching activities. This transition is done through measured adjustments and changes over time in teaching content, teaching curriculum, and teaching methodology. The cautious transition recognizes the complexity of transition in terms of students' cognitive development.

On the premises of mastering of the first language and its writing system (Tibetan), the pupils are introduced to the second language literacy (Mandarin Chinese), thus developing a firm linguistic basis for bilingual education. In principle, for this model, teachers of minority background should form the core teaching force and textbooks should be written by Tibetans or co-compiled by a mixed group of writers. All resources should be made to suit the teaching model. The bilingual teaching model with Tibetan as the main instruction language in content subjects and Chinese as a separate subject should not be seen as "exclusive education" as it is sometimes called. In the teaching process, the relationship between the two languages and the teaching objectives should be well understood and appropriately dealt with.

Effectiveness, Aims, and Operational Strategies of the Models Used in Gannan

This "priority alternative" approach is to adopt either the "Tibetan plus Chinese" model or the "Chinese plus Tibetan" model in primary and secondary education according the specific context. As described before, the former is often used in pasturing and agricultural-pasturing areas where people generally use Tibetan as the means for communication, whereas the latter is usually adopted in the mixed communities where all ethnic

Table 7.4 *t*-Test of pupils' scores in Tibetan, Mathematics, and Chinese

		Average	*Standard deviation*	*t*	*p*
Chinese	1.1	57.25	18.72	2.88	0.0005
	1.2	46.99	24.67	3.31	
Mathematics	1.1	68.72	13.27	3.31	0.001
	1.2	59.41	20.74		
Tibetan	1.1	49.23	21.31	−2.09	0.039
	1.2	56.92	24.00		

Note: 1.1, bilingual school following Chinese plus Tibetan model; 1.2, bilingual school following Tibetan plus Chinese model.

groups have at least a basic knowledge of Chinese and Chinese is often used as a lingua franca.

In order to see the effectiveness of the alternative models, Wan and Xing (1999) conducted *t*-test comparing examination scores of 421 students in three main school subjects. The following results (see Table 7.4) are obtained from the test showing statistic differences of the two models.

The difference of examination results in mathematics is hardly surprising as pupils in remote pasturing or agricultural-pasturing areas have traditionally been, will most probably continue to be scoring less in such examinations. This remains a challenge for minority education. What is surprising and encouraging is the means scored in Chinese and Tibetan by pupils taught by using the two different models. The results show that pupils taught with the "Tibetan plus Chinese" model are in no way linguistically inferior to those taught with the other model, despite the fact that many of the former group live in remote areas.

The "priority alternative" approach adopted in Gannan is now a characteristic of bilingual teaching in the region. The two parallel models have resulted from bilingual educators' years of teaching experience and educational research and practice in minority regions. The approach is a reflection of a macro-educational perspective, integrating traditional minority education with modern education. In view of minority psychology, the native language is always seen by a nationality as the foundation for learning any other language(s) and for carrying out all teaching activities, that is, the major channel for minority education in general (Wang, 1994). Socioculturally, this approach reflects the concern of sociologists and cultural studies scholars. They view bilingual teaching not only as an educational form but also as a perspective or channel to maintain and develop minority cultures. As a special instrument for minority culture transmission, the "Tibetan plus Chinese" model in Gannan is just a rewarding practice in this line of thinking.

Though differing in language as the main medium of instruction, the two models have the same teaching objectives. Both aim to achieve the goal of "having a command of the primary language, Tibetan, and acquiring a sound knowledge of the second, Chinese"; with strong competence in both languages learners taught in either model are likely to master the content of a common curriculum, to understand ethnic cultural heritage and to gain modern scientific knowledge.

Operational procedures

In primary schools that follow the "Tibetan plus Chinese" model, Tibetan is the medium of instruction for all the subjects from Grade 1 to Grade 3. Chinese is taught as a school subject. From Grade 4 onward, 4–5 teaching hours are added to Chinese language teaching each week while the time used for the Tibetan language subject is proportionally reduced. By the end of Grade 6, the Chinese proficiency of minority pupils is expected to reach the level a Chinese mainstream pupil can achieve after lower primary school (Grades 1–3) with other subjects to reach the same level as their peers in mainstream schools. The procedure and expectations are the same with those schools that follow the "Chinese plus Tibetan" model with only the roles of the two language reversed.

A very similar operational procedure and language expectations are found in secondary schools. In those schools where Tibetan is the main instruction language and Chinese as a separate subject, by the end of junior secondary (Grades 1–3), minority students' Chinese proficiency is expected to reach the level a Chinese mainstream student can achieve by the end of higher primary school (Grades 4–6) with other subjects to be the same level as their mainstream counterparts. When in senior secondary schools (Grades 4–6), the teaching hours for the Chinese language subject will be increased and those for Tibetan will be correspondingly reduced. By the end of senior secondary, students' Chinese proficiency is required to be the same level a Chinese mainstream student can achieve by the end of junior secondary (Grades 1–3) with other subjects to reach the same level as their mainstream counterparts. The procedure and expectations are the same with those schools that follow the "Chinese plus Tibetan" model, again with only the roles of the two languages reversed.

Operational strategies

Either model based on the "alternative priority" approach entail gradual increase of emphasis on the second language during the teaching process. In either model, the transition is a means, not an end. The purpose of the gradual increase of the second language is to enhance teaching effectiveness, not to put to an end the tasks of bilingual teaching. Throughout primary and secondary schooling, care is taken to appropriately deal with the relationship between the two languages, the course content, and the possible alternative use of the instruction languages. As to the textbook selection, in accordance with the different teaching models, the schools or classes with Tibetan as the main instruction language choose the textbooks co-compiled by the five provinces dominated by minority groups; the ones with Chinese as the main teaching language use textbooks following the national curriculum, except for the Tibetan language course that adopts the textbook co-complied by those five minority regions. As for teaching staff, different types of schools that adopt different models are expected to have minority and majority Mandarin speaking teachers in proportion.

The models used for bilingual education make available an operational paradigm for minority education in Gannan regions where Tibetan people reside. However, the actual implementation of the models is particularly complex because the "alternative priority" approach is operated in a context where two (in fact more than two) cultures meet. Therefore, more efforts are needed to explore ways to address the complexity of the "alternative priority" approach, which plays a vital role in bilingual education in Tibetan regions.

Significance of Tibetan–Chinese Bilingual Education

With the insight from the above analysis of bilingual education and Tibetan–Chinese bilingual teaching models, it is not difficult to see that bilingualism is both a linguistic and a sociocultural phenomenon. To meet the linguistic and sociocultural needs of the people, implementation of appropriate Tibetan–Chinese bilingual education is of crucial theoretical, educational, political, and sociocultural significance.

Theoretical significance

Current Tibetan–Chinese bilingual education models prove to be effective in language provision, and their implementation enriches bilingual teaching theories in China. The theoretical significance is twofold. First, the bilingual education models help create the needed space to promote the Tibetan language and broaden the scope for its development. Tibetan, one of the most developed minority languages in China, is the most important communication tool and the most effective thinking instrument for Zang people. It has played a vital part in transmitting Tibetan culture in Tibet's long history. Just as Tong Jinhua said in his *Survey of Tibetan Cultural Traditions*, since the creation of the Tibetan writing system, the wide spread and use of Tibetan has transcended time and space. The crucial role played by the language in recording, preserving, transmitting, communicating, and developing the Tibetan culture can never be overestimated. Numerous myths, folklores, stories, ballads, folk proverbs, and religions were all recorded and preserved with the language; many new creations such as epitaphs, epigraphs, historical documents, and religious works are produced; and a lot of Chinese, Indian, Nepalese, and Persian documents concerning medicine, religion, literature, and astronomical chronicles are translated into Tibetan. All these make the Tibetan culture capable of communicating with many other cultures and further drawing upon them for its development. The world-known Tibetan heroic epic, *The King Gesar*, in the form of ballad, has been spread widely and handed down until today through generations in considerable numbers of manuscripts and wood-cut copies. It is evident that Tibetan has played an important role in the transmission of *The King Gesar*. The famous *The Tibetan Tripitaka*, the valuable cultural heritage in the world, is not only a book of Buddhism but, in fact, an encyclopedia of various knowledge which includes many lost treatises of India. Most parts of it are translated into Sanskrit and some parts are translated into Chinese. The success of the book being preserved till now for contemporary scholars to use for reference should be of course attributed to the Tibetan written language. It is indisputable that Tibetan not only plays an invaluable part in recording, preserving, transmitting, communicating, and developing the Tibetan culture itself but also contributes to the preservation of cultural heritages of other nationalities and cultural groups.

We should never underestimate the functions of Tibetan in promoting minority cultures. In the era of reforming and opening up, it is impossible for us to continue rescuing, sorting, and promoting the Tibetan cultural heritages if we do not provide adequate opportunities to train enough personnel to be engaged in research and promotion of Tibetan language, which is the carrier and medium of its culture. We should be aware of and bring into full play both communicative and symbolic functions of Tibetan and further promote and develop the Tibetan culture (Fang *et al.* 2001). Appropriate models of Tibetan–Chinese bilingual education are the very means to this end.

Second, Tibetan is also the most effective tool in early learning stage and, for some, the whole compulsory education stage. Much primary education practice in Tibet or Tibetan residential regions has proved that it is more effective for the pupils to learn in Tibetan language when their Chinese is less proficient. This is the case for most pupils. According to recent statistics, among the 300,000 pupils in Tibet, nearly 70% live in the countryside, about 7% in cities, and 13% in towns. In terms of linguistic environment, about 90% live in the environment in which they are exposed to and familiar with only Tibetan. Tibetan is used by these children in most domains. Therefore, it is beneficial for these children to use Tibetan in learning at least in early primary education.

Educational, political, and sociocultural significance

Bilingual education in minority regions refers to the educational system in which both minority language and Chinese are used as instruction mediums in a planned way. Its purpose is to, through systematic bilingual education, enable minority students to first gain a good command of their native language and second to have good knowledge and competence in Chinese in order to be able to use Chinese for learning school subjects at higher levels and for communication with the majority and other nationalities. To some extent, we can say that implementing bilingual education in minority regions itself ensures the freedom of use and development of the minority language and transmission of the culture, which is conducive to the overall development of minority nationalities. From the above analysis of specific situations in Tibet and Tibetan communities elsewhere, it is clear that we should in most circumstances give priority to the minority students' proficient use and mastery of their native language. With a good command of native language, most minority students are more able to develop Chinese language skills with effective methods.

From an analysis of the historical development of bilingualism in minority regions, we can infer that bilingual proficiency will not only be beneficial to students' daily communication but also be favorable to their learning of advanced knowledge and culture. Therefore, in developing students Chinese skills, we should not only pay attention to their linguistic competence in Chinese, but more importantly, we should put emphasis on developing their academic language proficiency in thinking and expressing thoughts in Chinese. That is the ultimate aim of Tibetan–Chinese bilingual education. Only when educators have fully understood this point, can bilingual education for minority regions achieve desirable results and its objectives fulfilled.

Besides its educational aim, Tibetan–Chinese bilingual education is an important manifestation of minority nationality policies, nationality equality, and language equality in Tibet and Tibetan communities in other provinces. Language is an important boundary marker to distinguish different nationalities and is a major characteristic in forming an ethnic community. Language equality is the embodiment of nationality equality. Both notions are explicated in the constitution of the country as an indispensable part of ethnic nationality policies. The constitution and the laws for autonomous minority regions have made specific statements about the issue of teaching minority language and Chinese in schools. For instance, it has been clearly stated in Constitution that "every nationality has the freedom to use and develop its own language" (*The Constitution* ..., 2005). Article 37 in "The Laws for Minority Autonomous Regions" (*The Autonomous Laws* ..., 2005) stipulates that "in schools recruiting mainly minority students, textbooks in minority language, if available, should be properly used and lessons should also be presented in minority language; in upper grades of primary schools and secondary schools, the course of Chinese should be established to popularize standard Chinese." Bilingual education is of course an inevitable response to national minority policies and the implementation process itself, to a certain degree, mirrors the political realities in China.

On the sociocultural plane, Tibetan–Chinese bilingual education is beneficial to promoting and developing Tibetan culture, thus realizing the common prosperity among nationalities. A minority culture has been developed throughout its history of civilization. Each culture has features of its own and reflects values, beliefs, and norms of its people. Language is not only an indispensable part but also an embodiment of a particular culture. To promote bilingual education in primary and secondary schools is thus not only to maintain a minority culture but also to further develop it because pupils are able to draw upon knowledge and values from two or more languages and cultures, the process of which enables pupils to bring cultures into relationships and in turn to enrich their own culture(s). Especially nowadays, with the rapid development of science and technology and the progress of society, different nationality groups tend to learn from each other more consciously as they become more and more interdependent. Through fostering bilingual talents who are willing to explore the relationship between a minority culture and the majority Chinese culture, bilingual education makes it possible for minority nationalities to have more opportunities to learn from other cultures and to broaden their perspectives to view the world. That will in turn create a favorable environment for achieving the goal of common prosperity and national harmony.

Conclusions

As is argued throughout the chapter, Tibetan–Chinese bilingual education is beneficial for the development of Tibetan education, educational equality, and national unity. Bilingual education is an important part in minority education. Minority languages are not only a tool for minority groups to communicate and think but a symbol of their identity. People feel deeply attached to their mother tongue—historically, psychologically, and socioculturally. It has proved through years of bilingual education practice that, in many minority dominated regions, to implement bilingual teaching with a minority language as the main instruction language in primary and secondary schools is important with regard to encouraging parents to send their children to schools, increasing the attendance rate of school-age children and reducing drop-out rate. This is clearly a critical prerequisite for developing minority education. On the basis of a strong foundation of linguistic competence in their mother tongue and normal cognitive development, minority children are in a good position to use the native language as the medium to learn languages and cultures of other nationalities and to participate in social activities.

Language is a means of communication, a tool of mental activities, and a symbolic marker of ethnicity. The bilingual speakers' possession of two sets of communicative means and thinking tools means the increase of their individual potentiality. From the perspective of improving cognitive development of minority children, to promote minority cultures, and to ensure nationality equality, bilingual education in minority regions should be enhanced and strengthened.

References

Danzeng, J. (1996) Xizang shuangyu shijian yu tansuo [The practice and exploration of bilingual education in Tibet]. *Xizang Yanjiu* [*Tibet Study*] 1, 45–49.

Fang, J., Wang, J. and Linda, S. (eds) (2001) *Woguo dangdai shaoshu minzu shuangyu jiaoxue de shijian yu lilun* [Bilingual teaching practice and theory for contemporary minority nationalities in China]. Xi'an: Shannxi renmin chubanshe [Shaanxi People's Press].

Fei, X. (1989) Zhonghua minzu de duoyuan yiti geju [On the multiplex integrated setup of Chinese nationalities]. *Beijing Daxue Xuebao* [*Journal of Peking University*] 3, 1–6.

Han, K. (1991) *Xiwang zhiguang* [*Light of Hope*] (pp. 113). Lanzhou: Gansu Renmin Chubanshe [Gansu People's Press].

The Autonomous Laws for Minority Regions of People's Republic of China. On WWW at www.gov.cn. Accessed 12.9.2005.

The Constitution of the People's Republic of China. On WWW at www.gov.cn. Accessed 14.6.2005.

Wan, M. and Wang, J. (1997) Hanzang shuangyuzhe yuyan taidu diaocha [Study of bilingual attitudes of Tibetan-Chinese speakers]. *Xinlixue Bao* [*Journal of Psychology*] 3, 294–300.

Wan, M. and Xing, Q. (1999) Shuangyu moshi yu zangzu xuesheng zhili, xueye chengji guanxi yanjiu [A correlational study on bilingual teaching models and Tibetan students intelligence and academic records]. *Xibei Shida Xuebao [Journal of Northwest Normal University]* 5, 76–81.

Wang, J. (1994) Lun woguo shaoshu minzu jiaoxue de moshi [On bilingual teaching models in minority education in China]. *Xibei Shida Xuebao [Journal of Northwest Normal University]* 12, 70–74.

Yang, C. (1996) Zangyu jiaoxue dui fazhan mingzu jiaoyu de zhongyao xing [Importance of Tibetan teaching in the development of minority education]. *Xizang Yanjiu [Tibet Study]* 2, 56–60.

Part 3

Practices and Underpinning Principles

Chapter 8
Integrated English—A Bilingual Teaching Model in Southern China

ZENGJUN FENG AND JINJUN WANG

Introduction

Owing to a rapid process of globalization and internationalization of education, bilingual or multilingual human resources are in great demand. This is the most important reason why bilingual teaching is booming today.

As Tucker (1999) points out, there are many more bilingual or multilingual individuals today in the world than there are monolinguals and there are many more children who have been and continue to be educated through a second or a later-acquired language, at least for some portion of their formal education, than there are children educated exclusively via the first language. In many countries, the development of bilingual or multilingual proficiency is viewed as desirable by policy makers, educators, and parents. China is one of such countries.

Before the reform and opening-up policy, bilingual teaching in China mainly referred to helping minority people master both Chinese and their minority languages. However, bilingual teaching has nowadays extended to refer to using a foreign language (often English) as a medium for teaching content subjects in major cities and other developed areas. As Wang Xu dong (2003: 77) points out that, within basic education, especially within the area of compulsory education, this kind of bilingual teaching experiments are mainly being made available in major cities such as Beijing, Shanghai, Tientsin, Dalian, Guangzhou, Shenzhen, and Tsingtao. Most of these experiments aim to offer content subjects teaching in English (Liu, 2002). For instance, the education department in Liaoning Province proposed to offer bilingual teaching in such content subjects as maths, science, arts, and selective subjects in primary schools (Wang, X.D., 2003). Uptil now, the People's Education Press has published some bilingual textbooks such as physics, chemistry, geometry, and algebra for junior high schools, and physics, chemistry, history, and biology for senior high schools.

Though a new phenomenon, bilingual teaching varies in China in terms of approach. In Tientsin, Zhang (2002: 29) proposes a "transitional model" for "bilingualism, biculturalism, and bi-competence" in which the use of English for teaching school subjects is progressively increased from 30% at the preschool level to 60% at the senior high school level. In Xi'an, a "partial-immersion bilingual program" in which pupils are immersed in English language environments for about 15 hours per week is adopted (Qiang & Zhao, 2000, cited in Feng, 2005: 538). In Shanghai, according to Wang, L.Y. (2003: 23), a near-total "immersion model" is adopted at lower grades in primary schools, shifting to a partial-immersion bilingual teaching at higher grades aiming for additive bilingualism. In Guangdong Province, there are a few different bilingual teaching models such as those used in Shenzhen and Shunde. The Integrated English (IE) model, which is the focus of this chapter, is one of them. Taking the advancement of international bilingual teaching and the advent of China's reform and opening-up policies as the background and applying international experiences of bilingual teaching to the context of China's foreign language teaching, IE has been developed as a bilingual teaching model which suits the developed areas of China.

IE and Bilingual Teaching in China

Although disagreement still exists about what bilingual teaching is, many people agree to a working definition given in *Longman Dictionary of Applied Linguistics* (Richards *et al.*, 1985). It takes bilingual teaching as the use of a second or foreign language in school for the teaching of content subjects. There are also different ideas about what bilingualism is. At one extreme end of the definition, Bloomfield (1993, cited in Romaine, 1995: 11) specifies "native-like control of two languages" as the criterion for bilingualism. Haugen (1953, cited in Romaine, 1995: 11) draws attention to the other when he states that bilingualism begins when the speaker of one language can produce complete meaningful utterances in the other language. Therefore, any person can be bilingual to some degree, and bilingualism is a continuum. In China, Zhu (2004) states that for Chinese students bilingualism refers to the ability to use English to satisfy the basic need of English for future study, work, and life.

Different conceptions of bilingual teaching result in different bilingual teaching models such as immersion program, maintenance bilingual education, transitional bilingual education, etc. According to Tucker (1999), the use of multiple languages in education may be attributed to numerous factors, such as the linguistic heterogeneity of a country or region, specific social or religious attitudes, the desire to promote national identity, or innovative language education programs implemented to promote proficiency in international language(s) of wider communication together with proficiency in national and regional languages. Take the immersion program, which originated in Canada, for example. Around 1975, Canada's first French immersion programs came into being because Canadians realized English-speaking students were not acquiring enough French to attain satisfactory grades in school and to find jobs in French-speaking parts of Canada. However, in Finland, languages involved in bilingual teaching include French, German, and Swedish besides Finnish and English because of its favorable multilingual environment and government's encouragement (Feng & Ke, 2003: 64).

China has seen rapid development in bilingual teaching in recent years. Some local governments encourage high schools, primary schools, and kindergartens to make bilingual teaching experiments that take English as a medium of instruction for content subjects. There seem to be three main driving forces behind this. First, it results from the aspiration of internationalization of education. All learners in the experimental schools are majority language (Mandarin) speakers who do not need to "cross the bridge that helps them be proficient in their native language and in English" (José, 2004: 126) in order to "make a smooth transition into English instruction." That is to say, most subjects are taught in Chinese rather than English, which is just a foreign language in China. However, English is the most widely used language in the world. In China no one seems to doubt that he or she can communicate with people from every part of the world after having mastered English. Second, the ultimate target of bilingual teaching in China is to improve the effect of English teaching. In China, people always complain about the result of EFL teaching. They want to find an alternative that is more effective to substitute for EFL. Third, bilingual teaching in China is believed to be a kind of additive bilingual teaching, because it aims "to develop first and second language proficiency fully" (Latham, 1998: 79), not to thwart in any way the development of the first language.

As we mentioned above, many people in China accept the definition of bilingual teaching given by Richards *et al.* (1985), and therefore Canada's French Immersion Program is always taken as the most effective model (Lu, 2005: 190; Wang, B.H. 2003: 82). Yang (cited in Huang, 2004: 5) concludes that international tendency of bilingual teaching is to teach maths, physics, chemistry, biology, and computer first in a second language. However, does the immersion model suit the context of China? To answer this question, we must investigate the status quo of China's education, especially that of China's foreign language teaching. First, we must bear in mind that the National College Entrance Examination is the supreme target of China's basic education, at least for the time being. Examination-oriented education and testing have been the main characteristic of China's compulsory education. Bilingual teaching in China must take this factor into consideration while trying to improve the pupils' English levels. Second, much more importance is attached to EFL in China. English is one of the core subjects whether in primary schools, high schools, or universities. However, many university students who have learned English over 10 years cannot speak English fluently. This kind of phenomenon declares itself as the failure of traditional EFL teaching in China. Third, China is a developing country which lacks educational resources, including financial support and qualified bilingual teachers. What is more, China is a developing country which runs the largest-scale education in the world. Therefore, bilingual teaching in China must take cost effectiveness into consideration. Fourth, China is a developing country with a vast territory. A deep gap exists between China's eastern areas and western areas. Immersion programs mean a high requirement for financial and human resources such as equipment, authentic textbooks, and qualified teachers (Wang, B.H., 2003: 87) and a breakaway from an examination-oriented curriculum. It is obvious that neither traditional EFL teaching nor immersion programs can solve these problems, and therefore they do not suit the context of China. Hence, a new model to teach English must be established in China to address the contextual factor listed above. Under this condition, IE was established on the basis of careful studies and experimental experiences of 5 years. It absorbed the successful experiences of a wide range of bilingual teaching, combined them with the context of China's developed areas, and abandoned traditional EFL teaching methods such as learning by rote and grammar-translation approach.

IE stresses taking English as the language tool and integrating language with content. It falls under the rubric of content-based instruction according to Met (1999). As a typical language-driven program, IE advocates teaching contents in English to enrich or reinforce instruction in the student's native language, but not substituting for it. In fact, the responsibility for content learning in its academic sense lies with other content subject teachers. English teachers may, but unnecessarily, consult with colleagues in other disciplines to determine which, when, and how content will be integrated with language. Language activities and tasks for language practice may be drawn from many disciplines in a single lesson or unit, but all of them should focus on one topic. A topic can be taught in IE through different aspects. For example, if the topic of a unit is vegetables, it may be taught through such activities as classifying vegetables (from the aspect of botany), drawing pictures of vegetables (from the aspect of fine arts), buying vegetables in a supermarket (from the aspect of economics or mathematics). That is to say, IE belongs to theme-based courses, which are language-driven: the goal of these courses is to help students develop L2 skills and proficiency. Themes are selected based on their potential to contribute to the learner's language growth in specific topical or functional domains. What is taught in English classes is not only the language itself. It includes all kinds of knowledge areas arranged by themes, such as language, maths, geography, history, literary, civic virtues, music, art, science, society, etc. However, students (and their teachers) are not necessarily accountable for content mastery. Indeed, content learning is incidental.

IE consists of three main features. First, as any content-based model, it is an integration of content with language but gives prominence to the practice of language through learning knowledge of content subjects. Second, it stresses integration of interdisciplinary theories. IE incorporates contemporary psychological and pedagogical developments or achievements into bilingual teaching. For this reason, as Feng and Ke (2003) point out, IE aims at application and development of such theories as Lozanov's suggestopedia, Howard Gadner's multiple Intelligences, etc. Third, a group of experts from different research fields often work together to research psychological and cognitive characteristics of learners and characteristics of language learning. Their theoretical insights constantly feed into curriculum planning and practice. As we can see, IE is based on, but goes beyond, content-language integration to take other theories and methodology into consideration. It is further enhanced through ongoing reflections and research.

There are some similarities between IE and CLIL (content and language integrated learning), which have an important role to play in ensuring the attainment of EU objectives in the area of language learning (*The European Council. . .*, 2006). Both integrate content with language. Nevertheless, there is a difference. CLIL is aiming to enable pupils to study a non-language-related subject in a foreign language and so the subject knowledge becomes the end, while in IE content subject knowledge is not the end but the means to learn English. Sometimes, in IE, a small part of the non-language-related subjects is taught in English, often through the cooperation of bilingual teachers and non-language teachers. For example, an English teacher may cooperate with a physical education (PE) teacher to give a PE class in English, but the English input only takes a small part of PE class time.

A Brief History of IE

The first period: Failure of "immersion programs"

After the return of Hong Kong to Chinese sovereignty, Hong Kong was taken as an education base of English teaching by the Mainland. Fortunately, the International and Comparative Education Research Institute of South China Normal University in Guangzhou was chosen by Shenzhen Educational Bureau to undertake the task of introducing the experience of Hong Kong's bilingual teaching in Guangdong Province. In 2000, we began to introduce "immersion programs" in southern China. A few primary schools and kindergartens were invited to join in a pilot program. We planned to begin with partial immersion (teaching PE, music, arts, and maths in English at the first stage) and move to total immersion eventually. However, we soon found it impossible to succeed in immersion programs in China. After all, we had very few bilingual textbooks of content subjects for primary school pupils, and hardly any qualified bilingual teachers either, which are preconditions for immersion programs. As a consequence, just a few months later, all experimental schools and kindergartens lost interest in this program. The first experiment was a clear failure (Feng & Ke, 2003).

The second period: Adapting international experiences of bilingual teaching to suit the context of China

In order to find our way out of the difficult situation, we started to search for a bilingual teaching model that suits the context of China. This idea got support from all experimental schools and our cooperating experts in America, Finland, and Hong Kong, and strengthened our cooperation with bilingual teaching researchers at home and abroad. We invited native speakers (American experts from the University of Cincinnati and the University of Nevada), bilingual experts in Europe (experts from the University of Helsinki), and experts in Hong Kong (from the Hong Kong Institute of Education and Hong Kong Baptist University) to participate in our research project. In 2001, a group of reputable scholars from America, Finland, Hong Kong, and Macao gathered together in Guangzhou and decided to set up a new bilingual model which suits the context of Guangdong Province (the most developed province in China). It was the consensus of all attendant experts that English should be taken as a language tool, and must be integrated with content, and the new bilingual model must be open to the other models to absorb reasonable ideas from them. For this reason, this newly established model was named Integrated English.

The third period: Moving forward

Once the conceptual model was developed, several measures were taken to put the model into application. First, as IE stresses the importance of bilingual teachers as researchers, we explicitly encourage the notion of teacher as a researcher. Since 2001 we have held academic symposiums every year and awarded some teachers for their outstanding classroom teaching, teaching plans, research papers, or courseware. We encourage bilingual teachers of IE to do research on bilingual teaching and advocate intercommunication among experimental schools. The aims of the first few symposia were to do action research on the general principles of bilingual teaching. The latest symposiums start to focus on the IE approach itself, especially on IE teaching activities and on how to use the experimental textbooks effectively. Second, we have established a strict experimental system, set up a research center of IE, and built an IE website (http://www.integratedenglish.com). Third, we have laid emphasis on theoretical research. We have published such theoretical books as *A Handbook for IE Primary School Teachers* (Luo, 2002), *Bilingual Teaching and Integrated English* (Feng & Ke, 2003), *Teaching Methods of Integrated English* (Yuan, 2005), and *An Introduction of IE Teaching Model* (Feng *et al.*, 2006). Now we are planning to publish the following books: *The Principles of Bilingual Teaching and Integrated English* and *Teaching Activities of Primary Integrated English*. Furthermore, the second edition of our experimental school textbook, *Primary Integrated English* (Wang *et al.*, 2005), has been published with the multimedia courseware of this version. Some reference books to aid the bilingual teaching of our experiment have also been written and a collection of experimental teaching plans is under compilation. All these are meant to provide our teachers with "sharp weapons" and the feedbacks from stakeholders are usually positive.

Theory of Integrated English

Three rationales of bilingual teaching

IE emphasizes that bilingual teaching must abide by three rationales: the rationale of children's development of cognition, the logic of children's development of language competence, and the principle of language teaching.

Bilingual teaching involves not only linguistics, but also psychology and pedagogy. For this reason, IE stresses interdisciplinary insights from pedagogy, psychology, and linguistics. A group of experts in these three fields often work together to analyze psychological and cognitive characteristics of learners and characteristics of language learning. When making a decision, IE experts will consider from three aspects: linguistics, cognition, and intelligence. For example, when allotting unit topics to textbooks for different grades, the cognitive ability of pupils in each grade must be considered. Such topics as *body parts, family members* can be taught in Grade 1, but such topics as *states of matter* must be taught after Grade 3. Topics of the latter group clearly require higher cognitive thinking skills than those in the former. Another example is whether phonetic symbols should be taught at the beginning period. The teaching of them will enhance the learning of English, especially from the point of view to look up the pronunciation of new words in dictionary. However, learning of phonetic symbols will aggravate pupils' cognitive burdens, and may make them lose interest in English learning. Therefore, IE opposes teaching pupils phonetic symbols at the beginning period.

IE stresses the role of acquisition in language learning and proposes that bilingual teaching should be based on children's mother language, cognitive ability, and comprehension ability. According to Vygotsky (1978), there exists a "zone of proximal development" (ZPD) between what a child can do with help and what he or she can do without guidance. Therefore, in bilingual teaching, we must consider what children have already learned, and expand what they have known. For instance, pupils in Grade 1 (about 6-year old) have known such simple shapes as triangle, circle, and rectangle, but they know little about the features of them and find it difficult to differ square and rectangle from trapezoid. Then the unit about shapes in IE textbook begins with familiar shapes like circle and triangle, and expands children's knowledge to some new shapes such as oval and trapezoid, and helps them to distinguish one kind of shape from another.

IE does not exclude any useful teaching approaches. However, it advocates abiding by principles of communicative language teaching (CLT) in bilingual teaching. In addition, IE stresses that English be taught as early as possible in order to develop children's language and thinking abilities, because the development of children's intelligence takes place concurrently with the development of language (Feng & Ke, 2003). The learning of a second language at an early age through a mainly CLT approach will not impede but will enhance the development of intelligence and the acquisition of the first language.

Six beliefs in bilingual teaching

There are six beliefs of bilingual teaching in IE. They are starting English learning at an early age, teaching totally in English, focusing on listening and speaking first, acquiring English subconsciously, developing fully the abilities of English learners, and integrating content with language.

Learning English at an early age

It is a commonplace observation that (young) children are faster and better second language learners than adults. Children seem to acquire a second language without any effort and they generally attain high levels of proficiency. It is therefore often recommended that children start learning a second language as soon as possible. As they grow older, they will gradually lose this unique capability. The concept of "critical period" was proposed by Lenneberg (1967) for first and second language acquisition. Lenneberg assumed that there is a lateralization of the brain for anyone, which is finished at about puberty. Although there are doubts on this assumption, many people believe that there is a sensitive or optimal period for the acquisition of certain second language skills, especially pronunciation, and the social and psychological distance between the learner and the target community may be smaller for younger learners (Appel & Muysken, 1987: 94–95). For the above-mentioned reasons, IE advocates starting to learn English early.

Teaching English totally in English

IE objects to teaching grammatical rules directly. It stresses the internalization of language rules and regards it as an effective way to get language sense and form a habit to think in English. We accept the conception that a man cannot really master what is taught without internalization. Only through internalization can the newly learned knowledge be conversed from explicit knowledge into tacit knowledge. This requires explicit knowledge be embodied in action and practice through simulations or experiments to trigger learning-by-doing processes. This pedagogical philosophy is reflected by the notion we come up with for IE, that is, language cannot be mastered through teaching but learning. To master a language, the pupils must engage themselves in activities conducted in English.

But the occurrence of internalization needs a certain amount of input in English. Mackey (1978) mentions in his classic work, *Language teaching analysis,* that the estimated time in school for second language teaching is about 250 hours per year, while the total time for a baby to learn his or her first language during the first 5 years at home is about 25,000 hours. This indicates that a certain amount of time is the prerequisite to mastering a language. In China, it is hard to find a favorable bilingual environment for students to learn English. If an English teacher taught English in Chinese, his or her pupils would have less time to expose to English. For this reason, an IE teacher is required to teach his or her pupils totally in English in class, and even talk with the pupils in English after class. When a teacher finds it difficult to explain something in English, body language, visual aids, or material objects are suggested for use. For instance, pupils in Grade 1 find it hard to understand the meaning of "same" and "different." Then an IE teacher may draw two pictures of ducks and two pictures of rabbits. Then he will classify them into two groups and help students understand that one duck is the same with the other and one rabbit is the same with the other, but the two ducks are different from the two rabbits. This will help pupils understand the meaning of "same" and "different," but avoid the explanation in the first language. Moreover, what the pupils learn in the process of explanation is much more than the meaning of the two words. They get more opportunities to contact with English, especially the English out of textbooks.

Focusing on listening and speaking first

The acquisition of one's first language tells us that listening and speaking happen earlier than reading and writing, because no one can read or write before he or she can listen and speak his or her mother tongue. Furthermore, one's oral vocabulary is usually larger than his or her reading vocabulary. Thus, IE regards listening and speaking as the first step in bilingual teaching. It suggests a focused curriculum for developing listening and speaking skills with less emphasis on direct instruction of reading and writing at lower grades. This focus gradually shifts from the former to reading and writing skills at higher grades.

Why do we focus on listening and speaking first? Research on first language learning shows that verbal communication of parents with their children is a strong predictor of how rapidly children expand their language learning (Cuevas, 1996). It is widely believed that parental speech to young children is so redundant with its context that a person with no knowledge of the order in which parents' words are spoken, only the words themselves, can infer from transcripts, with high accuracy, what was being said. For this reason, IE teachers are encouraged to speak as much English as possible in their classes and after class even if the pupils may not understand them completely. We call this teaching strategy "Die Die Bu Xiu" (keeping on talking). With this strategy, a bilingual teacher in IE experimental schools is expected to speak English centering on a topic rather than repeating a few words or sentence patterns. For instance, a teacher can talk about spring outing, the trees, flowers, water, sky, kite, dressing, food, weather, activities, animals, the color of a flower, the width of a river, the price of a skirt, or even the number of swallows when he or she is teaching a unit about spring. He or she should never limit his or her language input within a few words (e.g. season, spring, rain, swallow) and expressions (e.g. Spring is coming.) about spring. Speaking is encouraged at any time in IE classes. At the beginning period, a period of silence is permitted, which may last for 1 or 2 months. After the silent period, pupils will have a strong desire to open their mouths. They may initially respond to the simple questions with "Yes" or "No." Gradually, with the encouragement and help of the teacher, most pupils will talk more and more. For instance, when talking about a cat, an IE teacher may ask "Do you like a cat?" or "Do you have a cat?" Pupils may answer simply with "Yes" or "No." The teacher may then help pupils with visual aids and words such as "This is a black (white) cat." In this way, the pupils will at least utter a few words about the color of a cat.

Acquiring English subconsciously

Pupils are more interested in activities (e.g. hands-on activity) than in learning English words, sentences, and grammatical rules. Thus, IE advocates not to teach vocabulary and grammar directly but to use techniques to enable pupils to acquire them subconsciously through activities or tasks. This is why IE stresses language acquisition and task-oriented learning.

Language learning and language acquisition are different. The learning of one's first language is a kind of acquisition. It is something "every child does successfully, in a matter of a few years and without the need for formal lessons" (Pinker, 1995: 135). Nevertheless, the learning of one's second language is so hard, even with the help of textbooks and teachers. Language is a tool and is different from other content subjects like maths or history. A man cannot master a language through learning the knowledge about language itself but through using a language to do something, because language is a tool in nature. For instance, when teaching something about "poster," in IE classes, pupils will be encouraged to make some English posters. In the process of making them, pupils can learn much more than a few words and sentences about a poster.

Hidden curriculum is an important part of a school's curricula today. It is also called latent curriculum or implicit curriculum, and "is taught by the school, not by any teacher... something is coming across to the pupils which may never be spoken in the English lesson or prayed about in assembly. They are picking-up an approach to living and an attitude to learning" (Meighan, 1981). IE stresses the mutual complementarity of overt curriculum and hidden curriculum in order to increase the effectiveness of English learning. In the campus of an IE experimental school, you can find many English posters, slogans, and signs. Pupils and teachers would greet each other in English and speak some daily English. There are many kinds of English activities including English salons and English corners. All this can help the pupils feel like studying in a favorable environment of English learning, and exert a subtle influence on pupils' acquisition of English.

Developing fully the abilities of English learners

IE opposes teaching English in Chinese or dismembering English into pieces and then feeding learners with them. It focuses on the full development of a learner's language abilities and stresses that language teaching should satisfy the overall needs of children's language development. It advocates taking English as an entire system instead of a collection of vocabulary and grammar that can be dissected and then individually taught. This can liberate foreign language teachers from the teaching method of rote learning to teaching more for meaning and less for forms. This is the essence of the CLT approach developed by scholars such as Hymes (1972), Canale (1983), and Beale (2002). IE stresses the full development of language skills, especially the communicative competence of pupils.

IE highlights thematic activities (teaching activities must center on a topic), the interest of learners, and the characteristics of life. Teachers adopting the IE approach are expected to try their best to create an authentic setting for pupils to contact English. To create a vivid and natural environment of English learning, they are often found to use such teaching methods as Total Physical Response (TPR), CLT Approach, Audiolingual Method, Community Language Learning, and Natural Approach. For example, in using the Natural Approach, a teacher would accept a "silent period" which could last a few months. During this silent period, output of language is not required. Therefore, pupils "absorb language without the stress of audio-lingual-type listen and repeat drills" (Oebel, 2001). For TPR approach, it combines information and skills through the use of the kinesthetic sensory system. This combination of skills allows the pupils to assimilate information and skills at a rapid rate. As a result, this leads to a high degree of motivation. In short, different teaching methods are integrated in IE classes. The purpose of such integration is to achieve the best teaching results and develop fully the language competence of English learners.

Integrating content with language

As Met (1999) points out that the integration of language and content has been a growing phenomenon in language teaching since the early 1980s and continues to be a tendency of bilingual teaching in the world. As we mentioned before, IE is based on content-based approach by integrating content with language. However, to facilitate cognitive development and to enhance mother-tongue competence, we do not encourage any school participating in IE experiment to use English as the only medium of instruction for teaching a school subject. As Flood *et al.* (1996: 356) state that the "failure to realize the potential benefits of native language instruction has kept us from focusing on the most effective ways to teach children." Cummins (1989) and Krashen and Biber (1988) also insist that instruction in the students' native language simultaneously promotes the development of literacy skills in both the native language and a second language. The use of the native language to develop the academic skills of students acquiring English appears beneficial for helping students avoid cognitive confusion and underachievement in their school performance (Hakuta & Diaz, 1984; Krashen & Biber, 1988; Thomas & Collier, 1997).

Thomas and Collier (1997) found that postponing teaching of academically challenging concepts until students develop the academic proficiency in English is not educationally worthwhile. Individuals most easily develop cognitive skills and master content material when they are taught in a familiar language. Once cognitive or academic language skills of the target language are developed, content subject knowledge can readily transfer itself from one language to another (Tucker, 1999). Therefore, in IE experimental schools, the integration of content and language is in some sense limited in scope. The English classes do not substitute for any content subjects.

The ultimate goal of IE is to speak English freely and to talk about non-language topics freely. However, many English learners in China cannot achieve this target. The most important reasons may not be due to poor pronunciation or lack of grammatical knowledge but due to a lack of basic words and expressions used in content subjects. Once I asked the university students in my English lecture, "Do you know how to express $1 + 1 = 2$ in English?" Most of them could not provide a quick answer. On the contrary to EFL teaching, IE provides many chances in English classes to contact maths, physics, chemistry, arts, geography, music, PE, and so on. Pupils are expected to communicate freely about the general matters related to these subjects. Thus, in IE experimental textbooks, there are many topics from different content subjects, and under a topic related knowledge is taught upon. For example, there is a unit entitled *Wood and Iron*, a topic from physics about matters in the world. But in this unit some knowledge about chemistry (e.g. corrosion) can also be learned besides some physics knowledge such as properties of wood and iron. At the same time, pupils learn how to protect our environment, why to keep world peace, and so on. As a result, pupils in IE experimental schools are equipped with the necessary language skills and content knowledge to talk freely on that topic.

Three aspects of development accelerations

According to IE principles, bilingual teaching must meet the requirements of both bilingual teaching and developmental psychology. Most researchers believe that knowing two languages and two perspectives gives bilingual children a more diversified and flexible basis for cognition than their monolingual peers and provides them with an "excellent tool" to fulfill their academic and intellectual potential (Appel & Muysken, 1987). This was confirmed in IE experiments. As we mentioned above, the development of pupils' intelligence goes hand in hand with the development of language, and a pupil in an IE experiment can talk freely in English to a level nearing his native-language (Chinese) competence because she or he can express everything in daily life in English and IE applies theories of ZPD and $i+1$ into bilingual teaching experiment. For these reasons, pupils in IE experimental schools can accelerate their abilities of cognition, intelligence, and language competence. For example, a normal pupil in Grade 1 may know the names of a few kinds of flowers, but an IE pupil in Grade 1 may not only tell you the names of many flowers in English but also tell you the meanings behind the names and even something about ikebana in English.

Tangible achievements made so far

Achievements by pupils

Krashen and Biber (1988) concluded that children who participate in properly designed bilingual programs reach satisfactory levels of competence in all academic areas. Genesee *et al.* (2003) found that students in bilingual programs can develop academic skills on a par with, or superior to, the skills of comparison groups of their peers educated in English-only classrooms. August and Hakuta (1997) have also found that highly bilingual students reach higher levels of academic and cognitive functioning than do monolingual students or students with poor bilingual skills. How about IE? Can IE enhance the development of first language and second language? If yes, how do we measure effectiveness? In 2003, Ma (2003), an IE bilingual teacher, made a statistical study on the effectiveness of

IE on the development of academic skills. Her analyses of data collected show that IE can greatly improve English levels of pupils and enhance the development of pupil's academic skills simultaneously. Bilingual teachers from Huiyang Experimental Primary School report (Feng & Ke, 2003: 257) that "evaluation indicates that pupils have improved their English levels greatly and become more active and creative... some pupils even became the interpreters when their parents communicated with foreigners." In April 2006, the improvisational performances of pupils from Boluo Experimental Primary School were live broadcasted by local municipal TV station in Huizhou city. In the municipal park, these pupils debated with some foreigners in English and presented their oral compositions as soon as they got the topics from the audience. More than 10,000 people in the park watched the performance and were deeply impressed by the wonderful performance of the pupils.

Popularity of experimental schools

Guangdong is the most developed province in China. Radio Guangdong reports that Guangdong's GDP hit 2.17 trillion yuan (264.84 billion US dollars) in 2005, exceeding Singapore and Hong Kong, and the provincial per capita GDP was 2882 US dollars. Now in Guangdong there are many foreign-funded enterprises and sino-foreign cooperative enterprises. In recent years, learning English as a second language here is perceived by many parents as of great importance. They believe that their children can benefit a lot from learning English as early as possible. Parents in Guangdong could not agree more with Barratt-Pugh and Rohl (2001) that learning two languages seems to be most beneficial to anyone's future. Many parents therefore send their children to bilingual schools. A famous bilingual school can always attract a crowd of parents and pupils. For this reason, many schools claim to be bilingual schools. The number of experimental schools has increased rapidly in recent years, because IE is widely seen as an approach that is based on educational theories, coordinates bilingual teaching with full development of experimental schools, and meets the need of schools. Almost every IE experimental school or kindergarten is famous and popular in its respective communities now. For instance, Jiangmen Second Education Kindergarten in Jiangmen city has become one of the most famous kindergartens in China, and now it is planning to run a chain of kindergartens. Huiyang Experimental School has become one of the top-class schools in Guangdong Province in only 3 years after it was set up. Guancheng English Experimental School in Dongguan city enrolled more than 1,700 students only 1 year after it was built and half a year after it participated in IE experiment. Jiamei School in Zhaoqing city was about to close down before it decided to join in IE experiment. Only 1 year after it had joined in IE experiment, it became the most popular school in Zhaoqing city.

Raised quality of teaching resources

Our Integrated English Teaching and Research Centre runs a 1-week teacher training program every year, which aims at improving the teaching skills of IE teachers. In the past 5 years, more than 300 bilingual teachers have taken this training and become qualified IE teachers. This has accelerated the professional development of English teachers. Teaching qualities in the region, in general, are obviously improved in a short time span. Most teachers could voluntarily lay more emphases on the attainment of students' full development of language abilities and improve their theoretical understanding of language teaching through reading about pedagogy and linguistics. Many of them applied IE experimental theories to the analyses of their teaching activities. Some of them have become outstanding English teachers and got many prizes in various English teaching competitions.

IE experiment has not only improved the quality of English teaching of experimental schools, but has also pushed ahead the English teaching levels of nonexperimental primary schools. Almost every experimental school has held some large-scale English teaching forums in the city or county where it is located. For instance, in 2002, Boluo Experimental School held an English teaching forum in Boluo County. In 2003, the 3rd International Symposium of IE was also held in this school. Jianghua Primary School held an English teaching forum in Jiangmen city every year in the past 5 years. The other experimental schools such as Shiwan No. 1 Primary School in Foshan City, Huiyang Experimental School in Huizhou City, Longmen Primary School in Longmen County, Media Experimental Primary School in Foshan City, and Jiamei school in Zhaoqing City introduced and extended the IE experiment to local societies. All these helped IE experiment exert great influence on local societies, and also pushed ahead the English teaching levels of local schools and kindergartens.

References

Appel, R. and Muysken, P. (1987) *Language Contact and Bilingualism*. London: Edward Arnold.

August, D. and Hakuta, K. (1997) *Improving Schooling for Language-Minority Children: A Research Agenda.* Washington, DC: National Academy Press.

Barratt-Pugh, C. and Rohl, M. (2001). *Literacy Learning in the Early Years.* Buckingham, Philadelphia: Open University Press.

Beale J. (2002) *Is Communicative Language Teaching a Thing of the Past?* On WWW at http://www.jasonbeale.com/essaypages/clt_essay.html. Accessed 15.3.06.

Canale, M. (1983) From communicative competence to communicative language pedagogy. In J.C. Richards and R.W. Schmidt (eds) *Language and Communication.* London: Longman.

Cuevas, J. (1996) *Educating Limited-English Proficient Students: A Review of the Research on School Programs and Classroom Practices.* San Francisco: WestEd.

Cummins, J. (1989) *Empowering Minority Students.* Sacramento, CA: California Association for Bilingual Education.

Feng, A. (2005) Bilingualism for the minor or the major? An evaluative analysis of parallel conceptions in China. *International Journal of Bilingual Education and Bilingualism* 8 (6), 529–551.

Feng, Z.J. and Ke, S. (2003) *Shuang Yu Jiao Yu Yu Zong He Ying Yu [Bilingual Teaching and Integrated English].* Guangzhou: Zhong San Da Xue Chu Ban She [Sun Yat Sen University Press].

Feng, Z.J., Wang, J.-J., Luo, D. and Xiao J.-F. (2006) *Zong He Ying Yu Jiao Xue Mo Shi Gai Lun [An Introduction of Integrated English Teaching Model].* Guangzhou: Guang Dong Ren Ming Chu Ban She [People Publishing House of Guangdong].

Flood, J., Lapp, D., Tinajero, J. and Hurley, S. (1996) Literacy instruction for students acquiring English: Moving beyond the immersion debate. *The Reading Teacher* 50 (4), 356–359.

Genesee, F., Lindholm-Leary, K.J., Saunders, W. and Christian, D. (2003) *Educating English Language Learners: A Synthesis of Empirical Evidence.* New York: Cambridge University Press.

Hakuta, K. and Diaz, R.M. (1984) The relationship between degree of bilingualism and cognitive ability. A critical discussion and some new longitudinal data. In K.E. Nelson (ed.) *Children's Language* (Vol. 5, pp. 319–344). Hillsdale, NJ: Erlbaum.

Huang, L.N. (2004) *Xue Xiao Shuang Yu Ke Cheng [School Based Bilingual Curriculum].* Nanning: Guangxi Jiao Yu Chu Ban She [Guangxi Education Press].

Hymes, D. (1972) On communicative competence. In J.B. Pride and J. Holmes (eds), *Sociolinguistics.* Harmondsworth, England: Penguin Books.

José, L.R. (2004) Defining our transitional bilingual program. *IDRA Newsletter.* On WWW at http://www.idra.org/IDRA_Newsletters/January_2004%3A_Self-Renewing_Schools%E2%80%A6Bilingual_Education/Defining_Our_Transitional_Bilingual_Program. Accessed 28.1.06.

Krashen, S. and Biber, D. (1988) *On Course: Bilingual Education's Success in California.* Sacramento, CA: California Association for Bilingual Education.

Latham, Andrew S. (1998) The advantages of bilingualism. *Educational Leadership* 56 (3), 79–80.

Lenneberg, E. (1967) *Biological Foundations of Language.* New York: Wiley.

Liu, H.R. (2002) Shuang Yu Jiao Xue Yao Shen Zhong [Be cautious in bilingual teaching]. *China Education Daily,* 3 September.

Lu, D. (2005) *Xiang Gang Shuang Yu Xian Xiang Tan Suo* [*An Exploration of the Bilingual Phenomenon in Hong Kong*]. Hong Kong: Joint Publishing (H.K.).

Luo, D. (2002) *Xiao Xue Zong He Ying Yu Jiao Shi Shou Ce* [*A Handbook for IE Primary School Teachers*]. Guangzhou: Zhong San Da Xue Chu Ban She [Sun Yat Sen University Press].

Ma, C.W. (2003) Xiao Xue Zong He Ying Yu Jiao Xue Shi Yan Yan Jiu Bao Gao [A Report on Primary Integrated English Experiment]. On WWW at http://www.integratedenglish.com/teachersforum/teachersforum22.asp. Accessed 18.1.06.

Mackey, W.F. (1978)*Language Teaching Analysis*. London: Longman.

Meighan, R. (1981) *A Sociology of Educating*. London: Cassel.

Met, M. (1999) *Content-Based Instruction: Defining Terms, Making Decisions* (NFLC Reports). Washington, DC: The National Foreign Language Center.

Oebel, G. (2001) *So-called Alternative FLL-Approaches*. On WWW at http://www.hausarbeiten.de/faecher/hausarbeit/paq/20953.html. Accessed 28.1.06.

Pinker, S. (1995) Language acquisition. In L.R. Gleitman and M. Liberman (eds) *An Invitation to Cognitive Science* (2nd edn). Language (pp. 135–182). Cambridge, MA: MIT Press.

Richards, J., Platt, J. and Weber, H. (1985) *Longman Dictionary of Applied Linguistics*. London: Longman.

Romaine, S. (1995) *Bilingualism* (2nd edn). Oxford UK & Cambridge USA: Blackwell.

The European Council Gives its Support to CLIL/EMILE. On WWW at http://www.euroclic.net/index.php?inhoud=inhoud/news/main.inc. Accessed on 28th January 2006.

Thomas, W.P. and Collier, V.P. (1997) *School Effectiveness for Language Minority Students*. NCBE Resource Collection Series, No. 9. Washington, DC: National Clearing House for Bilingual Education.

Tucker, G.R. (1999) *A Global Perspective on Bilingualism and Bilingual Education*. Washington, D.C.: ERIC Clearinghouse on Languages and Linguistics.

Vygotsky, L.S. (1978) *Mind and Society: The Development of Higher Mental Processes*. Cambridge, MA: Harvard University Press.

Wang, B.H. (2003) *Shuang Yu Jiao Xue Lun Cong* [*Collection of Papers on Bilingual Teaching*]. Beijing: Ren Ming Jiao Yu Chu Ban She [People's Education Press].

Wang, J.J., Luo, D. and Xiao, J.-F. (2005) *Primary Integrated English*. Guangzhou: Guangdong Ren Ming Jiao Yu Chu Ban She [Guangdong Education Publishing House].

Wang, L.Y. (2003) You Nan Du Dan Bu Zhi Bu, Tian Liang Dian Rang Xue Zi Shou Hui [Continue in spite of difficulty, and stand out to benefit the students]. *Shanghai Jiao Yu* [*Shanghai Education*] (2), 22–23.

Wang, X.D. (2003) Guan Yu Shuang Yu Jiao Xue De Zai Si Kao (Rethinking About Bilingual Teaching). In Wang, B.H. (ed), *Shuang Yu Jiao Xue Lun Cong* (Collection of Papers on Bilingual Teaching) (77–100). Beijing: Ren Ming Jiao Yu Chu Ban She (People's Education Press).

Yuan, C.Y. (2005) *Zong He Ying Yu Jiao Xue Lun* [*Teaching Methods of Integrated English*]. Guangzhou: Zhong San Da Xue Chu Ban She [Sun Yat Sen University Press].

Zhang, Q. (2002) Zhong Xiao Xue Jiao Xue Yun Zuo Mo Shi De Jian Gou Fang Wei Yu Ban Kuai Lei Xin [The constructional orientation and plate types of operational bilingual models in primary and high schools]. *Tientsin Shi Jiao Ke Yuan Xue Bao [Journal of Tientsin Institute of Educational Science]* (5), 27–29.

Zhu, P. (2004) Shuang Yu Jiao Xue Jiang Zuo (I): Shuang Yu Jiao Xue De Ding Wei, Fen Lei, Ren Wu He Mo Shi [A course of lectures about bilingual teaching (I): The orientation, classification, mission, and model of bilingual teaching]. *Ji Suan Ji Jiao Yu Xue [Computer Teaching and Learning]* (3), 13–14.

Chapter 9

Implementing Language Policy: Lessons from Primary School English

ELLEN YUEFENG ZHANG AND BOB ADAMSON

Introduction

Following China's opening to the world and the launching of reforms in the aftermath of the Cultural Revolution, it has experienced rapid economic progress and has become increasingly active in globalization. As noted in this volume, creating a workforce with a high degree of bilingual competence in Chinese and English is viewed as highly desirable for the economic development of the nation. Competence in the language has become a crucial determinant for access to higher education inside and outside China and well-paid employment, especially in the commercial sector (Adamson, 2004; Dzau, 1990; Liu, 1995). As a result, English has become deeply embedded in the curriculum in educational institutions as well as the workplace and, increasingly, the modern culture of Chinese people. National policy recognizes the contribution that the English language can make to the realization of the Four Modernizations (the development of agriculture, industry, technology, and defence), a target elucidated by Deng Xiaoping in 1978, and to promoting the country's international status (Adamson, 2002; Lam, 2002). China's entry into the WTO in 2001 and winning the bid to host the 2008 Olympics created enormous interest in learning English all over the country, and this is reflected in official policies directed at schooling.

Primary and secondary schools have been tasked with making a major contribution to the development of the bilingual workforce. While this has long been true in the case of Chinese, the teaching of English was, until recently, mainly confined to secondary schools. However, in the National English Curriculum for Nine-year Compulsory Education, issued in 2001, English was made a compulsory subject from at least Grade 3 (children aged 8 or 9 years) in primary schools (Ministry of Education, 2001). A concurrent policy stream was concerned with the quality of education.

English teaching was targeted for reform because of concerns that the traditional teacher-dominated, knowledge-transmitting, and grammar-based pedagogy (Cortazzi & Jin, 1996; Hu, 2002; Ng & Tang, 1997; Rao, 1996; Tang & Absalom, 1998) were still prevalent in ELT paradigms in secondary schools (Ministry of Education, 2001) and affected the learners' competence to communicate in English. The pedagogical reform chosen by the Ministry of Education was task-based language teaching (TBLT), which had achieved popularity in a number of countries in the 1990s. The new curriculum, incorporating TBLT, was first tried out and implemented in 38 national experimental districts throughout the country. It was then implemented in provincial experimental districts in the autumn of 2002, which reached 10–15% of the entire student population. In 2004, its implementation expanded to 2576 cities or counties and 65–70% of students (Li, 2003). It was planned that the curriculum innovation would be implemented throughout the country by 2007 (Liu, 2004).

The two-pronged policy made major demands on primary schools. First, specialist English teachers were needed to teach the subject, and second, they would need to develop new ways of teaching. Furthermore, any national curriculum innovation, such as the TBLT innovation, is an extremely complex event (Zhang, 2005; Zheng, 2005), in that it is an interactive process involving different levels of curriculum development and different curriculum stakeholders (Adamson & Davison, 2003; Johnson, 1989). There is considerable potential for discrepancies between the policy-makers' intentions and the implemented reality to occur because the reform has to pass through different levels of curriculum development where the originally intended policies are likely to be reinterpreted, reconstructed, and reconceptualized by the other stakeholders (Adamson & Davison, 2003; Kelly, 2004; Morris, 1996; Zheng & Adamson, 2003). The major gatekeepers of pedagogical reform are the teachers, as they ultimately determine the implementation of reforms at the chalkface. Thus the success of the bilingual policy hinges, to some extent, upon the capacity of teachers undertaking the teaching of a new subject (primary school English) in an innovative manner.

This chapter traces the TBLT reform in the city of Shenzhen in southern China. It investigates how TBLT has been interpreted and implemented to date by stakeholders at all levels (see Figure 9.1): the intended curriculum level, where curriculum planning occurs; the resourced curriculum level, where teacher support materials are developed; the adopted level, where local strategies are deployed to facilitate the implementation of the initiative; the enacted level, where teachers interpret TBLT for use in the classroom; and the experienced curriculum, which refers to the learners' experience of the reform. Data collection comprised document analysis,

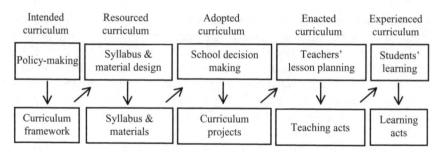

Figure 9.1 Stages in top-down curriculum decision making. (Adapted from Adamson and Davison, 2003.)

classroom observations, and interviews. At the intended curriculum level, official documents were analyzed to discover how curriculum makers interpreted TBLT. To study the resourced curriculum, training materials and textbooks were studied to determine how the teacher trainers or textbook writers interpreted and disseminated TBLT. To discern how teachers and learners implemented TBLT in their classroom teaching and learning, the study made use of naturalistic observation to study teachers' and/or learners' behaviors in classrooms. By means of purposeful sampling, three primary English teachers, who professed using TBLT but had different years of work experience and worked in different levels of schools and different districts, were chosen as case studies. The chapter raises important questions regarding the effectiveness of implementation of national language policies, and, in particular, the fitness-for-purpose of prevailing implementation strategies.

The Intended Curriculum

The origins of TBLT lie in the international literature. It was developed from the work of educational psychologists, such as Vygotsky, who emphasized social interaction as a powerful means of learning, and from language educators, such as Prabhu, who were attracted to TBLT because of its emphasis on realistic communication and active participation by learners in constructing their own language competence. The National English Curriculum in China follows the time-honored practice of grafting foreign ideas to the Chinese context, by incorporating TBLT into the curriculum and setting language standards that were intended to match national policy goals. The curriculum broke new ground by espousing a learner-centred approach and emphasizing that the curriculum should be based on learners' interests, life experiences, cognitive development, constructed knowledge, and holistic development achieved under the guidance of teachers, whereas the previous curricula had emphasized the central role of the teacher. According to the curriculum, traditional teaching methods overemphasized linguistic knowledge rather than the communicative competence that the workforce required to ensure the development of both the economy and society (Ministry of Education, 2001).

An initial complication with TBLT is establishing a consensus concerning the nature of tasks. Zhang (2005: 11–14) reviewed a broad range of definitions by various applied linguists and distilled the following common characteristics:

- a task is communication oriented;
- it involves a cognitive process;
- it is contextualized and authentic;
- it is primarily meaning focused; and
- its completion normally leads to a nonlinguistic product (e.g. a route drawn from a map, a conclusion reached, and so on).

Contrasting with a task is an activity that focuses on discrete linguistic forms, also called an *exercise* in some studies (Ellis, 2003; Littlewood, 1993; Tong, 2005; Tong *et al.*, 2000). Skehan (1998) and Ellis (2003) proposed a strong form and a weak form of TBLT. A strong form of TBLT takes tasks as the only unit of language teaching, in which learners acquire the target language by performing tasks in contextualized meaning-focused communication (Ellis, 2003). A weak form of TBLT considers tasks as an opportunity for learners to practice more freely the language items they have learned in a teacher-controlled way, and tasks are only supplementary activities before or after the form-focused instruction (Ellis, 2003). Tong *et al.* (2000) and Tong (2005) identify a medium form of task-based learning, which is situated between the abovementioned forms on the continuum. A medium form of TBLT involves tasks that balance holistic communication with a focus on linguistic forms.

When the National English Curriculum was published, it was written in Chinese. The term chosen to translate "tasks" was *renwu*, and "TBLT" was *"renwu xing jiaoxuefa"*. However, the document also uses *renwu* in the sense of "assignments" or "teaching objectives," thereby causing possible confusion to readers. There is little detail to help clarify the terminology, other than six general principles of designing tasks for teachers to follow, listed in the section "Recommendations on Implementation":

> Teachers should teach according to the general objectives and contents described in the curriculum. They should creatively design activities that are close to learners' real life to attract them and motivate them

to participate. Students finish their learning tasks by thinking, investigating, discussing, exchanging and cooperating.

When teachers design task-based activities, they should ensure that:

(1) the activities have definite and achievable purposes;
(2) the activities start from learners' life experiences and interests and contain authentic content and processes;
(3) the activities are beneficial to learners for them to learn English and cultivate language skills, so that their practical abilities to apply the language can be improved;
(4) the activities promote the integration and connection of English with other subjects, which can develop learners' whole-person development including the ability to think and imagine, aesthetic interest and experience of arts, spirit of cooperation and creation;
(5) the activities enable learners to get, exchange and use information, communicate with others in English and develop the ability to solve practical problems in English; and
(6) the activities are not limited to classroom teaching, but extend to learning and life outside learners' classrooms (Ministry of Education, 2001: 29, in translation)

These principles typify tasks as purposeful, authentic, life-related, holistic, process-oriented, and communication-oriented, and, as such, match the generic characteristics of tasks found in the broader literature (Zhang, 2005). However, the curriculum offers little guidance on how TBLT can be interpreted and realized in practice. This creates a space for other stakeholders, such as textbook publishers and teachers, to form their own interpretations and realizations. While it is sometimes useful to allow stakeholders some freedom and flexibility so they can enhance their ownership of an innovation, too much leeway can actually subvert the intentions of policy makers.

The Resourced Curriculum

The resourced curriculum is found in curriculum documents such as textbooks, teacher's guides, multimedia materials, which serve to translate policy into resources for teaching and learning. It is therefore a conduit for disseminating the innovation to the teachers and learners (Kelly, 2004). For previous reforms, curriculum dissemination in China had been characterized by a highly centralized centre-periphery model, in which there was only one series of textbooks for all schools in the country, published by the People's Education Press (PEP), a part of the Ministry of Education.

By the time the National English Curriculum was produced, the model had changed to one that featured a proliferation of centers (Xie, 2004). This model gave local education authorities greater responsibility, by allowing them to develop or choose teaching resources. Besides the official text-books published by the PEP, some education institutions (such as groups of university scholars), foreign commercial publishers, and different levels of education authorities also produced their own textbooks (Adamson, 2001). For example, the Shenzhen Teaching Research Office and Longman Hong Kong collaboratively wrote the textbook series, *Primary English for China*, which was published in September 2001.

A disadvantage of the new model was the distance between the center, where the policy was devised, and the periphery, where some of the teaching materials were developed. This led to a degree of slippage in interpretation of TBLT. Although many of the new textbooks claimed to be task-based, Zhang (2005) found that those used in Shenzhen actually adopted a weak form of TBLT, as the activities focused more on individual points of grammar than on holistic communication. The teacher's guides provided little assistance, with only a brief mention of TBLT.

A similar problem occurred in the design of training programs to support the new curriculum. After being prepared in Beijing, the curriculum document was disseminated throughout the country, through teacher-training programs for both primary and secondary teachers, organized and presented by local education authorities, teacher educators, or university academics (see Table 9.1). Zhang (2005) found that the dissemination of the TBLT initiative was limited, sporadic, unsystematic, and sometimes contradictory, for a number of reasons. First, although copies of the New English Curriculum were distributed to schools, there was no follow-up to ensure that teachers actually read and digested the contents. Those that did so reported that they found it too theoretical and abstract for practical application in their daily teaching.

Second, the in-service training programs were limited in terms of scale, frequency, and continuity. As with the New English Curriculum document, teachers complained that the content of the programs focused mainly on abstract theories instead of demonstrating the practical application of TBLT. Therefore, many teachers questioned the value of the sessions, feeling that they did not contribute to their professional development. Third, a tension arose between the recommended pedagogy and the assessment systems. Even though the local education bureaux claimed to promote the use of TBLT to teachers, they were also distributing form-focused tests and examinations for assessing learners. These tests and examinations concentrated on exercises that assessed learners' mastery of linguistic forms and

Table 9.1 Levels of curriculum disseminators in China

Level	Organization	Agent
Nation level	China's Ministry of Education (MOE)	Minister of Education
Province level	Provincial Education Bureau	Province Director
Municipal level	Municipal Education Bureau	Municipal Director
	Municipal Teaching Research Institute	Municipal Deputy Director
	Municipal Office of Teaching Research	Municipal ELT Researcher
District level	District Education Bureau	District Director
	District Teaching Research Centre	District Deputy Director
	District Office of Teaching Research	District ELT researcher

University scholars and teacher trainers are often invited as consultants or partners in different levels of curriculum dissemination.

involved very few tasks. The form-focused assessment tended to contradict the TBLT practices recommended in the new curriculum and had a negative wash-back effect on teachers' adoption of tasks.

Curriculum dissemination of TBLT is therefore problematic. Teachers are not well informed or prepared for the reform, and have been provided with textbooks and other resources that are not aligned with the strong form of TBLT advocated in the National English Curriculum.

The Adopted Curriculum

After an intended curriculum is introduced to schools and teachers through the resourced curriculum and the associated training programs, schools then make decisions as to how they handle the innovative practices. The process in schools is complex. The TBLT initiative, as with any curriculum reform, needs to be adopted and supported by schools' leaders before it can be successfully conveyed to teachers and learners in schools (McNeil, 1996). A supportive and collaborative school environment conducive to sustainable changes is required to facilitate teachers' acceptance of an innovation (Fullan, 1995; Fullan & Hargreaves, 1992; Hopkins *et al.*, 1994; Markee, 1997; Tong, 2005).

From interviews with school leaders, including school principals, school administrators, heads of departments, and school committees in the three case-study schools in Shenzhen, it appears that they pay more attention to the "value-added" effects of curriculum reforms on the marketability of their school rather than to the real benefits for teaching and learning. (For example, when one of the schools commissioned a university scholar to conduct a project in the school about the effectiveness of using a particular teaching method, the school leaders placed a bronze sign on the school gate proclaiming its participation in the project—even though the project simply consisted of a few abstract lectures by the scholar and a set of invented scores about learners' progress.) The motivation for adopting the TBLT reform was to enhance their schools' reputation of being innovative in English language teaching, but this noble aim has not been backed by the provision of a supportive environment for teachers, individually or collaboratively, to implement TBLT.

There are organizational and systemic factors that hinder the effective implementation of a reform that has been adopted by the case-study schools. Generally, teachers work in isolation without a collegial learning community to enhance professional development. With large class sizes (around 50 learners per class), teachers tend to use mainly teacher-controlled noncommunicative activities to avoid discipline problems—they are wary of pedagogical reforms that threaten or undermine the power relationships and hierarchical structures in the classroom, and which might give an impression to uninitiated observers that they cannot "control" their students. There is no English-speaking environment in schools where learners can use the language outside the class. Under the circumstances, the operationalization of TBLT becomes a personal choice for individual teachers to consider: they have little clarity and support from those charged with disseminating the reform. There is also a disjuncture between the pedagogical reforms promoted in the New English Curriculum and the epistemological underpinnings of public assessments that are used in the case study schools. Where the curriculum calls—albeit vaguely—for a focus on holistic communication, public assessment in English tests the learners' mastery of discrete linguistic items. Given the importance of public examination results for the marketability of the schools (and for teachers' promotion prospects), teachers face a dilemma in responding to the TBLT initiative.

The Enacted Curriculum

The implementation of a curriculum reform such as TBLT by teachers in their classroom teaching practice is called *the enacted curriculum*. The classroom implementation process is the most critical phase for change to take

Table 9.2 Personal data of the three teachers at the time of the study

Name	*Age*	*School*	*No. of classes*	*No. of lessons/week*	*Work experience (years)*
Fanny	23	District level	3	12	1.5
Gavin	29	City level	4	16	7
Helen	34	Province level	1	7	14

effect in school contexts, with teachers playing a crucial and pivotal role (Connelly & Clandinin, 1988). Here, the enactment of three Shenzhen primary school English teachers, namely Fanny, Gavin, and Helen (all names in the case studies are pseudonyms), is analyzed. Their personal data is shown in Table 9.2.

The period of data collection lasted for 1 month in each school and comprised lesson observations (all at Grade 3 level) and semistructured interviews with the teachers.

Fanny's TBLT implementation

Fanny had not received appropriate professional training in using TBLT. Although she graduated from college after the launch of the National English Curriculum in 2001, the lecturers in her preservice training course presented a form-focused knowledge-transmission approach to language teaching. Fanny had derived her interpretation of TBLT from the curriculum documents, but the interpretation displayed the confusion surrounding the term *renwu*, used in the documents to refer to both tasks and objectives. Fanny's version of TBLT involved setting teaching targets: she set objectives in terms of the number of linguistic items (vocabulary and grammar) to be mastered in the time allowed. Much of her class time (four 40-minute periods per week) was devoted to drilling her students in the linguistic forms, with a focus on the accuracy of learners' pronunciation and speech. She often gave the learners form-focused and grammar-based exercises to complete. The only strong tasks Fanny used were occasional role plays or adaptations of the surveys from the textbook, to provide the learners with freer practice in using the target linguistic items. For example, she asked the learners to find out the favorite sports of ten classmates and then report their findings. Her purpose was to practise the names of sports. In the postlesson discussion, it emerged that Fanny did not realize that this activity was actually a task. Overall, her teaching was mainly teacher-dominant, and displayed many characteristics of a weak form of TBLT.

Fanny's approach was reinforced by a number of contextual factors. She strongly believed that students were passive learners who should attend closely to teacher talk. With 49 students in the class, Fanny was concerned about potential discipline problems that might arise through her relinquishing some of her control of classroom events, and spent much time monitoring their behavior. In addition, her limited linguistic competence prevented her from communicating meaningfully with her students in authentic English. She used Chinese when giving instructions or explaining a point of grammar for convenience, rather than from a belief that the use of the mother tongue was an important support strategy. Another factor was the orientation toward a focus on form of the test papers distributed by the local education bureau that reinforced her own preference for a weak form of TBLT. Above all, as a relatively inexperienced teacher, she lacked guidance from colleagues in managing the practical problems that she faced in her classroom and exploring alternative approaches.

Gavin's TBLT implementation

Gavin's enactment of TBLT was similar in many ways to Fanny's. Although Gavin had 7 years of teaching experience, he had received limited preservice and in-service teacher training. Gavin oriented his teaching toward enabling learners to read, memorize, and write the vocabulary and passages in the textbook. His teaching approach was derived from his own experience of learning English through a focus on form and memorization, and from his perception that his students needed to build a linguistic foundation before they could communicate well. Gavin occasionally used communicative activities such as surveys and riddles but his teaching was mainly teacher-dominated, form-focused, and textbook-centered, and displayed many characteristics of a weak form of TBLT. Believing that Chinese was conducive to learning, he often used it to translate, clarify, and give instructions, which ran counter to the tenets of a strong form of TBLT, as it limited the learners' exposure to communicative English. Gavin also acknowledged that he was influenced by the form-focused test papers mandated by the local education bureau.

Nonetheless, Gavin felt the need for professional development and perceived curriculum initiatives such as TBLT as an opportunity to explore new approaches. Following up his interest, he read about TBLT and wrote an article for the school magazine describing ways in which games, songs, and other activities involving learning participation could be used within a TBLT framework. In the article, Gavin demonstrated an understanding of some of the characteristics of a strong form of TBLT. One of the vice-principals, Mr Fan, read the article and was impressed. However, when he discovered that TBLT was promoted in the National English Curriculum, Mr Fan forcefully told Gavin that he needed to create a new pedagogy of his own, not to borrow from one that had already been promulgated. Mr Fan's advice was based on the system of *teji jiaoshi* (master teachers), whereby pedagogical pioneers are identified and provided with an official platform to promote their ideas (Ko, 2002). Gavin became discouraged by this negative response from a school leader and no longer pursued his interest in TBLT, reverting to his long-standing teaching approach.

Helen's TBLT implementation

Helen was an experienced teacher. Her practice, even before the introduction of TBLT, demonstrated her belief in the value of learner-centred, life-related, and communication-oriented teaching. Helen's approach stemmed mainly from her empathetic personality and her experience as a student counsellor, which enhanced her understanding of primary students' needs and characteristics and improved her ability to organize students effectively and cater to their needs in their learning. She sought to stimulate learners' interest and to boost their confidence in learning English. She often allowed learners to make decisions about their own learning—this was also facilitated by the relatively small class size of 39 learners and the generous allocation of English lessons (seven 40-minute periods per week). Helen's qualities as a teacher were greatly valued by her principal, who was very supportive of her learner-centred approaches and experiments in innovative pedagogy.

Helen admitted her understanding of TBLT was limited. She equated it with problem-based teaching, which had similar epistemological roots but which focused on only one learning process as opposed to the variety of learning processes that TBLT accommodates. Her textbook did not include any tasks, so she designed all the tasks she used in her teaching. Finding it time-consuming, she did not use them in every lesson. However, her existing teaching practice actually matched some of the fundamentals of a strong form of TBLT. Having a good command of English, she was able to expose students to natural, meaning-focused communication in English in her classroom teaching much of the time. Overall, although Helen's pedagogy did not fully embrace the innovation, her practice reflected a medium-to-strong form of TBLT, mainly because of her predisposition to student-centered learning.

The three cases show that teachers' enactment of TBLT is shaped by the culture of their schools, their understanding of TBLT and the curriculum innovation, their professional development process, their own experience of learning English, their competence in the language, their perceptions of learners, and systemic forces, such as the nature of formal assessments. These contextual influences need to be taken into consideration in the policy-making process to ensure that language policies can be implemented effectively by teachers.

The Experienced Curriculum

There have been limited studies on learners' experience of TBLT in the literature (Carless, 2002). For this study, six primary school students (two from each of the three schools) were interviewed about their experience and views of TBLT. It was found that none of the learners was familiar with the term *renwu* in the sense of "tasks." Unsurprisingly, given the lack of precise knowledge displayed by their teachers, the learners did not have any idea of TBLT, nor were they aware of any conscious attempts by their teachers to use tasks in their lessons.

The learners accepted the use of form-focused, grammar-based teaching, as they understood that their teachers had identified the learning of linguistic items such as vocabulary and grammar as crucial to their language development. The learners found that this approach to language meshed with their experiences of learning Chinese, where memorization of characters is a key feature of the primary school curriculum, and adopted similar strategies in their English learning. They focused on memorizing and reciting vocabulary items and sentence patterns by reading them aloud and writing them over and over. Another common characteristic was that they all valued a classroom atmosphere that was conducive to study. For example, the learners disliked the use of surveys, the most common form of TBLT in the textbooks, as they tended to generate a lot of off-task behavior. On the other hand, the learners appreciated the value of communicating in English. They said that they took the initiative to talk to foreigners when they had the opportunity to meet them and if given the choice, they would prefer life-related communication-oriented tasks to decontextualized form-focused exercises, provided that classroom discipline was maintained. They differed in their views on the use of Chinese in English lessons. Fanny's and Gavin's students regarded Chinese as a necessary translation tool, while Helen's students were comparatively more communication-oriented in their formal English learning. Believing that English was the only language that should be used in class, they tried as often as they could to communicate in English with Helen and their peers.

These reactions show that learners, like teachers, are influenced by the context in which they operate. Their preferred styles of teaching and learning are located close to those which they regularly experience and which are therefore comfortably familiar.

Conclusion

This chapter demonstrates how the top–down TBLT innovation in mainland China is interpreted and reconstructed by all levels of change agents, from top-level policy makers and disseminators to middle-level school leaders, and finally to grassroot teachers and learners. It indicates that the message of the TBLT innovation becomes progressively weaker as it descends through the various levels of stakeholders (see Table 9.3). Although TBLT is recommended in the intended curriculum in 2001, there is only sporadic dissemination of TBLT in the resourced curriculum, and limited dissemination and support to prepare schools and teachers for the practical implementation. Consequentially, although TBLT is adopted in the National English Curriculum in the hope of developing learners' English communicative competence—a key component of the state's bilingual policy—its effective implementation is uncertain and certainly not guaranteed.

This study supports Adamson and Davison's (2003) position that the implementation of top–down educational change is a complex and context-bound process, which is shaped by the interaction of all levels of stakeholders, as well as by complicated contextual factors. To advance a student-centered approach such as TBLT, all levels of change agents must understand the challenges that exist at the chalkface. First, large class sizes are likely to bring about problems when interactive group tasks are employed and teachers lack the necessary skills to manage their students. Second, TBLT places a very high demand on teachers in terms of their linguistic and pedagogic abilities. Third, since TBLT is oriented toward real-life use of English, there may be a need for an English-speaking environment in which to facilitate the use of the language beyond classroom learning. Fourth, many schools have only four periods of English lessons per week (as in the cases of Fanny and Gavin), which are limited opportunities for teachers to use a approach such as TBLT that requires a significant amount of time to design and implement in the classroom, especially when teachers lack appropriate teaching resources and external practical support.

Table 9.3 Implementation of TBLT by stakeholders at various levels

Stage	Degree of implementation
Curriculum policy makers	There was insufficient information and elaboration of TBLT in official documents.
Teacher trainers and textbook writers	There was very limited dissemination and promotion of TBLT by local education authorities: limited exemplification of TBLT in textbooks and prevalence of form-focused tests and examinations.
School leaders (principals, vice principals, and heads of English group)	There was a leadership vacuum in school adoptions of TBLT. There were unfavourable contexts for teachers' use of TBLT: little support for teachers' innovative practice, large class sizes, and no English-speaking environment.
Teachers	It was teachers' personal choice whether to put TBLT into practice; the three teachers had a limited understanding of TBLT and made little deliberate use of TBLT. Their teaching practices were shaped mainly by their understanding of TBLT, professional development process, their experience of learning English, and their perceptions of learners.
Learners	Learners had not heard of TBLT or tasks; their experience matched their teachers' pedagogical features. They often used memorization-based strategies in their English learning but wanted to experience a stronger form of TBLT in their English learning.

Overall, the early experiences of TBLT create concerns about the effectiveness of the language policy in China. The National English Curriculum takes bold steps toward the realization of bilingualism in China by introducing the learning of the language in primary schooling and by promoting a pedagogical approach that is intended to foster the communicative competence that is needed for the development of Chinese society according to the vision of the state. The intention of providing Chinese learners with a state-of-the-art, quality education is a laudable aim, but it can succeed only if supportive dissemination mechanisms are in place and that the characteristics of the contexts in which reforms are actually implemented and experienced are taken into consideration at the planning stage. Perhaps the answer is to take small steps toward the goal—to find a happy medium between weak and strong forms of TBLT, for instance—and to avoid great leaps forward.

References

Adamson, B. (2001) English with Chinese characteristics: China's new curriculum. *Asia Pacific Journal of Education* 21 (2), 19–33.

Adamson, B. (2002) Barbarian as a foreign language: English in China's schools. *World Englishes* 21 (2), 231–243.

Adamson, B. (2004) *China's English: A History of English in Chinese Education.* Hong Kong: Hong Kong Univ. Press.

Adamson, B. and Davison, C. (2003) Innovation in English language teaching in Hong Kong primary schools: One step forward, two steps sideways? *Prospect* 18 (1), 27–41.

Carless, D. (2002) Implementing task-based learning with young learners. *ELT Journal* 56 (4), 389–396.

Connelly, F.M. and Clandinin, D.J. (1988) *Teachers as Curriculum Planners: Narratives of Experience.* New York, NY: Teachers College Press, Teachers College. Columbia University.

Cortazzi, M. and Jin, L. (1996) English teaching and learning in China. *Language Teaching* 29 (2), 61–80.

Dzau, Y.F. (1990) Introduction. In Y.F. Dzau (ed.) *English in China* (pp. 1–10). Hong Kong: API Press.

Ellis, R. (2003) *Task-Based Language Learning and Teaching.* Oxford: Oxford Univ. Press.

Fullan, M. (1995) *Successful School Improvement: The Implementation Perspective and Beyond.* Buckingham, Philadelphia: Open University Press.

Fullan, M. and Hargreaves, A. (1992) *What's Worth Fighting for in Your School? Working Together for Improvement.* Buckingham, Philadelphia: Open University Press.

Hopkins, D., Ainscow, M. and West, M. (1994) *School Improvement in an Era of Social Change.* London: Cassell.

Hu, G. (2002) Potential cultural resistance to pedagogical imports: The case of communicative language teaching in China. *Language Culture and Curriculum* 15 (2), 93–105.

Johnson, R.K. (1989) A decision-making framework for the coherent language curriculum. In R.K. Johnson (ed.) *The Second Language Curriculum.* Cambridge, England: Cambridge Univ. Press.

Kelly, A.V. (2004) *The Curriculum: Theory and Practice* (5th edn). London: Thousand Oaks, CA; New Delhi: Sage.

Ko, P.Y. (2002) The notion of teaching excellence in the People's Republic of China: The case of Chinese language teachers. Unpublished PhD thesis, University of Hong Kong.

Lam, A. (2002) English in education in China: Policy changes and learners' experiences. *World Englishes* 21 (2), 245–256.

Li, J. (2003) Xin kecheng shiyan tuiguang paichu shijianbiao [The schedule of new curriculum experiments]. On WWW at http://www.ncct.gov.cn/jsp/detail/detail.jsp?detailID=631. Accessed 19.5.03.

Littlewood, W. (1993) TTRA in perspective. *New Horizons* 34, 4–8.

Liu, D. (1995) *English Language Teaching in Schools in China*. Paper presented at the International Language in Education Conference (December 13–15), The University of Hong Kong.

Liu, Z. (2004) The curriculum innovation in basic education faces the dilemma of "wearing new shoes and wailing on the old road". On WWW at http://www.yblxx.com/detail.asp?n_id=753. Accessed 2.2.05.

Markee, N. (1997) Second language acquisition research: A resource for changing teachers' professional cultures? *The Modern Language Journal* 81 (i), 80–93.

McNeil, J.D. (1996) *Curriculum: A Comprehensive Introduction* (5th edn).New York: Harper Collins.

Ministry of Education (2001) *Quanrizhi yiwu jiaoyu putong gaoji zhongxue yingyu kecheng biaozhun (shiyangao)* [*English Curriculum Standards for Full-Time Compulsory Education and Senior Secondary Schools (trial version)*]. Beijing: Beijing Normal University Press.

Morris, P. (1996) *The Hong Kong School Curriculum: Development, Issues and Policies.* Hong Kong: Hong Kong Univ. Press.

Ng, C. and Tang, E. (1997) Teachers' needs in the process of EFL reform in China—a report from Shanghai. *Perspectives* 9 (1), 63–85.

Rao, Z. (1996) Reconciling communicative approaches to the teaching of English with traditional Chinese methods. *Research in the Teaching of English* 30 458–471.

Skehan, P. (1998) *A Cognitive Approach to Language Learning.* Oxford: Oxford Univ. Press.

Tang, D. and Absalom, D. (1998) Teaching across cultures: Considerations for western EFL teachers in China. *Hong Kong Journal of Applied Linguistics* 3 (2), 117–132.

Tong, A.S. (2005) Task-based learning in English language in Hong Kong secondary schools. Unpublished PhD thesis, University of Hong Kong.

Tong, A.S., Adamson, B. and Che, M.M. (2000) Tasks in English language and Chinese language. In B. Adamson, T. Kwan and K. Chan (eds) *Changing the Curriculum: The Impact of Reform on Primary Schooling in Hong Kong.* Hong Kong: Hong Kong Univ. Press.

Xie, Y. (2004) Curriculum situation and strategies: The case study on the curriculum implementation of English in primary schools. *Curriculum, Teaching Material and Method* 24 (2), 60–66.

Zhang, Y.E. (2005) The implementation of the task-based approach in primary school English language teaching in mainland China. Unpublished PhD thesis, University of Hong Kong.

Zheng, X. (2005) Pedagogy and pragmatism: Secondary English language teaching in the People's Republic of China. Unpublished PhD thesis, University of Hong Kong.

Zheng, X. and Adamson, B. (2003) The pedagogy of a secondary school teacher of English in the People's Republic of China: Challenging the stereotypes. *Regional Language Centre Journal* 34 (3), 323–337.

Chapter 10

Challenges and Prospects of Minority Bilingual Education in China—An Analysis of Four Projects

HEIDI COBBEY

Introduction

In this chapter I will give a brief introduction to the current bilingual education situation in certain minority areas in China, particularly in the provinces of Guizhou, Yunnan, and Gansu. I will also present challenges to implementing bilingual education programs and address these challenges specifically in the minority situation in China. Four separate bilingual education projects are also briefly introduced to give examples on how these challenges are being met.

I have been living and working in the People's Republic of China since the end of 1996 with the East Asia Group of SIL International. The East Asia Group is committed to a goal of working with local people to develop sustainable language development programs in their own communities and languages. I have worked in cooperation with local education offices to implement bilingual education projects in two different minority language areas.

Bilingual Education Among Minorities

In discussing bilingual education among the minority peoples (non-Han Chinese) of China, it is first necessary to address what is meant by bilingual education. A UNESCO publication (2004) discusses bilingual education among minorities in Asia. It states that "bilingual education means using two languages of instruction. In most cases, one of these languages will be the official national language and the other will be a regional or local language" (p. 4). There are many ways to implement bilingual education, depending on when the two languages are introduced, which one is taught first, which subjects are taught in which language, and how long each language is used for instruction. The UNESCO report states that it is most effective to use the local language for the first few years of schooling, and then introduce the national language orally followed by literacy in the national language. Finally, a transition is made to the national language for instruction.

One research study in Malawi and Zambia, where English is generally the language used for schooling but not the mother tongue of most students, concluded,

"A more radical suggestion than simply encouraging initial literacy in a local language would be for the local language to be used as the sole medium of instruction throughout primary schooling, with English taught, but only as a subject, from year 3 onwards. This would allow literacy skills to be established in the local language, and would also help more children to understand what is going on in the classroom. There might also be some people who would object that children would learn less at primary school, if they did not learn in English: however, the reality for most pupils is that the English language, far from being a bridge to knowledge, is in fact a barrier." (Williams 1998: 62)

China presents an even more unique situation, since unlike English, the national language writing system of Mandarin Chinese is a fairly complex system. Therefore, it almost seems inconceivable that 6 years of primary school education in the minority language, with Chinese only taught as a subject would be sufficient to transition to the national language for further education. However, the underlying principle still holds that the more developed the mother tongue language and literacy is, the better the transition to the national language and literacy will be.

It is generally agreed that all citizens of a country need to be effectively literate in the national language if they are to participate fully in national economic and social development. For minority people groups, to get to this point is not always easy. One study sought to find successful programs where a language other than that spoken by linguistic minorities had been used in their early education.

In researching this report, we looked for programs where the language of wider communication had been used successfully for initial education. We did not find any such examples in programs addressing underserved groups of the developing world. This is not surprising. When parents are not literate and when children and adults never hear [the language of wider communication] except in the classroom,

children are unable to learn, repeat their grades, and drop out of school
before reaching Grade 3 of the primary cycle. (CAL 2001: 19–20)

The use of the local language for schooling has many advantages. Children's performance on examinations will be improved if they have started
their education in their mother tongue (UNESCO Bangkok, 2004). In addition, their parents are more likely to participate in school affairs and to
encourage the learning process if the local language is used. The local community will be more supportive of basic education in the local language
because it will reflect local culture and knowledge. Children who learn
initially in their mother tongue are less likely to become frustrated and
drop out of school. Local language instruction also helps to preserve and
to revitalize the local language, many of which are seriously endangered.

China's Situation—Challenges

China has 55 officially recognized ethnic minority nationality groups.
This accounts for approximately 8% of the population and 50–60% of
the territory. By a conservative estimate, they speak around 80 distinct
languages (Zhou, 2000). Other sources estimate as many as 236 languages
(Gordon, 2005). The bilingual education discussed here consists of
education in one of these minority languages and the national language,
Mandarin Chinese.

There are many factors and challenges to consider when introducing bilingual education. The following will be addressed: national language and education policy, local culture, writing systems, community
readiness and involvement, curriculum, teacher training and instructional
materials, and funding.

How do these factors and challenges play out in China?

National language and education policy

China's national language policies are generally favorable toward bilingual education. In the Chinese Constitution, there is a clause that states
the minority nationalities have the right to develop and use their language
(Zhou, 2000). However, in some ways this conflicts with the national language policy that Mandarin Chinese or Putonghua be promoted in the
society as a whole and specifically used and taught in schools. Local education bureaus make the decisions on the makeup of the class schedules
in their areas. And, in practice, it is up to the local schools to decide what
programs and curriculum are best for the student population of their individual schools.

This is where *Min-Han Jiantong* education, or simultaneously using Chinese and the minority language, comes in. One educator in Xishuangbanna prefecture said,

> In brief, in minority areas, the *Min-Han Jiantong*'s bilingual education system not only helps to preserve and continue to develop the people's traditional culture, but it also helps minority students to stride across language and cultural barriers, and in the midst of today's social and economic circumstances to gain even greater development. (Ai, 2001: 165)

One of the main goals for bilingual education among most educators I have talked with in China is to improve the children's Chinese ability in order to enable them to have better opportunities for higher education, as well as to be able to participate more fully in mainstream society. This satisfies the national language policy as well. Bilingual education is seen as a tool for reaching this goal. It also provides the schools the opportunity to include more of what is already familiar to the students by allowing them to develop and use their own language within the school system. Currently, this means that at some point the minority language and/or culture is involved in the classroom in ethnic minority language areas. How it is implemented is different in different situations. At this point, the only way to determine the results of bilingual education is through Chinese examinations. The national and provincial education departments only keep statistics on the examination results for high school or university levels. The examinations are for Chinese language and Mathematics. The statistics kept are for how many students passed the entrance examinations to get into high school and university. They are ranked by which area they come from and what ethnic group they represent. The preparation for passing these examinations is done in the lower grades—elementary and junior high. The prefecture and county education departments are responsible for creating the appropriate examinations for their students. The national and provincial government places emphasis on Chinese examination results. There can be no national examination results for the minority languages since there are so many different languages. However, in the areas where minority language speakers live, the challenge for the education system is how to prepare the students to pass the examinations to enter high school. So far, no official system is in place to give minority language examinations at any level, with the exception of more established bilingual education programs among larger minority groups, such as Korean and Uyghur. Also, in the *Dong* project to be mentioned below, examinations are given in the minority language. As a national policy, it is not seen as a need to test the reading and writing ability of the minority languages. However, various officials I have talked with are open to this idea. At the end of the Spring semester 2006, in Jinghong county they began to implement simple tests in Dai for the kindergarteners who have had 1 year of Dai language study.

Culture

Different minority cultures in China value education differently. Certain minorities have traditionally had their own education system, e.g. the Dai of Xishuangbanna prefecture in the province of Yunnan. Traditionally, only Dai males were taught in the temples. The boys would enter the temple at around age 8 and learn from the older monks. It is only in recent years that girls are educated as well, and both boys and girls now go to the national schools, although many boys still study as well at the local temples. Where these traditional education systems differ from the national education system, conflicts can arise that make it difficult to introduce a bilingual education project. However, recent policies encourage schools to start programs that add something of the minority culture to the classroom. I recently visited a special project in one school in an Akha area in Xishuangbanna. The main goal of the sponsors of the project is protection of the environment. This is being attempted through training the students to learn about the local wild plants and vegetables and how they are traditionally used in their local culture. The children are also taught their traditional handicrafts as well. This project is being highly praised because of the inclusion of the people's culture. Currently, the project is entirely in Chinese, including the curriculum.

Writing systems

In China, orthographies must be approved by the government if they are to be officially used in published materials. Approximately 30 languages have written forms (Zhou, 2000), and only 10 are used in schools (Mooney, 2004). In 2003, SIL International was invited by education authorities to cooperate in starting a bilingual education program among the Jinuo people group, but because the Jinuo do not have an officially recognized script, it would be impossible at this point to create curriculum in Jinuo for a bilingual education program. The teachers will continue to use the Jinuo language orally in the classroom to explain the Chinese textbooks, but all textbooks are only in Chinese.

Another issue to consider in China is that Chinese characters are quite different from most other orthographies. In China, the minority scripts vary as well, with both Roman and non-Roman scripts being used.

Minority language speakers will need to learn two different writing systems to become completely biliterate.

Community readiness and involvement

Polls conducted among minorities in China show that parents ideally want their children to be bilingual. The problem is that no one has come up with a way to achieve both goals. Conventional wisdom says that it's important for students to maintain their native languages. (Mooney, 2004: 12)

In my own informal surveys among the Dai communities in Xishuangbanna, when asked if they would support a bilingual education program in their area, most parents and community leaders immediately respond "yes." However, when asked further questions, it becomes apparent that they are not really sure what this means. They are certainly interested in their children learning to read and write in Dai because they say it represents their history and culture. The parents are also keenly interested to learn to read and write Dai themselves. When asked whether she herself would want to study the Dai script, one 36 year-old Dai woman from Manguanglong village in Jinghong county said, "I am interested. If I would master the old Dai script, I could then read the traditional scriptures and learn from the stories about children's education. I would also be interested in reading traditional stories and singing songs." It is important to build on this interest by continuing relationships with the local communities, including local leaders as well as parents of school children. Adult literacy classes in the local language would be one way to stimulate continued interest. Continuing to dialogue with the communities about their interests as well as involving them in events at the schools helps to sustain interest and promotes the local language. Mobilization of communities is one key to any successful bilingual education program.

Curriculum

A new national curriculum went into effect in 2005 that allows schools to dedicate 16–20% of their class time to a school-based curriculum and teach about the local environment and things more relevant to the lives of students. Currently, three types of curriculum are allowed in China: (1) national curriculum, which everyone must use all across the country—each school can decide how many hours per week for each subject, depending on the needs; (2) area curriculum—a whole region may have a specific curriculum that is relevant just for that area, which could include language curriculum not relevant in another language area; and (3) school-based curriculum—schools may decide that they want to try a project using a certain type of curriculum. The above-mentioned Akha project is an example of a project using a school-based curriculum. Four other projects are briefly described next, which also use a school-based curriculum. At this point, school-based curriculum is not common, according to local education officials in Xishuangbanna. The schools do not need permission in advance to use a school-based curriculum, but they must report on what they are doing.

Policy makers and education officials are beginning to place more emphasis on the importance of curriculum in any type of bilingual education program. To be literate in Chinese society means to be literate in Mandarin Chinese. Literacy statistics for China are broken down by ethnic minority groups, but the statistics reflect the literacy rates for Mandarin Chinese. This is, therefore, reflected in curriculum design and classroom teaching. There is no national plan to design curriculum specifically for certain language groups.

However, provinces with the greater populations of minorities are seeking to better address the problems facing minority children in the current education system. One way China has tried to solve the problem of minority children not understanding Chinese is to translate language textbooks. Yunnan province, in particular, has translated the national Chinese language textbooks for first and second graders into 14 different languages. The third grade textbooks are currently being translated. These textbooks have the Chinese and the minority language side-by-side and are used mainly as diglots. The focus is on having the minority language as an aid to help the children understand the Chinese texts. Usually, the children are taught the alphabet in their mother tongue so that they can sound out words. However, there is no plan for curriculum or literature solely in their own language for further developing their reading and writing skills in their own language. No additional materials in the mother tongue are being produced for use in schools. The exceptions here are again the Korean and Uyghur programs. The man responsible for overseeing any bilingual education among minorities within Jinghong County in Xishuangbanna states that the training given for using the translated textbooks is that the Chinese language is considered primary and the minority language is only to assist.

Teacher training and instructional materials

In the past few years, China has made many changes in teacher training. They have begun to emphasize the student-centered approach, as opposed to the traditional teacher-centered approach. A new national education reform policy began implementation in 2002 and finished in August 2005. This incorporated training in new methodology as well as new curriculum training. The reforms included in this policy took effect at different times in different provinces and counties. In Xishuangbanna prefecture, Jinghong County, the training for these reforms was implemented in 2003. In the remaining two counties within the prefecture, the training has just begun. The benefits expected through these reforms are listed as follows: (1) teachers will have transformed ideas about education and teaching; (2) students will move around creating a lively classroom; (3) dynamic unprecedented educational research; (4) new evaluation system; (5) raised education standards; and (6) mature teachers. Starting in 2005, there is also a new education reform in process in China. The teachers are expected to study on their own to raise their own teaching standards, as well as to transform their ideas on education. This new reform is supposed to be in process for the next 4 years (Jinghong County Education Department, 2005).

In addition, in certain minority areas training is also provided for bilingual education teaching. Teachers are trained in reading and writing the minority language of a given area. Up to this point, not much emphasis has been placed on how teaching in a bilingual education situation might be different from teaching in a monolingual situation. Training does include, however, that it is acceptable for the teachers to use the minority language for explanations for the younger grades.

In Chinese, when you say "bilingual education," the words used only imply oral language, not written language. There is a separate way to emphasize biliteracy, or shuangwen (双文) as well as oral bilingualism, shuangyu (双语). This has not been emphasized in teacher training up to this point because there has been no curriculum available in the minority languages. Currently there is some curriculum available, but training in using these translated textbooks is only now beginning. Generally, the teachers are told to read the texts to the students in the minority language first so that they will understand the content of the Chinese texts. In classrooms, I have observed where these textbooks are used; the children cannot actually read the minority language texts themselves. Also, teachers are not yet trained in how to teach Chinese as a second language to the children before using Chinese as the language of instruction. However, the education departments are beginning to place more emphasis on these types of teacher training. When I was asked to begin the project I now work in, one of the main things the education department requested help with was teacher training.

Funding

Outside a few larger minority groups (Korean, Uyghur, Mongolian, etc.), most bilingual education programs in China are experimental, and as such, they are funded by outside NGOs and other funding agencies. They are generally seen as short-term, as "trying out" a new approach to bilingual education. These types of programs are generally carried out in a limited area, that is, in just a few schools. If the results are not satisfactory, it does not matter because it was an experiment to test a new method or new curriculum. However, if a project was seen to be successful by reaching the goals of the education departments, the local budgets could be changed to incorporate bilingual education into the school systems. The education departments themselves generally do not have any extra money in their budgets, and that is why they apply to outside agencies for funding for "special projects." However, at least in Xishuangbanna where I now work, the schools themselves often have money. Different schools own different amounts of land, and the principals of the schools are in charge of how the land is developed and how the profits gained from the resources are to be used for the schools. One principal told me that if he felt that the bilingual education program was successful, he would be willing to use the resources at his disposal to support the project.

The need for long-term bilingual education

So, what outcomes would satisfy educators that a bilingual project is successful? Obviously, improvement in the students' Chinese ability is crucial. And, as mentioned above, the way to test this is through the students' scores on examinations in Chinese. In order to reach this main goal, any means possible to get the students to have higher scores on the Chinese examinations should be looked into. There have been various attempts at bilingual education programs off and on for more than 20 years where I am working now, and they all showed that the students in these programs seemed to do better in school overall. However, none of these programs was sustainable, due to lack of curriculum, teacher training, and funding.

If the students first learn to read and write in their own mother tongue, they will do better eventually in learning the second language, Chinese.

The most important conclusion from the research and experience reviewed in this paper is that when learning is the goal, including that of learning a second language, the child's first language (i.e. his or her mother tongue) should be used as the medium of instruction in the early years of schooling. The first language is essential for the initial teaching of reading, and for comprehensions of subject matter. It is the necessary foundation for the cognitive development upon which acquisition of the second language is based. (Dutcher & Tucker, 1996: 36)

Minority language students should first be given the chance to learn Chinese as a second language before they are expected to actually have content classes in Chinese.

> There is ample research showing that students are quicker to learn to read and acquire other academic skills when first taught in their mother tongue. They also learn a second language more quickly than those initially taught to read in an unfamiliar language. Early mother-tongue instruction is a key strategy to reach the more than 130 million children not in school—and help them succeed. (UNICEF 1999: 41, 45)

Professor Chen Mingxiang, head of the Education and Human Development, Department at Beijing University, says being successful does not mean traditional languages and cultures have to be abandoned, which could hurt a child's self-esteem. She favors a transitional model that offers native language instruction for the first 1–3 years, gradually phasing in Putonghua. To do this, she says, the whole curriculum would have to be changed, with new textbooks written and more emphasis placed on bilingual education (Mooney, 2004). Bilingual education programs that have plenty of material in both languages for the children to interact with will likely be the most successful. This is, of course, a problem among most minority groups in China because there is not much available in the minority languages. So, a big part of the projects I mention below is developing mother tongue curriculum that is relevant to the children's own culture. For an example of very successful bilingual education among a minority people group within China, we can look at the Koreans, who are one of the minority groups within China. The advantage they have is that there is a huge body of material available in Korean since this language also exists outside of China as a national language.

> The Yuanbian prefecture in Northeastern Jilin province has a system of fully integrated programmes for teaching Korean as the first language of Korean students. They have achieved integration of teacher training, textbook compilation and publication, and instructional support and research. . . . As a consequence, the Koreans are the highest achievers in education, exceeding the level of the Han overall. (Lin, 1997: 202)

What is available in a few of the minority languages is the translated Chinese textbooks. However, if the students cannot read their own language, these textbooks are of little value. That is why many schools want to have a preschool or kindergarten program to teach the children to learn to read their own language first. Also, preschool/kindergarten programs are more acceptable within the existing education system because they are not mandatory, but rather "extra." The idea is that the minority language can be taught within the 1 or 2 years of a preschool program. Then, the children can start using the national Chinese curriculum when they enter first grade. This will meet the requirements of studying the national language curriculum without needing to make changes within the primary school years. This is good, but the issue of teaching the children to understand oral Chinese first still needs to be addressed.

We, NGO educators, education officials, and teachers, cannot expect immediate results from bilingual education programs but rather we need to be patient. Studies elsewhere have shown that to really show results in language acquisition and how well students are doing overall in school, it is important to allow them ample time to learn in their own language first. These results show that in most cases students who start in one language and are allowed an extended period of time to develop in that language before and while transitioning to the second language actually do better in the second language over time.

> ... when students have the opportunity to do academic work through the medium of their first language, in the long term they are academically more successful in their second language. (Thomas & Collier, 1997: 48)

Examples of Bilingual Education Projects

As previously mentioned, most bilingual education programs among the lesser-known minorities in China are carried out using outside funding. Brief accounts are given next to four different programs in three provinces in China. Three of the languages, Dongxiang, Dong, and Bai, have only a brief history of orthography. Chinese linguists developed orthographies for two of these groups, Dong and Bai, in the 1950s, and a working set of writing symbols for Dongxiang was only recently approved in 1999. Despite the efforts by linguists, these three scripts are still considered unofficial. The fourth language, Xishuangbanna Dai, has a long history of orthography in and outside of China. However, in the 1950s, linguists developed a simplified orthography that is only used within China. These projects are all in different stages of development and carried out in slightly different ways. The common denominators are curriculum development in the mother tongue, allowing the children to learn to read in their mother tongue first and then transition to Chinese, and great emphasis placed on teacher training.

Dongxiang bilingual education project, Gansu province

The Dongxiang minority people group of China have a population of 530,000. They live in an arid, mostly mountainous, area of Gansu province in northern China. They are mainly agriculturalists, farming wheat and potatoes, combined with raising sheep on a small scale. The level of education and the literacy rate has always been the lowest among the officially recognized 56 people groups in China.

Because of the education situation, local educators and scholars took it upon themselves to address the difficulties Dongxiang students were facing learning Chinese at school. After more than a year's preparation, in the Fall of 2002 the bilingual education experimental class at Narisi Primary School began. The experiment was to be of 3 years, starting with a 1-year preschool class.

The project had three objectives: (1) students would learn the Dongxiang orthography so that they could read and write Dongxiang. (2) Mother tongue language comprehension would be implemented into the Chinese language learning process in order to enhance the efficiency of the training of the Chinese language in the areas of listening, speaking, reading, and writing skills. These language skills would enable the students to understand and participate fully in Chinese language classes. Students would be given the language foundation necessary to use the standard national Chinese curriculum starting in third grade, after completing the requirements for first- and second-grade Chinese language education. (3) Because of this new method of learning, students would have greater interest in school. They would then stay in school, which would improve enrollment rates, especially for female students. This would enable successful completion of compulsory education for the Dongxiang children and allow as many as possible to become useful, educated members of society (Qi, 2004).

The preschool class focused primarily on learning the Dongxiang orthography and also on oral Chinese. The first-grade curriculum included further learning of the Dongxiang orthography, a continuation of the preschool Chinese oral instruction, and teaching of the standardized national requirements for first graders' Chinese character recognition. The second-grade curriculum primarily stressed Chinese learning and also final strengthening in using the Dongxiang orthography. The intention was to pass students along to a Chinese level that allowed complete use of the national Chinese curriculum in the third grade. New stories as well as translated stories in Dongxiang were included in the curriculum.

This 3-year experimental project finished in 2005, and the educators and community were pleased with the results. From the start of the project, statistics were kept to compare examination results in Mathematics and Chinese between project students and another class that only used the national curriculum. The results showed that the students participating in the bilingual education program had higher test scores through both first and second grades (Dongxiang Bilingual Education Pilot Project Office, 2005). Discussions are underway now as to how to proceed. The officials hope to expand the project to 20 schools in the area. Revisions of textbooks and more specific training in methodology are needed, as well as funding.

Dong bilingual education, Guizhou province

The Dong minority people group numbers 2.9 million, with approximately 1.5 million speakers of the two dialects, northern and southern Dong. They are located in three provinces in southern China, Guizhou, Guangxi, and Hunan. The Dong are mainly rice farmers. Like other minority language speakers in China, the Dong mainly speak the Dong language at home and in their village communities.

> Some Dong leaders in positions of influence are strongly supportive of promoting Dong literacy to enhance literacy in Chinese and to sustain Dong culture. This was the first key in promotion of a bilingual education pilot project in Zaidang village, Rongjiang county, Guizhou. The second was the strong support of local leaders and parents in the village. This support has grown naturally from the encouragement of Dong and Han leaders from outside the village, and from recognition that the former educational status quo in the village could well be improved. (Geary & Pan, 2003: 282)

This bilingual education project differs substantially from the Dongxiang project. In this program, the children continue to study their mother tongue, Dong, all the way through sixth grade. The first year of the 2-year preschool program is entirely taught in the Dong language. The Dong project is currently changing so that oral Mandarin is introduced into the second year of preschool and national Grade 1 Mandarin textbooks will be used in Grade 1, as in other schools around the country. Starting in the second year of preschool, the amount of Dong begins to decrease and the amount of Chinese begins to increase. Figure 10.1 shows an approximation of the ratio between Dong and Chinese. As revisions are currently underway in the project, this should be taken as only a close approximation.

The Dong language curriculum is based on weekly themes, close to the children's culture. The language curriculum revolves around many stories in Dong for the children to read and to listen to. One hundred

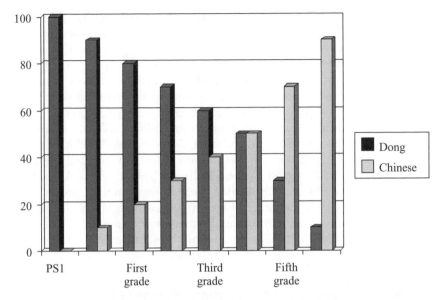

Figure 10.1 Transition model in the Dong project, Guizhou

and sixty stories were written for each of the first and second years of preschool. Creation of appropriate written materials is another key strategy for success of the bilingual education pilot project, after adequate teacher training. Most of the 500-plus stories already written for this pilot project are new stories. A common feature of the stories is that they are close to the familiar culture of Dong children.

This is a 9-year pilot project, due to finish in July 2009. It is a cooperative research project involving Rongjiang County Education Bureau, Guizhou University Southwest Minority Language and Culture Research Institute, and SIL International. Records are being kept on students' grades in all subjects to determine long-term results. Up to this point, the project is seen as successful in that the students are now completely fluent in reading and writing their own mother tongue, which the community is thrilled about. It has spawned adult literacy classes in the surrounding communities as well. The children have done better on their mathematics examinations than previous years of Dong students, as well as better than current students in nonproject schools. They are also making real progress in their Chinese language examinations. It is too early to predict long-term results in terms of Mandarin language learning, but current signs are good. Statistics are being kept from project as well as nonproject schools in the area in order for accurate evaluation to continue during and after the project. The intention is to follow project students out of the local elementary levels into the secondary levels to see what, if any, impact can be discerned at upper secondary levels when the national examinations are administered there.

A subproject of the Dong/Han bilingual education project began in October 2005, with a month of English teaching by a native English speaker to Grade 5 students. Another month of English teaching followed in April 2006, and another month is planned for October 2006. The Grade 5 students had not studied Dong before. The following year's Grade 5 will have studied Dong. The plan is to teach them 2 months of English and then compare the two classes with respect to their ability to learn English. According to theory, those children who studied their mother tongue Dong will be stronger in their third-language (English) acquisition. Study of English has become widespread throughout elementary schools in China, and an improvement in English learning would be significant to educational authorities.

Bai literacy project, Jianchuan County, Yunnan province

There are around 1.8 million people in the Bai minority people group located in west Yunnan province. There are three major dialects of Bai, with the largest (700,000 speakers) based on Jianchuan county Bai. In mountain areas where large numbers of Bai live, Bai is the only language spoken in the home and the village and the national Chinese language is only used with outsiders. As a consequence, children in these regions start school knowing no Chinese at all and are confronted by a common nationwide curriculum that uses exclusively Chinese texts.

The Bai Literacy project formally began in 2004, although preparations began in 2001. It is motivated by working with the support of local people and government leaders, diligent students, and a motivated group of bilingual workers. It is a 6-year cooperative venture between SIL International and the Yunnan Province Language Affairs Commission. It has the active involvement of the Jianchuan County Education and Culture Bureaus as well.

As a pilot program, the project is deliberately focused upon a single mountain village with high educational and economic needs, but one which is located at the strategic cultural center of Shibaoshan mountain. Consequently, the potential exists for the benefits of the project to receive wide publicity across the whole of the Jianchuan dialect group.

This program will train three groups of people in Bai literacy: (1) singers, artists, storytellers, and potential project teachers; (2) preschool children in a 2-year program designed to give them a grounding of literacy in Bai before they reach primary school; and (3) parents, particularly mothers, who have key influential roles in the home, but who have missed educational opportunities in the past.

Adult literacy classes have already been successfully established. Many of those initially trained have already begun to hold classes in the village for others interested in learning to read and write Bai. Writers' workshops have been held to train local people to write curriculum for the children's program. A local Bai newspaper has also begun to provide more reading material. Currently, curriculum is completed for the 2 years of preschool. Curriculum development used similar principles to the Dong program, with stories written based on weekly themes. The preschool program began in the Fall of 2006 (Billard, 2004).

Dai bilingual education project, Xixhuangbanna prefecture, Yunnan province

There are approximately 1.2 million Dai people living in China. One language spoken by the Dai nationality is Dai Lue whose speakers live in the Xishuangbanna prefecture of Yunnan province. The Dai people are well known in Yunnan for their rich and ancient culture. The Dai have had their own written script for centuries. In the 1950s, the old script was officially replaced by a new simpler version. The old script is still taught to Dai boys in Buddhist temples. There has been little chance for the new script to be adopted widely, as there have been relatively few publications using it. The Dai language is closely related to northern Thai. The Dai minority area borders with Burma and Laos and is close to northern Thailand.

The Dai bilingual education project is only in the beginning stages. This project is where the author currently works. The program is set to open in five schools in five different areas of Jinghong County in September 2007. Currently, curriculum is being developed in the Dai language. The plan is to have 2 years of preschool similar to the Dong program. Oral Chinese will be introduced in the second year. The children will begin to use the Chinese textbooks in first grade. We do plan to have the children continue to have at least one Dai class each week from first through sixth grades so that they will be able to continue to improve their Dai reading and writing skills. This will, of course, mean continued curriculum development, as well as developing outside reading materials. Although this will not be a significant amount of time for the children to continue studying their mother tongue, it is to be hoped that it will at the very least continue the interest in reading and writing Dai. The students will also continue to use the diglot-translated textbooks provided by the government. Also, the additional materials will add to a body of literature in Dai that others will have access to as well. Currently a weekly newspaper and a monthly magazine are available in Dai. Teacher training for the project is done in the holiday breaks, to first improve the teachers' reading and writing skills, then to begin to train them to use the curriculum that is being developed, as well as new methodology training.

Evaluation should be an important part of all bilingual education programs. Assessment can be made both qualitatively and quantitatively. Qualitative evaluation includes attitudes and perceptions about the program; teachers' performance; quality of curriculum and of reading materials; costs of the program compared to achievement of program goals; and costs of the program compared to learners' (or learners' parents') satisfaction. Quantitative evaluation would include numbers of students, teachers, classes, and materials over a period of time; learners' progress in achieving reading and writing skills; costs of the program compared to achievement of program objectives; and costs of the program compared to learners' progress through the system.

In the Dai project, informal surveys have been carried out in each of the five areas surrounding the project schools. Interviews have been conducted with education officials, teachers, local government officials, parents, and other members of the communities. There will continue to be dialogue with all these parties through the duration of the project. Also, as materials are developed, there will be ongoing assessment in each area to evaluate the appropriateness of the content and the interest of the communities.

As this project works closely with local education officials, plans are underway to collect baseline statistics on students, teachers, materials, and grades for schools in each project school area. Statistics will be included for schools during the period when bilingual education programs were previously carried out, as well as during the time when there were no bilingual education programs. Statistics will also be kept for the duration of the project for project schools as well as other schools within each area that are not participating in the project. Thus, there will be a control group with which to compare results.

Conclusions

There are many challenges to face in implementing successful bilingual education projects in any minority language community. Times are changing in China, and educators are doing their best to keep up with these changes. More value is now placed on bilingual education programs. The communities and the education bureaus in the four projects highlighted here have the goals of (1) better learning of Mandarin language and literacy for the students and (2) appreciation and maintenance of the learners' ethnic language heritage. The minority language learners will then be bilingual, biliterate, fully participating citizens of the multilingual People's Republic of China.

References

Ai, X. (2001) *Minzu diqu shishi shuangyu jiaoyu de biyaoxing* [The necessity of implementing bilingual education in nationality areas]. Xishuangbanna Prefecture Education Department. Unpublished report.

Billard, B. (2004) *The Bai literacy project.* Unpublished report.

Center for Applied Linguistics (CAL) (2001) *Expanding Educational Opportunity in Linguistically Diverse Societies.* Washington DC: Center for Applied Linguistics.

Dongxiang Bilingual Education Pilot Project Office (2005) *Dongxiangzu zizhixian narisi xiaoxue shuangyu jiaoxue shiyanban gongzuo jianjie* [Dongxiang Autonomous County Narisi Primary School Bilingual Education Pilot Project Brief Conclusions]. Unpublished report.

Dutcher, N. and Tucker, G.R. (1996) *The Use of First and Second Languages in Education.* Pacific Island Discussion Paper, 1, East Asia and Pacific Region. Washington, DC: The World Bank.

Geary, D.N. and Pan, Y.R. (2003) A bilingual education pilot project among the Kam people in Guizhou province, China. *Journal of Multilingual and Multicultural Development* 24(4), 274–289.

Gordon, R.G. (ed.) (2005) Ethnologue.*Languages of the World* (15th edn). Dallas: SIL International. Available at http://www.ethnologue.com/.

Jinghong County Education Department (2005) *Jiaoyu gaige* [Education reform]. Unpublished report.

Lin, J. (1997) Policies and practices of bilingual education for the minorities in China. *Journal of Multilingual and Multicultural Development* 18(3), 193–205.

Mooney, P. (2004) Language lessons; China's minority languages are in danger of disappearing. *South China Post.* On WWW http://www.pjmooney.com/minoritylanguagesscmp.shtml.

Qi, G. (2004) A report on the first year and a half of the bilingual education experimental class of Narisi primary school, Dongxiang Autonomous County. *China Education Forum Newsletter* 5(1), 3–8.

Thomas, W. and Collier, V. (1997) *School Effectiveness for Language Minority Students.* NCBE Resource Collection Series, No. 9. Washington, DC: National Clearinghouse for Bilingual Education.

UNESCO Bangkok (2004) *What have we learned?* On WWW http://www.sil.org/asia/ldc.

UNICEF (1999) The *State of the World's Children, 1999.* New York: UNICEF.

Williams, E. (1998) *Investigating Bilingual Literacy: Evidence from Malawi and Zambia.* Serial No. 24. London: DFID.

Zhou, M. (2000) Language policy and illiteracy in ethnic minority communities in China. *Journal of Multilingual and Multicultural Development* 21(2), 129–148.

Chapter 11

Facts and Considerations About Bilingual Education in Chinese Universities

PAN JIAZHEN

Introduction

In 2001, the Ministry of Education of China issued a document stipulating that universities provide 5–10% in English or another foreign language at the undergraduate level in 3 years (*Jiaoyubu*, 2001). The document encourages universities to adopt authentic textbooks from abroad and to send young and middle-aged subject teachers to internationally reputable universities to enhance their ability to teach and research. For those tertiary institutions where offering courses in English is found difficult, authentic textbooks in English are to be used at the initial stage with Chinese as the medium of instruction. This should move gradually to using the foreign language as the medium of instruction. This bilingual education policy is reaffirmed in a more recent document issued by the Ministry of Education (*Jiaoyubu*, 2005), which states that English–Chinese bilingual education should be further promoted both in terms of quality and quantity. Under the auspices of these documents, bilingual education has been enthusiastically pursued in many universities.

In order to promote bilingual education, the higher education department of the Ministry of Education decided to set-up a special committee coordinating bilingual education in tertiary institutions throughout the country (*Jiaoyubu Gaodeng Jiaoyusi*, 2004). The special committee is entrusted with the tasks of overseeing curriculum planning and teaching, managing resources, coordinating textbook compiling or importation from internationally famous universities and developing teaching methodology.

As we all know, bilingual education is flourishing not only in universities, but a phenomenon in the entire education system including primary and secondary schools. Here only are some examples given in Wang (2005):

- Guandong province announced that some high schools would provide some courses in English. But in fact around 100 secondary and primary schools have engaged themselves in bilingual education.
- Qindao city in Shandong province is extending English as a major medium of instruction to all middle and/or primary school.
- Shanghai municipality decided to set-up 100 trial bilingual schools a few years ago. In these schools, the bilingual courses were provided to primary pupils from Grade 1. The target of these schools was that the students are expected to be capable of communicating in English when they graduate from secondary school. Within only a few years, bilingual education has mushroomed from these 'trial schools' to a large scale 'mass experiment'.

In most schools in these developed areas, English is often used as the medium of instruction for science subjects such as maths, physics and chemistry. In some, social science or arts subjects such as geography, history, music, painting, physical education, handcrafts and arts work etc. are conducted bilingually. The percentage to use a foreign language for teaching is not less than 50% in most cases. Bilingual education no longer seems to aim at improving students' ability to speak English, but to enable them to become balanced bilinguals who are competent in both English and mother tongue across all situations (Baker, 2001).

Chinese-English bilingual education has developed at an amazing speed all over China (Feng, 2005). This chapter will centre on the development at the university level with a particular focus on bilingual teaching since 2001. As I have been personally involved in bilingual teaching in my own university, I will present a case study to illustrate how this development impacts on university teachers and students and on curriculum development in general.

Globalization and Higher Education

It is widely acknowledged that the tendency is more and more towards internationalization and globalization. Not only economy and trade are increasingly globalized, but higher education is also becoming more and more internationalized. The following facts about higher education both at home and abroad are commonplace observations:

- In all kinds of competitions the competition for human resources is perhaps the fiercest. Enterprises, national or international, desire the best personnel. Universities also want to enrol the best students, to train and foster excellent graduates to meet the challenges posed by globalization.

- Many developed countries provide scholarships to attract the best students from China in order to build-up strong international student profile.
- Chinese higher education authorities and institutions do not only strive to keep top quality students but also try to attract foreign students by providing scholarships particularly for those from the third-world countries. On campuses of Chinese universities today, it is easy to find many foreign students from various countries.

All universities have to internationalize their curriculum to meet the needs of multicultural student population. Bilingual education is inevitable as a precondition for internationalization and helps to cultivate the needed bilingual personnel for the globalising society.

EFL Teaching and Learning

English as a foreign language (EFL) teaching has long been seen as ineffective in China. Most pupils start English learning from primary school, through junior middle school, senior middle school, up to university. After more than 10 years, their English ability is often described as 'dumb English' or 'deaf English'. Very few can speak or communicate in English although some of them obtain good scores in English examinations.

According to the policy documents promulgated by the Ministry of Education of China, English proficiency tests are divided into several bands. They are called CET tests (Certificate of English Test) some of which are administered nationwide, such as CET-4, CET-6 and CET-8. Undergraduate students are required to pass the CET-4. About 50% of them can pass the test of CET-6. The latter is the requirement for graduate study. The CET-8 is the highest-level test for the students majoring in English.

It is reported in the website of Northeast News (www.nen.com.cn, accessed on 15.05.2005) that in the plenary meeting of 2005 National People's Congress, some delegates proposed to disassociate the bachelor degree with CET-4 certificates, due to a lot of drawbacks. Before the motion, the CET-4 is required by many universities as a prerequisite for graduation. As the aim of EFL education is to pass the examination, not to use the language for communication, the outcome is the abnormal phenomenon of 'graduates with high score but low ability'. Policy makers are increasingly aware that EFL education needs fundamental changes to rectify the phenomenon. Bilingual education has thus come to the fore and is believed to be the best way to get to the bottom of this problem.

As a result of the official concerns, many universities abandoned the policy of associating the CET-4 with the qualification of the bachelor degree. However, almost all universities made it explicit that such a measure is in no way a suggestion to lower the standard of students' English competence. On the contrary, students are expected to learn how to use the English language for communication. Bilingual education is believed to be of value to this end.

Growth of Bilingual Education in Universities

Bilingual education is rigorously promoted in Chinese universities. Take the website of Beijing University (2005) for example. One can find 104 items of information about bilingual education at the time of drafting this chapter. Many courses taught at Tsinghua University are conducted bilingually (News Tsinghua, 2005). As one of the most prestigious university in China, it invites worldwide famous professors of the first class universities to give lectures to students. Their aim is to enable their students to obtain fast, more advanced information and knowledge directly in English.

In Shanghai, on the website of Shanghai Jiaotong University (2005), there are 46 news items about bilingual education. Fudan University announced that the university will continuously develop the bilingual education for 3 years beginning from 2004. Fifty courses (62 teachers out of 156 applicants) were approved as the first batch to offer courses bilingually. As a financial incentive, the teachers would get 2000 to 8000 RMB yuan for each course they offer (Fudan University, 2004, accessed on 02.07.2004). In Tianjin, Tianjin University encouraged teachers to offer courses bilingually in graduate schools (Dan, 2001). It is stipulated that every college offer at least one bilingual course in every specialty as the first step.

Most universities in China promote and encourage bilingual education with similar measures. With regard to quality assurance and teaching objectives, in most cases, a bilingual course is expected to follow the procedure and meet the requirements as listed below:

• Applying with a sound bilingual curriculum and evidence of qualified human resources;
• Specifying whether authentic textbooks by a foreign university are adopted or teaching materials are self-compiled;
• Specifying the ratio of English and Chinese use in teaching, depending on the teacher's competence of the English language;

- It is usually required that the homework and the test be conducted in English;
- It is usually required that the blackboard writing or Power Point slides be in English.

A university usually provides some financial support for the approved bilingual programs. This support is aimed to help purchase authentic textbooks by foreign universities and reference materials, draw up teaching plans and subsidize the expenditures of preparing the course.

Specifying the ratio of English and Chinese use in teaching is deemed as very important for bilingual courses. It is interesting to note that some universities interpret the ratio in terms of teaching workload for tutors. For example, on the website of Shanghai University, the following figures are explicitly given to teaching bilingually (Shanghai University . . ., 2002):

- Hundred percent English teaching, that is, using an authentic textbook of foreign universities; giving lectures in English; and assigning homework and conducting tests in English. The amount of work can be calculated as three times as the workload of an equivalent Chinese course.
- Eighty percent teaching, that is, using an authentic textbook of foreign universities; 80% of teaching in English; blackboard writing in English; and 50% homework and test done in English. The amount of work can be calculated as 2.8 times as the workload of an equivalent Chinese course.
- Fifty percent teaching, that is, using an authentic textbook of foreign universities; 50% of teaching in English; blackboard writing in English; and 30% homework and test done in English. The amount of work can be calculated as 2.5 times as the workload of an equivalent Chinese course.
- Using an authentic textbook of foreign universities; teaching in Chinese; blackboard writing in English; and 20% homework and test done in English. The amount of work can be calculated as two times as the workload of an equivalent Chinese course.

The message of this calculation is clear: teaching bilingually is strongly encouraged. The more a tutor can use English as a medium of instruction, the more reward she/he will receive.

Bilingual Teaching Resources

Publishers and publication corporations are very active to promote bilingual education resources. The China National Publications Import &

Export (Group) Corporation and the China Educational Publications Import and Export Corporation work closely with many international publishers such as the McGraw-Hill Higher Education and Pearson Education, USA. They have held several international book exhibitions in recent years to introduce international textbooks to Chinese universities.

The Chemical Industry Press published a book titled *The Famous Textbooks of Famous International Universities* (Chemical Industry Press, 2002). This book lists 7 categories of textbooks with copyright and 12 categories of translated textbooks. Within 5 years, the press plans to publish 100 sets of textbooks written by reputable scholars from internationally famous universities in cooperation with international publication companies. The press is also planning to import textbooks related to the fields of chemistry, applied chemistry, chemical engineering and technology, material science and engineering, bioengineering, environmental engineering, pharmaceutical engineering, process equipment and control engineering, process automation, etc.

Furthermore, the Ministry of Education has set up several international university textbook centres in high-profile universities such as Beijing University, Tsinghua University, Nanjing University and Fudan University and authorized them to import and recommend authentic textbooks used by foreign universities to Chinese universities to promote bilingual education. The library of the East China University of Science and Technology (ECUST) in Shanghai was appointed as a Shanghai Centre of International University Textbooks (SCIUT) and has acquired textbooks from several world-famous universities such as Harvard University, MIT, Cambridge University and Oxford University. It displays the textbooks in universities around Shanghai regularly to facilitate textbook selection for bilingual education.

Case Study

Next, I shall give an account of how bilingual teaching is conducted at the ECUST, a university located in the vibrant metropolitan Shanghai that houses some 20,000 full-time students. As a faculty member at the university who is heavily involved in bilingual education, I shall begin with a brief description of what courses are offered bilingually in different schools and departments and what measures the university takes to promote bilingual education. To offer an insider's view, I shall describe how a particular course I have been coordinating is conducted in our department and my own experience and philosophy in developing this bilingual course. Challenges are briefly discussed towards the end.

At the ECUST, bilingual education has been vigorously pushed forward twice. The first time was in the year of 2003 when 30 courses were approved to be conducted bilingually (Table 11.1).

Two years later in 2005, 20 more courses were selected for such purposes (Table 11.2).

The courses listed in both the tables suggest that engineering, science and business schools and departments are more active or likely to offer courses bilingually than those of social sciences.

The University made initial plans to send 30 teachers to go abroad for a period of about one semester. The aim was to improve their English ability and familiarize the courses they would conduct bilingually. According to the information by the personnel department of the ECUST, during the past 4 years, though 27 teachers were chosen, 16 teachers have been actually dispatched to English-speaking countries, mainly to the United States and the UK, for a time span from 3 to 9 months.

The practice of sending university teachers to English-speaking countries for bilingual teaching purpose is by no means unique. In fact, many universities throughout the country have similar policies to provide opportunities for teachers to be trained for teaching various subjects using English as a medium of instruction.

Table 11.1 Bilingual courses provided from the year of 2003 at ECUST

No	Name of the course	School providing the course
1	Advanced Material Science	School of Material Science and Engineering
2	Foundation of Polymer Science	School of Material Science and Engineering
3	Ceramic and Compound materials	School of Material Science and Engineering
4	Polymer Physics	School of Material Science and Engineering
5	Data Structures	School of Information Science and Technology
6	Process Control Engineering	School of Information Science and Technology
7	C++ Program Design	School of Information Science and Technology
8	Organic Chemistry	School of Chemistry and Pharmaceutics
9	Instrumental Analysis	School of Chemistry and Pharmaceutics

Table 11.1 (*Continued*)

No	Name of the course	School providing the course
10	Modern Foundation of Chemistry	School of Chemistry and Pharmaceutics
11	Physical Chemistry	School of Chemistry and Pharmaceutics
12	International Economics	School of Business and Economics
13	Organization Development and Communication	School of Business and Economics
14	Management of Human Resources	School of Business and Economics
15	International Bidding	School of Business and Economics
16	Electronic Trade	School of Business and Economics
17	International Finance	School of Business and Economics
18	General Situation of Economy and Trade in English Speaking Countries	School of Business and Economics
19	General Description on Multinational Corporations	School of Business and Economics
20	International Business and Communication	School of Business and Economics
21	Strategy marketing	School of Business and Economics
22	Management of Human Resources	Sociology Institute
23	International Economic Law	Sociology Institute
24	Social Activities in Western Countries	Sociology Institute
25	Chemical Reaction Engineering	School of Chemical Engineering
26	Transfer Process and Unit Operation (Principles of Chemical Engineering)	School of Chemical Engineering
27	Microbiology	School of Biotechnology
28	Bio-separation Technique on Protein	School of Biotechnology
29	Heat Transfer	School of Resource and Environmental Engineering
30	Advanced Mathematics	School of Science

Table 11.2 Bilingual courses provided in the year of 2005 at ECUST

No	Name of the course	School providing the course
1	Mass Transfer and Its Application	School of Chemical Engineering
2	Advanced Ceramic materials	School of Material Science and Engineering
3	System Analysis and System Design Method	School of Mechanical and Power Engineering
4	Process Equipment Technology	School of Mechanical and Power Engineering
5	International Economy Cooperation	School of Business and Economics
6	Writing on International Economy and Trade	School of Business and Economics
7	Management Communication	School of Urban Administration
8	Economic History of Foreign Countries	School of Business and Economics
9	Introduction on Manage Information System	School of Business and Economics
10	Introduction on Tourism	School of Culture and Arts
11	Correspondence on Foreign Economy and Trade	School of Business and Economics
12	Research and Development on New Drug	School of Chemistry and Pharmaceutics
13	Polymer materials and Science	School of Material Science and Engineering
14	Sport device and materials	School of Material Science and Engineering
15	Automatic Control System	School of Information Science and Technology
16	Introduction on Software Engineering	School of Information Science and Technology
17	Mathematics Experiments—Mathematical Tools and Its Application	School of Science
18	International Business	School of Business and Economics
19	Management Accounting	School of Business and Economics
20	Organic Chemistry	School of Chemistry and Pharmaceutics

Note: The information in both tables is provided by the Teaching Affairs Office of ECUST.

Our university has over the past few years defined the scope and the objectives for bilingual education, three of which are listed below. According to 'The program for Evaluation of undergraduate courses at ECUST' (ECUST 2005):

- The definition of the bilingual education is using a textbook in a foreign language; 50% and above of the course is taught in a foreign language.
- In the fields of biotechnology, information technology, finance and law, the number of courses offered bilingually should be larger than 10%.
- Effective measures should be constantly developed to enhance the quality of bilingual education, and the number of courses should be gradually increased using English and Chinese as teaching media.

As a bilingual academic, I have been personally involved in bilingual teaching in the department of process equipment and control engineering of the ECUST in recent years. I have formed a team with five other teachers to undertake a specialized course 'Process Technology, Equipment and System' using the textbook with the same title by Thomas (2002). We chose this book as the first textbook for this course because it is plain, simple and easy to read and understand. There are 17 chapters of almost equal length. The range is very wide, containing the most basic content in each subarea of this specialty. At the start of every chapter, there is an outline, describing the key points in this chapter. At the end, there are review questions.

The book may not be an ideal textbook. A good course book, to me, should consist of some latest theories and principles as well as some basic concepts in a particular field. This book does not contain the former and thus looks like a technician's handbook. However, we think the book is suitable for bilingual education, especially at the beginning stage because the students can easily familiarize themselves with special terminology in this specialized field. It helps students to build-up a foundation to read literatures later in this area.

Our choice of an easy-to-handle, authentic textbook has been approved by both teachers and students, and its rationality is further confirmed by a recent panel meeting invited by the Ministry of Education of China to evaluate the applications for the nationwide textbooks to be published in the 11th 5-year plan. Experts in the panel rejected all the applications for writing textbooks for bilingual education. The reasons are

- Linguistically, the quality of the textbooks is not assured as writers are most non-native speakers of English.
- If writers extract contents from textbooks of foreign universities by only simplifying the language, there will be copyright issues.
- If the book is synthesized from different foreign textbooks, the integrity of the textbook is a problem besides the copyright issue.
- It is agreed that all the textbooks for bilingual education should be original copies published by foreign universities, instead of being written by bilingual teachers themselves.

We are aware that a well-selected textbook does not automatically lead to effectiveness of bilingual education. We have also taken measures to ensure high quality of a teacher team for the course. Within our team, there are two professors; others are all associate professors with PhD degrees. All associate professors are middle-age teachers. Only two professors have had experience abroad. The speaking competence of most teachers may not be so desirable, but the lectures are usually well prepared by the whole team. As most classrooms in the department are equipped with computer projectors, the bilingual lectures are given in PowerPoint slides and become very popular in the university.

As team leader, I see bilingual education as a transformation process for both students and teachers and as a means to achieve three main objectives:

- (for students) from passive to active learners
- (for teachers) from forced-feeding method of teaching to heuristic education
- (thus for students) from merely book learning to quality education through a holistic approach

Challenging as these objectives may be, I believe that they could be achieved through dialogue and cooperation between teachers and students.

Accordingly, for bilingual education, I suggest to the team that the most important criterion for measuring effectiveness is that a lecture is understood by students. Teachers should therefore use simple English and vivid language to ease understanding. Secondly, all the PowerPoint slides or blackboard writing are in English, but explanations could be given in Chinese. To me, this is the true bilingual education. The ratio of spoken English and Chinese actually used in the classroom should not be imposed on teachers. And last, all questions in exercises and tests are given in English and the students are encouraged to answer questions in English. I videotape every lesson by the teachers for the purpose to help inexperienced teachers to improving their teaching practices. Through reflection on their own performance, teachers can see weaknesses and strengths of their teaching practice.

At the national level, as Deputy Director of the Teaching Guiding Committee of the Process Equipment and Control Engineering appointed by the Ministry of Education of China, I organized a national bilingual education seminar in April, 2002 to discuss how to develop bilingual education in the specialty of Process Equipment and Control Engineering. About 40 academics from several universities that offer this specialty course attended the seminar. Several presenters including me (Pan, 2003) gave papers and workshops to demonstrate how to engage in bilingual education and shared ideas with delegates from other universities on how to develop bilingual teaching in this specialised area.

It is encouraging to note that evaluation by students who take the course at our department is consistently positive. Most students find our course helpful in terms of course knowledge and English competence development. One of my students (TGW) remarked that 'during the course I learned a lot of nomenclatures. The course helped me to read the literature and to engage in wide reading for writing up the dissertation for the bachelor degree'. Colleagues in the department are also found to make positive comments on the course. The popularity of the course is clearly shown by the fact that so far colleagues from more than 20 universities all over the country who teach the same course have contacted me showing great interest in details to run the course. Comments on the benefits for students could be summarized as follows:

- Bilingual education conducted as such can at the very least enhance students' familiarity with the terminology in English in the specialized area.
- It enables many students to read more extensively so as to gain professional knowledge in this field.
- This knowledge in turn can widen their vision to view this specialized area.
- Bilingual education increases their understanding of the process of internationalization of education.

Despite our efforts and positive feedback of our course, it is important to note that the challenges facing bilingual teachers in general are still enormous. As a faculty member in a highly responsible position for teaching administration comments, the results of bilingual education are not always encouraging as negative feedback from students is frequent (through personal communication). From the feedback of the students this faculty member has access to, bilingual teaching is often ineffective because

- Students meet a lot of specialized technical terms, and therefore they feel difficult to cope with the situation.
- The textbook is authentic, and therefore even teachers find it a real challenge as far as understanding of content is concerned.
- Students' understanding is often hampered by incorrect pronunciation of English of some teachers.
- Some teachers do not follow the textbook systematically. Some parts in the textbook may not be covered by the teacher while some content covered by the teacher in the class may not appear in the textbook.

Considerations

It is now widely agreed that traditional EFL teaching is ineffective. Bilingual education may be the best way to truly improve students' communicative competence. Bilingual education aims to teach language use and to enable students to learn another system of culture and ways of thinking. While English–Chinese bilingual education is flourishing in Chinese tertiary institutions, policy makers and bilingual educators are aware of the challenges they face and adopt pragmatic measures to deal with them.

In order to develop in students the ability to read in English and learn the knowledge of specialty in English, teachers must first of all have a very good command in the target language, as well as a thorough understanding of the courses they teach. Accuracy and fluency in both these languages and deep knowledge in specialized area are prerequisites to facilitate knowledge input in a bilingual classroom. It looks obvious that teachers with high-degree qualifications obtained from abroad are more likely to meet these challenges. Though they may lack teaching experience, they have the potential to provide quality bilingual education. In this sense, many universities have realized the challenge and taken measures to attract bilingual talents from English-speaking countries and send teachers abroad for training. These measures appear to be effective in most cases.

The second challenge is the issue of how far we educators can help (co)create a favourable environment for the students to use both languages and improve competence. It is commonplace observation that many pragmatic ideas such as 'English corners' on campuses, English drama or play activities and games in English are usually enjoyed by students. These activities can help students develop basic communication skill; however, they' are not enough for learners to engage in academic study. In some universities, as the student population is becoming more and more international (e.g. I personally supervise several foreign postgraduate students from Pakistan, Morocco, Congo and Nepal), students on these campuses have opportunities to use the English language as a lingua franca or Mandarin Chinese for real academic discussion. Some of the opportunities are created by students themselves and some are organized by teachers. In a bilingual course, I further suggest that in order to help students master the English language, they should be encouraged to communicate with their bilingual teachers in- or outside the classroom. As they try to express their academic ideas in English, they are likely to use higher-order thinking skills to theorize and conceptualize, to understand the meaning and eventually to develop what Cummins (1984, 2000) calls the Cognitive/Academic Language Proficiency (CALP). In this way, the students will not only be able to converse in simple English but also engage effectively in academic study.

Thirdly, it should be emphasized that bilingual education does not reject students' mother tongue Chinese. We should bear in mind that in bilingual education, Chinese is the dominant medium of instruction. Students still depend on Chinese to understand complex concepts and principles; most teachers are mainly Chinese-speaking teachers with limited exposure to the foreign language. Dazhi (2002) presents a statistic analysis of two departments of two high-profile universities. In the department of electronics and research institution of microelectronics, Tsinghua University, out of 163 professors and associate professors, only 15 have more than 2 years of experience abroad including 5 in non-English speaking countries. In the college of Guanhua school of management, Peking University, 13 out of 77 professor and associate professors have more than 2 years of studying or working experience abroad. This data to a certain degree indicates that even in top educational institutions the quality of courses conducted in English cannot be taken for granted.

For this reason, many educators such as Li (2005) and Chen (2003) argue against bilingual education. They maintain that lack of qualified teachers affects quality education. Liu (2004) and Lu (2002) insist that loss caused by bilingual education outweighs the gain. In their words, while students may gain some 'half-cooked' English, they lose their mother tongue competence and their cognitive thinking skills might be affected. However, I hope this chapter makes it clear that bilingual education is a new challenge posed by globalization of the worldwide economy and internationalization of education. We have to face it and we can provide quality bilingual courses by designing a practical curriculum, selecting appropriate teaching material, selecting suitable human resources for teaching and experimenting with effective measures and teaching methods to address specific contexts.

My own experience convinces me that while we should actively promote bilingual education, we need to be cautious in developing our own model and philosophy to suit the context of our own country. Though there is a large literature on bilingual education, teaching is a kind of art and teaching in another language is a real challenge. It requires the joint commitment, effort and creativity of bilingual education researchers, theorists, policy makers and frontline practitioners like me to develop appropriate models of bilingual education to meet the demands of the 21st century.

Acknowledgements

Thanks to Dr Anwei Feng, School of Education, University of Durham, for his valuable comments on an earlier draft of this chapter.

References

Baker, C. (2001) *Foundations of Bilingual Education and Bilingualism*. Clevedon: Multilingual Matters.
Beijing University (2005). On WWW at http://162.105.129.254, Tianwang.org.
Chemical Industry Press (2002) *The Famous Textbooks of Famous International Universities*. Beijing: Chemical Industry Press.
Chen, W. (2003) Shuangyu jiaoxue buneng yihong ershang [Don't rush bilingual teaching headlong into mass action]. *Xuhui Jiaoyu*. On WWW at http://www.xhedu.sh.cn/jwt/info/doc/2003-04/15/26455/index.htm. Accessed 15.04.2003.
Cummins, J. (1984) *Bilingualism and Special Education. Issues in Assessment and Pedagogy*. Clevedon: Multilingual Matters.
Cummins, J. (2000). *Language, Power and Pedagogy: Bilingual Children in the Crossfire*. Clevedon: Multilingual Matters.
Dan, L. (2001) Tianjin Daxue Shixing Yanjiushen Shuangyu Jiaoxue [Tianjin university's trial implementation of bilingual education in graduate schools]. People's Daily Overseas Version. On WWW at http://www.people.com.cn. Accessed 3.04.2001.
Dazhi (2002) Dui Gaoxiao Tuixing Shuangyu Jiaoxue de Sikao [Considerations on bilingual education carried out in universities]. On WWW at http://www.people.com.cn. Accessed 26.05.2002.
East China University of Science and Technology (ECUST) (September, 2005). *Benke jiaoxue shuiping pinggu gongzhuo Fang'an* [The programme for Evaluation of undergraduate courses]. The Evaluation Office for Undergraduate Studies, ECUST, Shanghai.
Feng, A.W. (2005) Bilingualism for the minor or for the major: an evaluative analysis of parallel conceptions in China. *International Journal of Bilingual Education and Billingualism* 8(6), 529–551.

Fudan University (2004) Fudan Daxue fafang shoupi shuangyu jiaoxue kechen jianshe jingfei [Fudan University grants financial support for the first time for bilingual course development]. On WWW at http://www.fudan.edu.cn.

Jiaoyubu Gaodeng Jiaoyusi, Guanyu chenli gaodeng xuexiao shuangyu jiaoxue gongzuo xiezhuozu de tongzhi [Notification on setting up a coordination committee for tertiary bilingual education] (2004). On WWW at http://www.moe.edu.cn/.

Jiaoyubu guanyu jiaqiang gaodeng yuanxiao benke jiaoxue gongzuo tigao jiaoxue zhiliang de ruogan yijian [Guidelines for improving the quality of undergraduate programmes] (2001) Zhonghua Renmin Gongheguo Jiaoyubu [Ministry of Education of the People's Republic of China]. On WWW at http://www.moe.edu.cn/.

Jiaoyubu guanyu yingfa "Guanyu jiaqiang gaodeng yuanxiao benke jiaoxue gongzuo tigao jiaoxue zhiliang de ruogan yijian" de tongzhi [Notification of the Ministry of Education on promulgating "Guidelines for improving the quality of undergraduate programmes"] (2005) Zhonghua Renmin Gongheguo Jiaoyubu [Ministry of Education of the People's Republic of China]. On WWW at http://www.moe.edu.cn/.

Li, Z. (2005) Shanghai gaoxiao wei xuewei zhenshu jianfu, siji buguo zhaona xuewei [Universities in Shanghai reduce the load for the bachelor degree; students can obtain the degree without having to pass CET-4]. On WWW at http://www.nen.com.cn.

Liu, H. (2004) *Shuangyu jiaoxue yao shenzhong* [Bilingual education should be cautious]. On WWW at http://www.sredu.net/Article/Xuexi/qwxy/yingyu/200409/862.html.

Lu, X. (2002). Zhiyi shuangyu jiaoxue [Query on bilingual education]. *Wen Hui Daily Newspaper*, 1 May.

News Tsinghua (2005) On WWW at http://news.tsinghua.edu.cn.

Northeast News (2005) On WWW at www.nen.com.cn.

Pan, J.Z. (2003) Shuangyu jiaoxue de neihan jiqi sikao [Implications and Thoughts on Bilingual Education]. *Higher Education in Chemical Engineering* (3), 48–51.

Shanghai Jiaotong University website (2005) On WWW at http://202.120.2.135.

Shanghai University website (2002) Available at http://jwc.shu.edu.cn/jwc/Message.

Thomas, C.E. (2002) *Process Technology, Equipment and Systems*. Berne, NY: Uhai Publishing Inc.

Wang, X.D. (2005) *Guanyu shuanyu jiaoxue de sikao* [The considerations on bilingual education]. On WWW at http://www.bilingual.com.cn.

Part 4
English Provision for Minority Students

Chapter 12

Teachers' Perceptions of Chinese–English Bilingual Teaching in Guangxi

BINLAN HUANG

Introduction

Due to China's increasing integration into the world, bilingual education has become a necessity for China's education to face the world, the future, and modernization. English–Chinese (E–C) bilingual teaching* (using both English and Chinese as mediums of instruction) has become a strategic means for China to develop high-quality talents in order to integrate into the global economy. In Guangxi, the autonomous region with the biggest minority group, the *Zhuang* nationality, and one of the least developed provinces/regions in China, it is widely believed that it is badly in need of *Guojixing Rencai* [international talents] to develop its economy (Guangxi University, 2003; Nie *et al.*, 2003). To produce these talents, importance has gradually been attached to the implementation of college E–C bilingual teaching. E–C bilingual teachers play a decisive role in the push for this form of teaching. Their attitudes toward and perceptions of the teaching have great effect on both the teaching quality and students' learning outcome.

It can be argued that success or failure of E–C bilingual teaching depends, to a larger extent, on the teachers. However, research on teachers' attitudes toward and perceptions of this new phenomenon hardly exists in the literature on E–C bilingual teaching. Therefore, empirical research is needed urgently to find out how college E–C bilingual teachers perceive, offer, and evaluate E–C bilingual teaching, how they see the relationship between E–C bilingual teaching and *Guojixing Rencai*, what policies have been adopted for E–C bilingual teaching, what approaches, models, and textbooks are used, and what difficulties exist in implementing E–C bilingual teaching. As Guangxi is chosen for my empirical research, it is also hoped that the study can shed new light on what position the minority *Zhuang* language finds itself in this push for E–C bilingual teaching. Through such empirical studies, better understanding will be gained of E–C bilingual teaching and more appropriate measures can be found to solve the existing problems in order to better implement E–C bilingual teaching for the prosperity of minority regions such as Guangxi.

Chinese Conceptions

Bilingualism is often used to designate the capability of using two or more languages. The use of a language can range from native speaker competence to minimal ability to survive in simple transactions and encounters. Weinreich (1968: 1) offers one of the shortest definitions: "the practice of alternatively using two languages will be called bilingualism." Mackey (1970: 555) incorporates and expands Weinreich's definition of bilingualism with the words, "we should therefore consider bilingualism as the alternative use of two or more languages by the same individual." However, bilingualism as a concept has an open-ended semantics. Earlier definitions tended to restrict bilingualism to equal mastery of two languages while recent ones have allowed much variation in competence (Edwards, 1994).

The concept of bilingualism in China has long been associated with the minority groups, and bilingualism is traditionally used to refer to the competence of linguistic minorities in using Mandarin Chinese as well as their home languages for communication (Feng, 2005). In the past decades, the literature on bilingual education has been therefore dominated by education of linguistic minorities. The purposes are both linguistic, to keep the minority languages from extinction or to train minority language speakers to master the majority language in order to communicate with the larger society, and political, to assimilate them into the mainstream society and to socialize them for full participation into it. To the Han majority that comprises about 92% of the total population, it remained largely a remote notion until nearing the turn of the century. In the last few years, however, bilingualism has been rapidly embraced by the Han majority as a useful tool for improving foreign language education, in particular English, and for developing human resources using such notions as *Guojixing Rencai [international talents]* or *Zhuanye Waiyu Fuhexing Rencai [all-rounded talents who possess both specialized knowledge and strong competence in a foreign language]*. In the whole country, particularly in major cities such as Shanghai, Beijing, and special economic zones like Shenzhen, a school system is being rapidly developed in which English as well as standard Chinese are used as the mediums of instructions. China's "open-door" policy, its fast economic development, its successful bidding for the 2008 Olympics Games, and its access to the WTO are catalytic factors in promoting this bilingual schooling which looks almost certain to reshape China's education system as a whole (Feng, 2005).

Models of Bilingual Teaching

To adapt to the rapid change of the society, China's Ministry of Education promulgated a 12-clause document in 2001 for enhancing its college education. In this document, every college and university is required to teach 5–10% of its curriculum courses in a foreign language within 3 years (Ministry of Education, 2001). This is the first formal official document of policy concerning university bilingual teaching of content subjects. Thereby, bilingual teaching becomes one of the important aspects of tertiary education.

Since then, E–C bilingual teaching has been initiated and implemented in most colleges and universities in China. Key universities, such as Beijing University, Tsinghua University, etc. took the lead in bilingual teaching. According to Huang and Wang (2004), Jia (2005), Ye (2005), in 2001, 54 out of 1440 courses of Tsinghua University used English as medium of instruction, covering courses for the first-year undergraduate students to postgraduate students. Tsinghua University has promulgated a plan to adopt authentic teaching materials (English textbooks that are compiled and published by publishing presses in the English-speaking countries) for as many as 500 core courses within 3 years (Ye, 2005). At Beijing University, over 20% of its content subjects are taught using authentic teaching materials. In Huazhong University of Science and Technology, bilingual teaching has been applied to nearly half of its curriculum courses. In 2001 alone, Shanghai Jiaotong University selected from its colleges and departments 25 bilingual teachers and sent them abroad for training on bilingual teaching. Due to regional differences in teaching facilities and conditions, availability of teaching materials, and teachers' and students' specialized knowledge and English competence, there exist roughly four models commonly found in E–C bilingual teaching in China (Table 12.1, models based on an overview of the most recent literature including Huang and Wang (2004), Jia (2005), Xu (2004), and Ye (2005)).

In general, E–C bilingual teaching at tertiary institutions in China has been developing fast. However, many problems remain to be solved before it could satisfy the needs of China's bilingual education. In some colleges and universities, bilingual teaching is still at the preparatory stage while at

Table 12.1 Models of bilingual teaching adopted at China's tertiary institutions

Model	Medium of instruction	Edition of teaching materials	Teaching method	Ways of evaluation
1	Basically in Chinese	Chinese edition or English edition with Chinese translation	Some English phrases/expressions on board, or a summary of the text in English, or some English books/articles assigned for complementary reading after class	Examination in Chinese, or assignment in Chinese with an English abstract
2	10–20% in English	English edition with Chinese translation or self-compiled materials in English	Some key points written in English on board, or teaching software or PowerPoint in English, but explanation mostly in Chinese	Examination in English with some difficult items or points in Chinese, and students could deal with it either in Chinese or English, or assignment in Chinese with an English abstract
3	20–40% in English	English edition published either at home or abroad, or self-compiled materials in English	Simple items/points explained in English, key points written in English on board, with English software or PowerPoint, but difficult items/points taught in Chinese	Examination in English, and students could deal with it either in Chinese or English
4	40–70% in English	Authentic teaching materials published abroad	Much written on board in English, and lesson taught mostly in English, but with difficult items/points explained in Chinese	Examination in English, and students deal with it in English, or assignment in English

some others where it is under way it is not running smoothly. According to Huang and Wang's statistics (2004) from a questionnaire conducted between September and October of 2002 on Liaoning's (a province in northeastern China) bilingual teaching, 42 out of its 71 colleges and universities had not implemented bilingual teaching for lack of teachers and other necessary resources. In some colleges and universities, E–C bilingual teaching started but has discontinued due to the large number of dropouts or lack of qualified teachers. Even Tsinghua, a high-profile university is not an exception. In 2001, more than 130 students started E–C bilingual teaching of physics, a compulsory course for four departments. However, the number of attendants dropped to 102 two weeks later. In Xi'an Jiaotong University, E–C bilingual teaching was implemented for mathematics and approximately 200 students selected the course at the beginning, but only 54 students managed to stick to the end (Huang & Wang, 2004; Xu, 2004; Ye, 2005). The same situation is also found at Guangxi University where the study is conducted.

As this large-scale E–C bilingual schooling is quite a new phenomenon, not surprisingly China's tertiary institutions, especially those in central and western China where financial and human resources are less favorable, have encountered many problems in its implementation. Discussions on this new phenomenon are often restricted to theoretical overview of concepts, with very few empirical studies. Up till now, no empirical study has ever been done on Chinese E–C bilingual teachers, whose attitudes and perceptions of the teaching have great effect on both the teaching quality and students' learning outcome. This research study is intended to fill in this gap and to contribute directly or indirectly to the development of realistic models that suits the context of less-privileged tertiary institutions.

The Current Study

This study focuses on teachers' perceptions of E–C bilingual teaching for senior undergraduate students at tertiary institutions in Guangxi, China. It aims, as mentioned before, to find out how college E–C teachers of Guangxi perceive, offer, and evaluate E–C bilingual teaching, how they see the relationship between E–C bilingual teaching and *Guojixing Rencai*, what policies have been adopted toward E–C bilingual teaching, what approaches, models, and textbooks are used, and what difficulties exist in implementing E–C bilingual teaching. Besides, it also wants to find out the position of Zhuang language in this push for E–C bilingual teaching since Guangxi is one of the five least-developed provinces with the biggest minority group, Zhuang nationality, in China. Semi-structured interviews were chosen to

Table 12.2 Core questions for semi-structured interviews

Q1	How do you interpret/define bilingual teaching? What do you think should be the goal/perceivable learning outcomes of English and Chinese bilingual teaching?
Q2	Many scholars and policy makers say the aim of E–C bilingual teaching is to develop *Guojixing Rencai [international personnel]* or *Zhuanye Waiyu Fuhexing Rencai [all-rounded talents who possess both specialized knowledge and strong competence in foreign languages]*. How do you define these *Rencai*? How do you see the relationship between bilingual teaching and *these Rencai*?
Q3	What is the status quo of bilingual teaching in your university? And what policy(ies) is(are) adopted toward bilingual teaching in your university?
Q4	What approaches and models are adopted in your implementation of bilingual teaching? And what sort of textbooks is/are adopted?
Q5	How do you evaluate the effectiveness of bilingual teaching of your class(es)?
Q6	What difficulties exist in implementing bilingual teaching in your university? And what measures have been/should be taken to overcome these difficulties?
Q7	What is the position of Zhuang language in this push for E–C bilingual teaching?

collect data for two reasons: perceptions are best explored in depth with such a qualitative instrument (see the Instrument section below) and the small population of E–C bilingual teachers in Guangxi. The questions listed in Table 12.2 were formulated to achieve these objectives.

The Informants and Instrument

Based on voluntary principles, 18 informants from five colleges and universities of Guangxi were interviewed. Among them, 10 are from Guangxi University, which is usually described as the most important and comprehensive university in Guangxi and thus supposed to take the lead in E–C bilingual teaching. The other eight informants were from four other colleges and universities: three from Guangxi College of Nationalities, one from Guangxi Medical University, two from Guangxi Teachers' Education College, and two from Guangxi Chinese Herbal Medicine College. The age of the informants ranged from 31 to 56, with four informants under

35. The informants held either the doctor's degree or the master's degree. Twelve informants held full professorship, and 15 informants had been abroad for further study for 1–3 years. It is worth mentioning that 10 of them were holding the position of dean or vice dean of department or faculty. All the informants had been teaching E–C bilingual courses for senior undergraduates for 1–3 years.

The decision to use the qualitative method for the research was made by considering several factors for its appropriateness. As many methodologists agree, qualitative research focuses on understanding meanings and depth and patterns of relationships whereas a quantitative method emphases causes and relationships demonstrated statistically (Babbie, 1983:537). One of the rationales for qualitative research has been that it takes into account the "native or insider point of view" by including quotations from informants, but maintains the researcher's interpretative perspective. The central goal of qualitative research is often seen as providing analytical, theoretical, or in-depth description (Cohen *et al.*, 2000; Silverman, 2000). As the aim of the study is to evaluate and analyze how the respondents perceive E–C bilingual teaching at tertiary institutions, it represents human reality and phenomena and only in-depth and intensive interview studies in the fieldwork could provide new insights for understanding, perceiving, and reflecting on their perceptions.

Data Collection and Analysis

To ensure the fitness of the questions for purposes and that the questions are clear to the informants, a pilot interview was first carried out with an E–C bilingual teacher of Guangxi University. The core questions were later revised according to the pilot interview and the focus of the study. Informants were then contacted by emails and phone calls and told the purpose of the study. After seeking permission from the informants, the core questions for the semi-structured interviews were sent to them by e-mails beforehand to familiarize them with the content of the interview. This was to reduce their anxieties. To obtain accurate information on the status quo and the informants' perception of E–C bilingual teaching, the interviews were conducted in Chinese and recorded with a recording pen. Data shown in this article are English translations. E-mails were sent again to the informants when more information had to be added or confirmed. The interviews from 18 informants were collected and transcribed. These qualitative data were grouped and coded according to certain categories based on the core semi-structured interview questions. Results of the analysis along with the quantitative data were used as evidence to show the status quo of E–C bilingual teaching and how E–C bilingual teaching was offered and viewed at tertiary institutions in Guangxi.

Results and Discussion

Awareness of and attitudes toward E–C bilingual teaching

During the time when the study was conducted, Guangxi had successfully held the first China–ASEAN (Association of South-east Asian Nations) Exposition, which Chinese Premier Wen Jiabao proposed would be held annually in Nanning, the capital city of Guangxi, from 2004. To host the yearly international event more successfully, Guangxi has opened its door wider and made great efforts to attract more international exhibitors and investors so as to bring about more business opportunities for businessmen and enterprises for both China and ASEAN countries. Against this background, professional personnel who possessed not only knowledge in their specialized areas but also strong competence in foreign languages, particularly English, were highly valued and badly needed. This constitutes a social foundation for the implementation of E–C bilingual schooling and provides the background for the series of interviews. The following statement by Interviewee B, a Professor of Mathematics, clearly demonstrated the awareness and attitude shared by others:

> *As a strategic means to further enhance quality education at tertiary institutions and to develop human resources for Guangxi's economy, it's absolutely necessary and important to implement E–C bilingual teaching. Actually, we've been left far behind by colleges and universities in the developed or coastal provinces and cities in this regard. The economic development of Guangxi needs more talents who are both good in professional knowledge and competent in English. We have the responsibility for cultivating more such talents, so we're willing to do something for E–C bilingual teaching.*

Definition and perceivable outcomes of E–C bilingual teaching

The informants interpreted E–C bilingual teaching in various ways. On the one hand, some took it as "using authentic teaching materials and teaching the content subjects partly (50% or more) in English and partly in Chinese." Some who stayed abroad for over a couple of years defined it with a view to student motivation, as "using English and Chinese alternatively or using English completely as the medium of instruction to teach the content subjects, so as to satisfy students' instrumental motivation or integrative motivation." However, most informants adopted a flexible view by defining all teaching that involves the use of two languages as bilingual teaching. They thought when both English and Chinese were used as mediums of instruction for part or a certain stage of the teaching process—lesson planning/previewing, lecturing, blackboard-writing, question-answering/reviewing, homework, examination—then such teaching could be termed E–C bilingual teaching. In this way, E–C bilingual teaching became something that was within easy reach, which could be encouraging and give both teachers and students impetus and confidence to get ahead. Then when conditions were favorable, a higher-level model with more English exposure could be adopted. They did not think it practical to set or impose the same high demand or standard on all colleges and universities in implementing E–C bilingual teaching regardless of conditions and environments. The following comment by Interviewee M, Professor of Finance and Banking, represented the above viewpoint of these informants:

> *We are still at the beginning or exploratory stage of implementing E–C bilingual teaching, so people should be tolerable with the models, approaches, and materials we adopt. It's definitely not practical to set the same standards on all the students and universities regardless of different conditions and environments. Take my students as an example. When I taught them Finance in Chinese last term, nearly one fifth found it hard to learn and failed it. As is required, this term I choose an original textbook from the United States. Though I teach them 90% in Chinese, 10% in English, about one third of the students still find the course too hard because of their low competence of English. They have complained to the school authority and asked to revert to the old practice.*

With respect to the effectiveness of E–C bilingual teaching, the informants agreed that after 2 years' E–C bilingual teaching, students' interest in and level of English in general were raised and stimulated through such teaching. They further remarked that ideally upon graduation, at least 15–25% students would become *Guojixing Rencai* who possessed specialized knowledge and were able to browse the Internet, read authentic books, journals, materials, etc. directly in English for the latest professional knowledge and development in their specialized areas, and to communicate in English with foreign colleagues or experts for information or exchange of opinions. However, since E–C bilingual teaching was developing slowly and at a low level at present in Guangxi, they believed it would take at least

3–5 years before such outcome could be obtained. Here was the remark by Interviewee G, Professor of Physics:

> *In the case of Guangxi, we need to implement E–C bilingual teaching gradually. It's true we need more and more Guojixing Rencai with both rich specialised knowledge and strong competence of English for its economic development. But it will take some time, I think at least three to five years, before we could implement E–C bilingual teaching more smoothly and achieve better outcome.*

Aim of E–C bilingual teaching and its relationship with Guojixing Rencai

If Guangxi wants to become integrated into the global economy for more stable and faster development, most informants believe that it is important to train more innovative talents of high quality, especially *Guojixing Rencai*. The informants demonstrated a considerable degree of uniformity in the view that the ultimate goal of college E–C bilingual teaching was to develop for Guangxi's economy *Guojixing Rencai*. They defined these *Rencai* as graduates who not only had rich specialized knowledge the ability to keep up with the new development trends and to innovate and create in their specialized domains, but also had strong competence and good communication skills in English. They considered that the specialized knowledge should be placed in the first position, and English competence in the second in E–C bilingual teaching. Otherwise, these *Rencai* could not be termed *Guojixing Rencai* because they would be the same as those students whose major was English. Therefore, in their opinion, in E–C bilingual teaching students should never sacrifice specialized knowledge for the sake of fluency and competence in English. Specialized knowledge is the goal of E–C bilingual teaching, while English competence is the means to reach the goal. The following comment by Interviewee C, Professor in Mechanical Engineering, represents this view:

> *In the era of economic globalisation, it won't do for universities to produce traditional students who have only specialised knowledge with little English competence to communicate with the outside world, or vice versa. Guojixing Rencai is the new aim imposed on universities and colleges. I think the goal of E–C bilingual teaching is to develop such Rencai. Through bilingual teaching, students can further improve their English competence, and meanwhile learn the latest specialised knowledge, advanced experimental/research methods and innovative concepts. So we should work out how to implement this teaching well.*

Status quo of E–C bilingual teaching in Guangxi

E–C bilingual teaching was implemented only in one or two universities in Guangxi in the year 2001 when China's Ministry of Education promulgated the national document on bilingual teaching. However, when this requirement was set in 2002 as one of the important criteria in the evaluation of undergraduate teaching quality and level (cf., Guangxi University, 2003), most colleges and universities in Guangxi responded quickly and began to offer some E–C bilingual courses for senior undergraduate students because evaluation by the Ministry of Education would be carried out between 2003 and 2005. In their words, they had to offer a certain number of E–C bilingual courses if they wanted to get a "Pass" or a "Good Pass" or an "Excellent Pass" in the evaluation. This was considered closely related to the reputation of a university, or something of "life and death" for a university, in the words of Interviewee O, Professor of Education.

Thereby, this official policy was imposed on all tertiary institutions as a tall order despite some reluctance from individuals. Colleges and universities had to make the best out of their inadequately prepared staff and hardware. As Interviewee D, Professor of Physics, said, E–C bilingual teaching was something like "driving a duck onto a perch" (a Chinese saying, which means making someone do something entirely beyond his/her · capability):

> We are not ready for the implementation of E–C bilingual teaching yet. We're asked "to drive a duck onto a perch." There is lack of qualified teachers who are both strong in specialised knowledge and competent in English. Worse still, the students' level of English, their interest and motivation in learning content subjects in English are all too low. However, since it is something that is required, then we have ways to deal with it. We can guarantee the quantity of 10%, but not the quality (of teaching).

Data show that few colleges and universities in Guangxi had made strategic plans, short-term or long-term, for their E–C bilingual teaching yet, nor had they made any evaluation criteria. The departments had their own say as to what to do with their E–C bilingual teaching. They asked the teachers they thought good in English, especially those who had been abroad to open certain E–C bilingual courses. Usually the Dean or vice-Dean of the department or teachers with full professorship or a doctoral degree had to take the challenge themselves. Without guidance and unified criteria, these bilingual teachers made decisions all by themselves about what models, approaches, and teaching materials to use, how to evaluate the students, etc. This implies that E–C bilingual teaching at tertiary institutions in Guangxi is left to be self-regulated by each school authority and individual teachers.

Models adopted for E–C bilingual teaching

As mentioned above, teachers were free to decide on almost everything for their E–C bilingual teaching. Of the four models summarized in Table 12.1, nine informants adopted model 1, three used a model somewhat between Model 1 and Model 2, four used Model 2, while the other two used Model 3. The two informants who adopted Model 3 taught students majoring in such popular subjects as law and computer science. These students scored higher in the National College Entrance Examinations and apparently had stronger competence in English. Both informants took great pains to prepare for their teaching materials and lesson plans. They used software, Power Points, etc. to enhance their teaching effect. The rationale for teachers to choose different models was guided by certain pragmatic principles as Interviewee A, Associate Professor of Economics, said

> *We choose the model we think fit for our students' level of specialised knowledge and English competence. And our limited English competence also plays a part. We have to be very careful in selecting the right materials and teaching approaches in order to obtain a certain effectiveness of teaching and to meet the students' practical needs. Most students want to earn credits from the course. They are not very interested in improving their English, in fact. So to achieve the best result of teaching, we instruct the course mostly in Chinese. Since the school authorities do not know much about this sort of teaching, you could make your own decisions and make them think you're doing the right thing!*

Effectiveness of E–C bilingual teaching on students

Data show that the informants on the whole were optimistic about the present implementation of E–C bilingual teaching, though the teaching effect was not satisfactory enough. For example, through E–C bilingual teaching, the students' awareness of the importance of possessing both rich specialized knowledge and strong English competence had been raised. According to the statistics the library assistants of the five university libraries provided through personal communication, the number of science and engineering students borrowing authentic journals, reference books, etc. for specialized knowledge had increased by about 15–20% as compared with that of 3 years ago. However, as Interviewee K, Lecturer of

Mathematics, pointed out, for students whose general quality and English competence were relatively low and limited, E–C bilingual teaching was time-consuming and served mainly as a means of learning about certain foreign cultures, rather than acquiring knowledge on science and technology. On the other hand, the teachers' weak communicative ability in English also rendered it difficult to carry out interactive teaching in class, making two-way communication more difficult and affecting the teaching quality. Furthermore, lack of extracurricular reading materials or reference books was another factor to hinder the smooth implementation of E–C bilingual teaching. The following comment by Interviewee G, Professor of Physics, gives us some idea of the effectiveness of E–C bilingual teaching at tertiary institutions in Guangxi:

> *Even when the course is instructed in Chinese, more than 10% of the students fail it every year. More students fail it after we adopted bilingual teaching. Students need to spend twice the time and energy on the course: they have to look up in the dictionary for clearer definitions of words and expressions, translate the sentences into Chinese to understand the points. They do not feel safe enough for fear of failing the course, so they make complaints and ask the teacher to instruct the course in Chinese. The limited resources and facilities also make it difficult for students to learn the course better. Of course, we teachers have responsibility too because our English is not good enough to express ourselves sometimes. However, through E–C bilingual teaching, students could learn about some latest developments in the specialised fields, and their English learning has improved more or less since they could keep up their English study by learning the English texts or reading complementary materials assigned.*

The data showed that some bilingual courses in Guangxi University had discontinued because of unsatisfactory teaching quality, as was the case in other four colleges and universities. The number of students signed for the bilingual courses was too small for certain courses to reopen, said Interviewee C, Associate Professor of Electrical Engineering. However, he added, to reach the national criteria of teaching 10% bilingual courses of the curriculum, these temporarily discontinued courses would be made compulsory and reopened soon, and all students were required to take them in order to graduate. Coercive measures, according to the Interviewee F, Professor of Medicine, would be adopted at the university level in implementing E–C bilingual teaching in Guangxi. The teachers and students would not have much say. With respect to students' complaints, the common practice for the authorities to deal with them, according to Interviewee P, Professor of Chinese, was to increase pressure on teachers to improve their teaching. The bilingual teachers are caught in this crossfire. They could do nothing else but to adopt various strategies to cater to the students' needs. For example, they would reduce the amount of English if students complained about the degree of language difficulty, or make examinations easier to pass to please the students, etc.

In spite of the difficulties, E–C bilingual teaching did get started, which is an important step forward in Guangxi. Furthermore, there were certain successful cases of bilingual teaching, too. Take Interviewee E (Associate Professor of Law) as an example. She said she had chosen the right course (Introduction to British and American Law) for bilingual teaching, which was relatively easier with less technical terms; second, she was willing to spend time and energy amending the teaching materials, deleting the difficult and out-of-date contents, and upgrading the important parts according to her students' level of English and specialized knowledge. In addition, she used PowerPoint, software, and other interactive teaching approaches to stimulate her students' interest and participation. Both her and her students' English competence was strong enough to carry out effective two-way communication in class, with over 85% of her students having passed the national College English Test Band 4, a passing rate of about 50% higher than other bilingual classes other informants taught. Both she and her students were satisfied with the course. She said

> *We need a careful and scientific plan for the E–C bilingual teaching. For example, we need to choose the right textbooks or materials, and the right approaches of teaching according to the students' level of English and specialised knowledge. And we need to select the right course, as not every course is suitable for E–C bilingual teaching. We even need to think about the academic hours needed for each bilingual course, the number of students for each bilingual class, etc. There are many factors we need to consider to make a bilingual course successful. Most important of all, more support and understanding are needed from the school authority and other teachers.*

Interviewee E's case certainly has many implications and should prompt us to deep thought for the improvement of E–C bilingual teaching.

Major difficulties in implementing E–C bilingual teaching

E–C bilingual teaching is still at the trial stage of its development at most tertiary institutions in Guangxi, and therefore it is natural that there exist difficulties or obstacles to its implementation. According to the informants, one of the most outstanding problems with E–C bilingual teaching is that no unified standards and models have been set up. As a result, they were usually at a loss as to what to follow, what model to adopt, etc. What they could do was to follow their own intuition and judge by their own feeling of what was right or wrong.

The second major difficulty lies in the students' weak English competence. Interviewee R's (Professor of Chinese Herbal Medicine) comment clearly demonstrates this:

> *You know, during the first two years when students learned College English, they learned it in big classes which were teacher-centered and examination-oriented. They learned "dumb English" with little communication and inter-action in class. Now when they become senior students and E–C bilingual teaching is implemented, their English competence becomes a bigger problem since they have to learn the specialised knowledge through English. Two-way communication and classroom interaction are very difficult due to their limited vocabulary and poor communicative ability. They're actually not ready for E–C bilingual teaching yet, so very often we teachers assume the role of translators.*

Shortage of teaching materials suitable for students' level of specialized knowledge and English competence presented another big challenge. The limited materials available in the home market were either difficult or out of date in content. Those imported from abroad were generally so expensive that most students could hardly afford. According to Zhuang and Sun (2004), the authentic edition of a textbook introduced by Beijing University and Tsinghua University usually cost as much as 30 to 50 US dollars. For most Zhuang students at tertiary institutions in Guangxi, whose monthly expenditure on food and daily necessity is only about RMB 200 yuan per person on the average, 50 US dollars for a textbook is really too much for them. Because of these factors, many teachers had to compile the teaching materials by themselves. However, as they had little experience and there was hardly any coordination between them, coupled with their limited proficiency in English, the quality of the materials they compiled could hardly be guaranteed. From the comment by Interviewee J, Professor of Medicine, we will see the problem more clearly:

> *Originally we planned to use a foreign edition, but it was too expensive for most students. Then we chose a home edition but dropped it very soon because the contents were not new enough. So I had to compile the material by myself. To tell you the truth, my English is not good enough though I have been abroad. On the one hand I have to make sure the English is not too difficult; on the*

other I need to cover the necessary specialised knowledge. It's really hard and time-consuming as I lack experience and need guidance in this regard too. I once thought of giving up the course.

The shortage of high-quality E–C bilingual teachers is another major factor influencing the outcome of E–C bilingual teaching (Wang, 2004) and a bottleneck hindering the development of E–C bilingual teaching at tertiary institutions (Luo and Wang, 2004). It is usually the case that teachers (usually the junior ones) with strong competence in English are weak in their specialized knowledge, while teachers with rich professional knowledge (usually the senior ones) are not good enough in English. Worst of all, no bilingual teacher-training plan has ever been made or implemented at any tertiary institution in Guangxi according to the informants. Some informants, usually the senior ones, admitted that it was difficult for them to communicate with students when it came to impart specialized knowledge in English. As far as specialized knowledge is concerned, some younger informants said they lacked experience and professional knowledge and found it hard to keep up with the latest development trends at the leading edge of their own domains. Hence, when it came to choosing or compiling teaching materials for bilingual courses, they found it difficult to decide on the appropriateness of the contents.

Finally, the imperfect management system and shortage of incentive mechanism have also rendered it difficult to implement effective E–C bilingual teaching. Nine out of 10 informants expressed dissatisfaction with the present management system of bilingual teaching. Curriculum arrangement was unsatisfactory; an effective evaluation system was not established. Worse still, though bilingual teachers' workload was much heavier—they had to spend more than twice the time and energy preparing for the courses and dealing with issues concerning the relatively new courses—their work was not well recognized. They had the feeling that they were doing a hard but unrewarding job. Some informants mentioned that they would not try any new model or teaching method or teaching material, which would cost them more time and energy without doing them any good. The following comment by Interviewee F, Professor of Ecology, is representative:

Actually, our workload is heavier and harder, but our work is not very well recognized here. The time and energy we spend on the bilingual courses double those of the non-bilingual courses. Bilingual teaching is very demanding indeed. You need to have rich and latest specialised knowledge in your field because the materials or textbooks adopted are imported from abroad. On the other hand, you need strong English competence. Otherwise you won't be able to understand the materials or textbooks well enough to impart the knowledge or to communicate with the students. A good management and incentives system is badly needed to motivate and encourage the bilingual teachers to get further ahead.

The position of Zhuang language in this push for E–C bilingual teaching

Guangxi is the biggest Zhuang Autonomous Region in China, with the largest group of people from the Zhuang nationality, most of whom speak Zhuang language. When asked about the position of Zhuang language in this push for E–C bilingual teaching, 10 informants said they had never thought about this issue. They commented that even if they had, they could not afford the time to take care of the local language and culture. Three informants did not think Zhuang language had much to do with bilingual teaching. Here is the comment by Interviewee I, Associate Professor of Chemistry:

Well, I don't speak Zhuang language, and I guess it has little to do with bilingual teaching. You know, whatever language a student speaks, he/she needs to learn specialised knowledge in order to get a job in the future. And he/she also needs to learn English since it is an international language. He/she needs to be equipped with both: sound specialised knowledge and strong English competence, if he/she wants to integrate himself/herself into this global world and become Guojixing Rencai.

Some informants mentioned that they did notice Zhuang students' spoken English and Mandarin influenced greatly by their strong Zhuang accent and guessed that these students' inactive participation in class activities was partly due to their strong Zhuang accent, which was often laughed at by other students. Zhuang students were usually found to be at a disadvantage "because of their strong accent" when it came to language learning. The Zhuang language, culture, and tradition were often taken as something backward or unfavorable or hindering factors in language learning. Some commentators such as Xu (2004) thus argue that bilingual teaching may result in loss of minority culture and measures should be taken to address this problem.

Among the interviewees, only Interviewee L, Associate Professor of Computer Science, belongs to the Zhuang nationality and speaks Zhuang language. When asked how he viewed the position of Zhuang language in bilingual teaching, he said

> *Yes, most Zhuang students speak Mandarin and English with a strong accent, which is sometimes laughed at by other students, intentionally or unintentionally. Sometimes I am a victim, too. I myself don't care about this. However, many students are psychologically hurt to some extent. In my class, about one third of the students are of Zhuang nationality. Most of them seat themselves at the back of the classroom, and assume a passive role in class. Their motivation is low, affecting their learning outcomes. They are obviously in an inferior position in E–C bilingual teaching. Some students said if the bilingual course had been a selective one, they wouldn't have taken it. I encourage them now and then by showing them videos of some Indians communicating fluently and successfully with native English speakers, though they have strong Indian accent.*

Obviously, the position of Zhuang language in bilingual is neglected by the school authorities, educational planners, and most teachers as a whole, which has produced negative effect on the Zhuang students' learning motivation and enthusiasm and may lead to low effectiveness of E–C bilingual teaching. To solve the problem, strong awareness and coordination and cooperation from both students and teachers are needed, but most important of all, the school authorities, educational planners, and policy makers should take some concrete and effective measures to figure out how to create a favorable learning environment for the Zhuang students.

Summary and Conclusion

The results of this study aim to contribute to an in-depth understanding of how E–C bilingual teaching is offered and viewed by content subject teachers in Guangxi, China. As shown by the results of the data analysis, most informants first of all hold a positive attitude toward E–C bilingual teaching, are highly aware of the importance of, and willing to implement this teaching. They view it as a necessity and a strategic means for Guangxi to develop human resources and become integrated into the global economy. Second, given that neither teachers' nor students' competence in English was strong enough, they think bilingual teaching should be flexibly defined and implemented step by step. They predict that in about 3–5 years, perhaps 15–25% of graduates would become *Guojixing Rencai* with strong English competence and specialized knowledge. They agree unanimously that the ultimate goal of E–C bilingual teaching is to develop *Guojixing Rencai*, which they define as those who possess rich specialized knowledge with English competence as an effective means to that end.

Thirdly, they remark that the national criterion of teaching 5–10% bilingual courses of the curricular is not difficult to meet in quantity but in quality due to various factors, including lack of qualified teachers, lack of teaching materials, poor English competence of teachers and students, etc. And because of these barriers, it is found that most informants adopt Model 1 or Model 2, the lower levels of E–C bilingual teaching. Furthermore, the study shows, surprisingly, that most informants think that Zhuang, the mother tongue of Zhuang students in the Autonomous Region, is not an issue in bilingual teaching. But in fact, the data shows that students from the Zhuang nationality are perhaps further marginalized in this bilingual teaching movement "because of their Zhuang accent." Their self-esteem and cognitive development are thus affected. Owing to the issues listed above, effectiveness of bilingual teaching is in general unsatisfactory, though teachers and students are aware of the importance of E–C bilingual teaching.

The current study was the first attempt to explore the perceptions of content subject teachers of E–C bilingual teaching at tertiary institutions in Guangxi. More in-depth or longitudinal studies look necessary to investigate how E–C bilingual teaching functions in enhancing students' quality, what effect it has on the local economy, when is the best time for the implementation of E–C bilingual teaching at tertiary institutions, how teachers' language competence is related to the teaching effect on students, and what effect local languages and cultures have on this teaching. Results from these studies will hopefully help shed new lights on the issues and in turn improve E–C bilingual teaching in Guangxi, which will be beneficial to the local economic development.

The author of this chapter is aware of the limitation of the study such as the relatively small size of the sample. However, tentative suggestions can be drawn from this study. First, long-term plans, teaching curricula, assessment criteria, and management mechanisms need to be made or established based on conditions in different colleges and universities. Second, E–C bilingual courses should be made optional especially at the early stage. According to the informants, E–C bilingual teaching is more easily and effectively implemented for some introductory or theoretical courses since they are relatively easier with fewer technical terms or less specialized knowledge. Thirdly, great importance should be attached to the professional training of E–C bilingual teachers, which in practical terms in the Guangxi context may refer to financial support for research projects, reduced routine workload, and academic promotion. Thus, more teachers with higher qualifications will be motivated to contribute to bilingual teaching. Furthermore, preferential conditions should be created for students in the form of extra credits or scholarships to stimulate their interests and enthusiasm in taking these courses. In addition, special funds should be made available each year for experts to compile or modify teaching materials and experiment with various teaching approaches in order to enhance the quality of teaching. Finally, special attention should be paid to the impact of E–C bilingual teaching on minority students and measures should be taken to create a favorable learning environment for them.

Note

*I am aware that many authors, including those in this volume, use the phrase—Chinese-English bilingual education—in their discussions. I also use this phrase in the chapter title to keep the language consistent in the book. However, in the text I use the phrase, English-Chinese (E–C) bilingual education, instead; this is to remind readers that the former is not a universally adopted notion. Many other authors do place English before Chinese in their discussions. This word order, followed unconsciously or consciously, reflects the fact that English has become the focus of attention in bilingual education to many people.

Acknowledgement

I am deeply indebted to Dr. Anwei Feng at the School of Education, University of Durham, who has offered me throughout the process of this study generous and encouraging help with invaluable advice and insightful ideas. Without his help, this study would not have been possible.

References

Babbie, E. (1983) *The Practice of Social Research*. (3rd edn). Belmont, CA: Wadsworth.
Cohen, L., Manion, L. and Morrison, K. (2000) *Research Methods in Education*. London: Routledge.
Edwards, J. (1994) *Multilingualism*. London: Routledge.
Feng, A.W. (2005) Bilingualism for the Minor or for the Major: An evaluative analysis of parallel conceptions in China. *International Journal of Bilingual Education and Billingualism* 8(6), 529–551.
Guangxi University (2003) Guanyu Benke Jiaoxue Shuiping Pingguo Gongzuo De Yijian Yu Jianyi [Opinions and suggestions on the assessment of undergraduate students' teaching level], official document.
Huang, J.G. and Wang, X.H. (2004) Gaodeng Xuexiao Shishi Shuanyu Jiaoxue De Xianzhuang Fenxi Ji Duice [Bilingual teaching in colleges: present conditions and measures]. *Journal of Jinggangshan Normal College* 25(2), 89–91.
Jia, M.F. (2005) Dui Guo Nei Shuangyu Jiaoxue Xianxiang De Fenxi [An analysis of the phenomenon of the bilingual teaching in China]. *Journal of Xi'an International Studies University* 13(2), 25–27.

Li, J.W. (2004) Gaodeng Yuanxiao Zhuanye Kechen Kaizhan Shuangyu Jiaoxue De Ruogan Wenti Fenxi [Problems of implementing bilingual teaching in specialized courses in higher learning institutions]. *China Higher Medical Education 3*, 14–15.

Luo, L.CH. and Wang, J.H. (2004) Guanyu Putong Gaodeng Yuanxiao Shuanyu Jiaoxue De Sikao [Reflection on bilingual teaching in universities]. *Theory and Practice of Education* 24(9), 59–61.

Mackey, W.F. (1970) The description of bilingualism. In J. Fishman (ed.) *Readings in the Sociology of Language*. Mouton: The Hague.

Ministry of Education of the People's Republic of China (2001) Guan'yu Jiaqian Gaodeng Xuexiao Benke Jiaoxue Gongzuo Tigao Jiaoxue Zhiliang De Rugan Yijian [Opinions on strengthening the teaching and improving the teaching quality for university undergraduate students]. Official document.

Nie, H., Huang, B., Chen, N. and Fang, W. (2003) Guanyu Shuanyu Jiaoxue Huo Caiyong Waiwen Jiaocai Shouke de Sikao [An inquiry into the practice of exercising course books in foreign languages and bilingual instruction within higher education]. *Journal of Guilin University of Electronic Technology* 23(2), 80–82.

Silverman, D. (2000) *Doing Qualitative Research. A Practical Handbook*. London: Sage.

Wang, L.P. (2004) Yingxiang Shuanyu Jiaoxue De Zhiyue Yinshu: Shizheng Fenxi Yu Duice Jianyi [Restricting factors in bilingual teaching: a positivist analysis and solutions]. *Journal of Yangzhou University (Higher Education Study Edition)* 8(1), 77–80.

Weinreich, U. (1968) *Language in Contact*. Mouton: The Hague.

Xu, K.Q. (2004) Shuangyu Jiaoxue Zhong Ying Guangzhu Zhonghua Mingzhu Wenhua Yishi Wenti [The popularity of bilingual teaching and the loss of the Chinese traditions]. *Foreign Language Education* 25(3), 86–89.

Ye, J.M. (2005) Zuo Hao Daxue Yingyu Jiaoxue Xiang Shuangyu Jiaoxue Guodu De Jiekou Gongzuo [Properly Tackling the work of the interfaces between bilingual teaching and college English teaching]. *Foreign Language World* (2), 69–72.

Zhuang, D.L. and Sun, Ch.P. (2004) Zhiyue Gaoxiao Shuanyu Jiaoxue De Zhuyao Yinshu Ji Duice Tantao [Obstacles to the implementation of bilingual teaching and corresponding solutions]. *Journal of Hefei University of Technology (Social Science)* 18(4), 177–181.

Chapter 13

EFL Education in Ethnic Minority Areas in Northwest China: An Investigational Study in Gansu Province

QIUXIA JIANG, QUANGUO LIU, XIAOHUI QUAN AND CAIQIN MA

Introduction

The linguistic development of bilingual students has been extensively treated in the literature of the last three decades. Most research in this field focuses either upon subtractive bilingual education for immigrants, or upon additive bilingual education for some balanced or unbalanced bilingual communities (Beardsmore, 1986; Grosjean, 1982; Hamers & Blanc, 1989; Huguet *et al.*, 2000; Li, 1996; Milk, 1981; Purdie & Oliver, 1999; Romaine, 1989; Scheu, 2000; Tucker, 1991; Zentella, 1981). Relatively little literature, however, has been devoted to the trilingual education in those communities in which English is taught as a FL but not spoken as L1 or L2 (Jan *et al.*, 2005; Modood & May, 2001; Pluddemann, 1999; Webb, 1999). To teach EFL in a trilingual context is very different from that in a bilingual context because involvement of three languages makes EFL education in a trilingual context all the more complex. This gives the very reason for carrying out educational research on the former. Just as Cenoz and Jessner (2000: ix) point out

> Third language acquisition or TLA is a more complex phenomenon than second language acquisition (SLA) because apart from all the individual and social factors that affect the latter, the process and product of acquiring a second language can themselves potentially influences the acquisition of a third. Third language learners have more experience at their disposal than second language ones do, and have been found to present more strategies and a higher level of metalinguistic awareness.

Trilingualism becomes even more complicated in consideration of the fact that there have been potential and continued disadvantages and new forms of exclusion of racial and ethnic minorities in national educational system (Tomlinson, 2003).This research is based upon EFL education in ethnic minority areas of Gansu Province in Northwest China. Gansu Province is a region in Northwest China with 54 ethnic minority nationalities, among which 16 are indigenous groups. Bordered by the Xinjiang Uiyghur Autonomous Region, Ningxia Hui Autonomous Region, and Inner Mongolia Autonomous Region, the province is inhabited by the Han majority and other ethnic minorities, and hence an ideal location from which a sample of mixed ethnic groups can be selected for research on minority education.

From the beginning of this century, China has started a thorough curriculum reform in primary and high schools (Ministry of Education of the People's Republic of China, 2001). The reform is launched against the EFL education tradition, which overemphasizes the importance of grammar and vocabulary but understates the comprehensive linguistic competence of using EFL. The reformation involves fundamental ideological changes. The reform document states that EFL education aims

(1) to be inclusive and character-education-oriented;
(2) to be open, integrative, and flexible in designing teaching objectives;
(3) to be learner-centered and respect learners' individual differences;
(4) to learn in activity and participation;
(5) to foster learners' development through continuous assessment; and
(6) to develop and widen curriculum resource.

Meanwhile, the reform is designed to stratify the learner's EFL development into nine grades in nine years' compulsory education and senior high school education. According to the new syllabus (Ministry of Education of the People's Republic of China, 2001), the aim of EFL education is to develop learners' comprehensive linguistic competence in foreign languages. Linguistic competence is defined to consist of five interactive components: linguistic skill, linguistic knowledge, affect and attitude, learning strategy, and culture awareness. The reform involves systematic changes of all elements in EFL education, ranging from teachers' professionalism to learners' activeness, from pedagogical philosophy to ways of classroom life, and from teaching materials to equipment and hardware to facilitate EFL education.

The reform in ethnic minority areas has met with various challenges due to the shortage and professional proficiency of EFL teachers and the complexity of EFL education in the trilingual context. Our investigation was conducted against this background and also against the backdrop that China had just started a long-distance education project in rural primary and high schools since 2003 (http://www.yuxianedu.com/dy2005/Article/Class6/Class26/200501/74.html). Some schools in the minority areas of the province had been equipped for the pilot project. Therefore, we were interested in finding out to what extent the reform and the project had impacted on the EFL education in minority areas and what outstanding problems in the application of the equipment are, and whether ethnic minority learners can truly benefit from the long-distance educational resources.

In China, systematic implementation of EFL education for ethnic minority learners has been a new concern and some research has been carried out in this regard. The research has either been focused upon the investigation into the status quo of and strategic solutions to EFL education in ethnic minority learners (Jiang *et al.*, 2006), or dealt with theoretical reflection upon such issues concerning EFL education planning (Yang & Duan, 2003, Ding & Zhou, 2004), or inquired into the characteristics of some cognitive factors of EFL learning, such as EFL learning styles of ethnic minority learners (Liu, 2005). Some research also treated such issues as EFL education in a trilingual context in ethnic minority areas of China (Liu, 2005). However, the paucity of research just underlines the important need for further research on the issue under discussion. Many factors involved remain academically unknown in China. The present research was conducted to fill in this gap and to provide a descriptive analysis of the status quo and some influential factors in Chinese context, thus aiming to advance some possible strategic solutions to the issues.

Research Design

Research questions

The investigational study is designed to answer the following questions:

(1) In what way is ethnic minority learners' EFL learning different from that of majority learners? How do L1 and L2 affect their EFL learning?
(2) What are the current challenges for the EFL teaching staff in ethnic minority areas? How much do they want to be further trained?
(3) To what extent does long-distance educational equipment facilitate and foster EFL education? And what are the possible problems ethnic minority learners may have with the long-distance resources mainly designed for the majority?

Instruments

We studied EFL education in ethnic minority areas from three perspectives: of EFL learners, of their teachers, and of the administrative staff. Thus, three questionnaires were developed respectively. The questionnaires for learners and teachers were composed of two parts: one took the form of statements with responses on a Likert Scale of five points (1 = strongly disagree, 2 = disagree, 3 = undecided, 4 = agree, and 5 = strongly agree); the other had open questions. The items in the questionnaires ranged from EFL learning, EFL teaching ideas and approaches, cultural awareness in EFL learning and teaching, to the use of the resources and equipment already available for EFL education.

Interviews and classroom observations were also used in the investigation. Interviews were carried out with learners (one male and one female in each school), teachers (one in each school), and headmasters (one in each school), and classroom observations were made focusing on EFL teaching performance.

Subjects

In the investigation, samples were selected from four ethnic minority areas of Gansu Province, namely Linxia County and Dongxiang Autonomous County of Linxia Hui Autonomous Profecture, Tibetan Autonomour County of Tianzhu, and Yugu Autonomous county of Sunan. Considering the striking differences between rural and town schools in these areas, we further divided the sample schools in each sample area into two categories: rural schools and town schools. According to the duration learners are exposed to EFL, from each category we further chose as subjects one class from Grade 2 in junior and senior high schools, respectively, and Grade 5 in primary schools. The design involved administering the questionnaire to all the EFL teachers in the sample schools and interviewing EFL teachers of subject classes. Besides, one of the administrative staff or the headmaster from each sample school was interviewed.

Altogether 896 EFL learners were investigated, among which 567 were non-Han ethnic minority learners, and 325 Han learners, with the other 4 unspecified in nationality. Among the four non-Han minority groups, the Hui take Chinese as their mother tongue, and all the other three have their own mother tongues other than Chinese.

Procedure

Before the implementation of the investigation, we contacted the local educational departments for authorization for the investigation into the sample schools. With that, we visited the sample schools to make the aims of the investigation clear and chose the sample classes, teachers, and administrators. We first distributed questionnaires to EFL teachers and administrative staff as well as learners. Then interviews were held and classroom observations were conducted to get a direct understanding of the EFL classroom teaching.

Results and Discussion

A clearer picture of EFL education emerged with the progress of the investigation, and our understanding of the situation is deepened with the analysis and processing of the data collected. Results are presented in the following two parts: characteristics of EFL learning of ethnic minority learners and current problems for EFL teaching staff in the areas.

EFL learning of ethnic minority learners

The learners' questionnaire was designed to measure their learning motivation, linguistic attitudes and cultural awareness, as well as trilingual transference in EFL learning. Comparative analysis of the investigation results indicates that minority learners are lower in motivation, weaker in cultural awareness than their majority peers, and their learning is negatively affected by transfer from their L2, Chinese, to the target language.

Lower motivation

Brown (2001) argues that motivation is probably the most frequently used catch-all term for explaining the success or failure of virtually any complex task. In the present investigation, the questionnaire for motivation consists of 32 items describing the question "Why do you learn English language," each measured with a five-point Likert Scale (1 = strongly disagree, 2 = disagree, 3 = undecided, 4 = agree, and 5 = strongly agree). Analysis of the data shows that EFL learning of ethnic minority learners is characterized by a low level of motivation. The mean score for each minority is listed in Table 13.1.

Descriptive statistics in Table 13.1 indicate that Han and Hui learners score higher in the motivational level while the others score quite low. Hui learners live and learn in a culture much assimilated by the Han culture, for the two share the same mother tongue, and their EFL learning happens in absence of a second language. The other minority learners, however, are faced, first of all, with the task of learning both their own mother tongues and Chinese as their second language. These findings seem to suggest that

Table 13.1 Mean and standard deviation of motivation of Han and non-Han minorities

Nationality	Mean	N	Std. Deviation
Han	80.1802	268	14.40417
Tibetan	77.2465	142	13.12147
Hui	81.2439	82	15.19223
Yugu	79.5217	46	15.50303
Dongxiang	79.4080	150	14.68683
Others	77.0667	15	13.34416
Total	79.4374	703	14.37188

the extra undertaking of learning the mainstream language may affect EFL learning motivation.

As one of the vital non-intelligent variables affecting EFL learning, motivation accounts for the purposes and degree of self-initiation in EFL learning. Brown (2001) suggests that it is sensible in second language learning to claim that a learner will be successful with the proper motivation. Interviews reveal that minority learners' EFL learning motivation is relatively instrumental, though they are adjacent to their Han-minority counterpart in the continuum of motivation level. The finding is compatible with that reported by Fitzgerald (1978) that the motivational disposition of L2 learners among ethnic minorities is more likely to be instrumental.

For the ethnic minority learners involved in the investigation, a command of EFL means competence to communicate and bargain with foreign tourists. Places of tourist and religious interests can be found in most sample areas, and, as a result, tourist and religious activities there are relatively frequent. Although the correlative model between instrumental motivation and L2/FL success is still controversial (Au, 1988; Brown, 2001; Gardner & MacIntyre, 1991; Gardner *et al.*, 1992), investigation and interviews show that learners do not attach so much emphasis to the cultural and humanistic value of the EFL as to its instrumental significance. Furthermore, the low motivation is related to the local educational system in which EFL is sometimes only taught as an optional course, and is not obligatory in the entrance examination to colleges and universities. Perhaps because of this, EFL learners' motivation cannot be fully stimulated. The consequence of this is that, once they gain entrance to the university, they will find themselves at a disadvantage in adapting to EFL education.

Weaker cultural awareness

Cultural awareness is a term often used to refer to knowledge and interests in cultural differences and relationship to otherness (Risager, 2000). Studies on bilingualism and multiculturalism are enlightening in understanding EFL learners' cultural awareness in a trilingual context. Scheu (2000) holds the view that it seems impossible to develop a second language (L2) without being affected culturally in some way. Under the assumption that L3/FL learning also involves the process of developing cultural awareness, we examined minority learners' EFL cultural attitude and acceptance with questions in the form of a Likert Scale (1 = strongly disagree, 2 = disagree, 3 = undecided, 4 = agree, and 5 = strongly agree). The ratio of mean acceptance value between Han learners and non-Han learners is 2.8:2.6. The finding shows that non-Han minority EFL learners demonstrate lower acceptance of a foreign culture. Further interviews indicate that, strategically, non-Han minority learners make little comparison between the two languages and cultures in their EFL learning. The isolations of EFL from L1, and language from culture, suggest weaker cultural awareness of the minority learners, as can be seen in their negligence of the cultural value of EFL. Minority EFL learners do not conceptualize EFL learning as an indispensable process of cultural awareness. As Brown (2001) argues, second language learning is often second culture learning. This is the case with EFL. When EFL is learned together with its culture, it is more likely to be successful.

L2 negative transference

Transfer is defined as the carrying over of learned behavior from one situation to another. Positive transfer is learning in one situation which helps or facilitates learning in another later situation, while negative transfer is learning in one situation which interferes with learning in another later situation (Brown & Miller, 1980; Richard *et al.*, 2000). The findings of the investigation show that non-Han minority learners find themselves at a disadvantage in EFL learning partly because their learning is negatively affected by their extra undertaking of learning the mainstream language. Theoretically, negative transference is assumed to be partly caused by cognitive immaturity of the learners in learning through three languages. Our study, however, reveals that EFL teacher's classroom language might be responsible for the negative transference. Interviews and classroom observation show that ethnic minority young learners are relatively poor in their L2 competence, and most EFL teachers are from the Han majority with little knowledge of the learners' mother tongue; thus, EFL classes are mainly conducted in Chinese. The disparity between the competence of learners and teachers in three languages prevents them from full communication and interaction in class, and as a result constrains the development of EFL competence. The failure very often arises when the instrumental language in class cannot be fully accepted by learners, and the teachers' relative incompetence in the learners' mother tongue makes impossible effective decoding of meaning in class. Furthermore, most learners identify more similarities between their L1 and the EFL than between their L1 and L2, while their L2 Chinese is regarded as rather different either from their mother language or from English. Using Chinese as the only interlanguage in class does no good for facilitating learning of the target foreign language. Meanwhile, the interference of Chinese makes their cognition an indirect process in which three linguistic codes are involved. In this "zigzag" process, learners can be slower in understanding and learning. In an interview, a 26-year-old Han EFL teacher described her experiences of teaching Grade 5 Tibetan EFL learners in primary school as follows

> . . . Some Tibetan students are poor in Chinese. Although they can communicate in it, they have trouble in understanding my classroom language, either Chinese or English, which is a little formal in style. To teach a complex idea or abstract concept, I will see some puzzled faces. In this case, a code-switching to Tibetan always works. Unfortunately, I do not speak Tibetan, and then I have to ask some students good at Chinese for help. Their explanation in Tibetan will help me when I am in trouble with the Tibetan language . . .

The findings serve to qualify Cummin's BICS/CALP distinction and argument. The two notions BICS (basic interpersonal communicative skills) and CALP (cognitive academic language proficiency) are used to address the issue regarding how much proficiency in a language is required to follow instruction through that language (Cummins, 2000). If Cummins is right in his argument that there is a gap of 7 years, on an average, between the attainment of peer-appropriate fluency in L2 and the attainment of grade norm in academic aspects of L2 (Cummins, 2000), the challenges young ethnic minority learners meet within an EFL classroom can be accounted for with this argument. The findings also highlight the fact that L2 proficiency is one of the major factors in the creation of academic difficulties for young ethnic minority EFL learners in China.

EFL teaching staff

Our data suggest that inadequate EFL teaching resources in ethnic minority areas is one of the key issues encountered in English language education. There is a serious shortage of qualified EFL teachers. The positive side according to our findings is that most of the teachers who are at the forefront are, however, eager to be further trained.

Status quo

In the past decades, Northwest China has suffered greatly from a severe shortage of EFL teachers. The situation in ethnic minority areas is even worse due to the poor economic conditions and multi-sociocultural context. Furthermore, when young learners in primary schools began to learn English as required since the last decade of the 20th century, the demand for EFL teachers increased considerably. Despite great efforts from educational authorities, the shortage remains one of the constraints of EFL education in minority areas.

Ethnic minority areas are sparsely populated, and, as a result, rural schools are distributed far away from each other. The shortage of the EFL teachers is partly reflected in a teacher's workload. According to the investigation, 16.2% EFL teachers in ethnic minority areas teach four or more classes and 25.0% teachers will teach more than 15 hours per week, in addition to the time spent on homework marking, lesson preparation, class tutoring and management, and other duties. In some disadvantaged areas, EFL teachers have to travel several miles between schools to provide a peripatetic EFL service. Overloaded EFL teachers, therefore, can hardly get round to improving their teaching performance and developing their professionalism.

As mentioned above, EFL teachers in these areas are usually inadequately educated and lack professional training. China has set as an ideal that primary school teachers should receive junior college training; teachers in junior high schools should receive undergraduate education; and some postgraduates should be included in the teaching staff in senior high schools (Wang, 2003). The investigation, however, shows that many EFL teachers in Northwest minority areas are far from being qualified in their educational backgrounds.

As is illustrated in Table 13.2, the educational backgrounds of EFL teachers are rather unsatisfactory in the minority areas in Northwest China, with only 15.4% EFL teachers in the sample having received 4 years' college training, mostly in the form of self-taught education or correspondence courses. So far, none of the graduates from normal universities has joined the teaching staff in the minority areas after their graduation.

What is more, 24.2% EFL teachers in the sample have received no professional training. To meet the urgent need of EFL education in these areas, some graduates with backgrounds other than TEFL have become EFL

Table 13.2 The educational backgrounds of EFL teacher subjects

	Frequency	*Valid Percent*
Self-taught B.A.	8	15.4
Junior college graduates	23	44.2
Normal secondary school graduates	16	30.8
Others	5	9.6
Total	57	100.0

teachers to fill the vacancies. Through classroom observations, we found that some of these teachers are clearly struggling with English phonetics and grammar themselves, and linguistic mistakes and errors occur quite frequently in EFL classrooms.

Data collected in the investigation indicate that 73.0% teachers in the sample areas have been trained for less than 3 months and 81.1% EFL teachers list the wish for training opportunities as one of their most urgent needs. When questioned about their attitude and assessment of New Syllabus Standards, 64.8% of the sample EFL teachers strongly agree or agree that "although it sounds good, it is very hard to be put into practice." According to the findings, in-service EFL teachers hope to be further trained in the following aspects: the reform of educational ideology and teaching approaches (59.5%), EFL professional proficiency (48.6%), and the improvement in the application of IT technology (51.3%).

A work force without trilingual competence

Since most learners in ethnic minority areas take Chinese as their second language, their EFL learning, we believe, involves the process of cognitive processing and code-switching among three languages. Ideal EFL teachers in these areas should, therefore, have a command of three languages (L1, L2, and FL) and practice trilingual teaching in the EFL class. A trilingual teacher will better understand the intertransference of the three languages under study and thus be able to switch their classroom languages to facilitate learning. However, due to the shortage of competent trilingual teachers, trilingual teaching is insufficiently practiced in schools that minority pupils attend. The study shows that 62.9% EFL teachers surveyed are Han, with little knowledge of minority languages. Classroom observations also indicate that most EFL teachers fail to switch their languages in EFL classrooms when necessary, and thus fail to cater to the learning demand and cognitive particularity of the learners of different nationalities and linguistic backgrounds.

It should be noted that for the ethnic minority learners whose mother tongue is not Chinese, classroom language use is much more complex and thus deserves special attention. In classroom teaching, EFL teachers with trilingual competence are likely to switch their languages between L1, L2, and EFL. Nonetheless, how this trilingual code-switching facilitates language learning is rarely discussed despite the abundant literature and research on code-switching in a bilingual context. Therefore, it is of great theoretical and practical significance to research this phenomenon so as to construct trilingual EFL education models for specific contexts.

Classroom observations also show that only a few non-Han trilingual teachers are able to make effective use of code-switching among three languages in the light of the classroom situation, linguistic literacy of EFL learners, and topics being taught. For the easy topics shared by EFL learners and teachers, English or Chinese may serve as a major instrumental language, while in treating some complex concepts and ideas, EFL or L2 may be replaced by the learners' mother tongue. Trilingual code-switching thus serves as a dynamic strategy in accordance with the difficulty of topics dealt within an EFL class. Meanwhile, learners' responses to the instrumental language also determine code-switching in the EFL classroom. When learners look slow to understand the chosen language, the EFL teacher will seek to choose another language to facilitate their cognition.

Hardware without users

The past decade has witnessed the implementation of various educational projects in ethnic minority areas financed by the Chinese government. Some schools have taken advantage of the projects and have been equipped with IT teaching facilities. The hardware will be further improved in the near future, for, since 2003, China has started a long-distance educational project in rural primary and high schools, from which ethnic minority education will benefit to a great extent. However, our data show that the equipped teaching facilities have not been put into full use, partly because local EFL teachers are unfamiliar with educational applications of IT. The answer to this issue is not as simple as it looks. The dilemma EFL teachers are facing is that though they are in urgent need and willing to be further trained, the shortage of EFL teachers prevents this from happening.

Multilingual and multicultural context

EFL education inevitably involves the transmission of its culture (Brown, 2001; Scheu, 2000). In the ethnic minority EFL class, both teachers and learners are exposed to three cultures, namely their mother language culture (L1 culture), second language culture (L2 culture), and foreign language culture (EFL culture). In a multicultural system, both learners' and teachers' attitudes toward the three cultures may be represented in a mental multicultural system in which each one is located in some place ranging from kernel to margin corresponding to its relative value. In the trilingual classroom context, both teachers and learners find themselves in a multilingual system in which each language has its own status and position, and the relative position of each culture in the system may affect learners' acquisition of the culture.

Furthermore, the three cultures coexist and interact in a dynamic system. Under the interaction of the three cultures, the EFL class may develop its distinctive multicultural class pattern, which goes far beyond the simple addition of the three. As the different cultures may integrate or conflict in a multicultural system and make the EFL classroom culture develop and change in a dynamic fashion. Integration and conflicts are two fundamental phenomena of cultural contact in the classroom. In the ethnic minority EFL class, this becomes even more complicated for the cultural integration and conflicts arise among three cultures. It is in this multicultural context that the learners reconstruct their cultural outlook and attitude.

Suggestions

In this chapter, we have merely offered general descriptions of the most conspicuous issues concerning EFL learners and teachers in the sample areas, for we have had to be selective due to space. On the basis of these findings, we wish to speculate about the causal factors of these problems and make some recommendations to address the issues. The contributing factors of these problems are twofold: first, without successful and effective trilingual teaching models and approaches, minority EFL education cannot be conducted with universal efficiency; second, the lack of the trilingual EFL teachers calls for immediate EFL professional training. Accordingly, we suggest some possible solutions which may work to improve the situation.

As has been stated above, ethnic minority EFL learning is, in the trilingual and multicultural context, characterized by particular complexity. Although there are studies on multilingualism in the European, North American, and Hong Kong context (Bentahila & Davies, 1995; Hamers & Blanc, 1989; Huguet et al., 2000; Huss-Keeler, 1997; Jan et al., 2005; Li, 1996; Pedersen, 1997; Purdie & Oliver, 1999; Riley, 2005; Rollin-Ianziti & Brownlie, 2002; Tucker, 1991), unfortunately, little is known about EFL learning mechanisms and cognition in the multilingual and multicultural context in China. Literature devoted to this field is rather limited (Hasen, 1999; Jiang *et al.*, 2006; Johnson, 2000; Postiglione, 1999; Wang, 2003). Code-switching among three languages is rather frequent in non-Han teachers' EFL classes. The interaction and transference among the three languages can either be positive or negative, depending largely upon the context in which it occurs and the linguistic competence of EFL learners and teachers, respectively. Therefore, academic efforts should be made to find out in what circumstances trilingual teaching or trilingual code-switching fosters positive transference and how it leads to negative transference. With the knowledge of interactive transference, EFL teachers will be well-informed to make decisions to minimize the negative effects while maximizing the positive outcome.

Inter-language transfer of L1 to L2 and FL has been discussed in some publications (Bouvy, 2000; Cenoz & Jessner, 2000). Our findings challenge the idea that L1 always exerts a negative influence upon EFL learning. For beginners of EFL, as is the case of young learners in primary schools, classroom trilingualism may facilitate learners' construction of a referential system among three languages. Beginners' EFL learning is largely a constructive process of semantic equivalents among three languages. In this sense, the establishment of a trilingual referential system may facilitate beginners' EFL learning to a certain extent.

We have revealed that EFL teachers in ethnic minority areas are small in population and most of them have not undertaken formal education and professional training. Local economic and educational conditions are not likely to attract enough qualified EFL teachers in the short term. For in-service EFL teachers, despite their strong desire to be further educated, the opportunities of receiving full-time training are largely reduced by the shortage of local EFL teachers. Against this background, one of the best solutions is to develop a long-distance teacher-training program.

Due to limited formal education and limited chances for professional training, EFL teachers find it challenging to adjust to the EFL curriculum reform in China. Therefore, the present condition of teachers proves to be one of the most important constraints of the EFL education. The implementation of the New Syllabus calls for qualified EFL teachers, and makes the need for a training program even more urgent. In working out the teacher development program, the demands of the teachers should be taken into consideration. Further education for EFL teachers in ethnic minority areas should be based upon current needs such as the improvement of EFL pronunciation, EFL pedagogy, linguistic communicative competence, etc.

In the long run, the program should aim to train qualified teachers for a better minority EFL education.

Although an increasing number of teaching software and educational resources will become available with the progress of the long-distance educational project in rural primary and high schools, the resources are developed for Han majority EFL learners and have to be adapted and supplemented to suit the minority context. This is because, as stated before, the unique trilingual situation faced by minority children is not taken into consideration in the long-distance educational project designed for the majority Han children. The resources should be localized to address this dimension.

All in all, our study indicates that EFL education in these areas is of special complexity in that not only are three languages involved in the FL learning process, but in many cases learners are forced to operate in their second language rather than their mother tongue in this learning process. This is clearly the main issue that may potentially challenge the existing theories on EFL education, trilingual cognitive process, trilingual classroom code-switching, and trilingualism in general. Without doubt, future research into and theoretical discussions on this issue is needed to enrich and deepen our understanding of EFL education in ethnic minority regions.

References

Au, S.Y. (1988) A critical appraisal of Garder's social-psychological theory of second language learning. *Language Learning* 38, 75–100.

Beardsmore, H.B. (1986) *Bilingualism: Basic Principles* (2nd edn). Clevedon: Multilingual Matters.

Bentahila, A. and Davies, E.E. (1995) Patterns of code-switching and patterns of language contact. *Lingua* 96, 75–93.

Blommaert, J., Collins, J. and Slembrouck, S. (2005) Space of multilingualism. *Language and Communication* 25, 197–216.

Bouvy, C. (2000) Toward the construction of a theory of cross-linguistic transfer, In J. Cenoz and J. Ulrike (ed.) *English in Europe: The Acquisition of a Third Language* (143–156). Clevedon: Multilingual Matters.

Brown, E.K. and Miller, J.E. (1980) *Syntax: A linguistic Introduction to Sentence Structure*. London: Hutchinson.

Brown, H.D. (2001) *Principles of Language Learning and Teaching*. Beijing: Foreign Language Teaching and Research Press.

Cummins, J. (2000) Putting language proficiency in its place: Responding to critiques of the conversational/academic language distinction. In J. Cenoz and J. Ulrike (ed.) *English in Europe: The Acquisition of a Third Language* (pp. 54–81). Clevedon: Multilingual Matters.

Cenoz, J. and Jessner, U. (2000) Introduction. In J. Cenoz and J. Ulrike (eds)*English in Europe: The Acquisition of a Third Language* (pp. vii–xii). Clevedon: Multilingual Matters.

Cenoz, J. and Jessner, U. (2000) Expanding the scope: Sociolinguistic, psycholinguistic and educational aspects of learning English as a third language in Europe. In J. Cenoz and J. Ulrike (eds) *English in Europe: The Acquisition of a Third Language* (pp. 248–260). Clevedon: Multilingual Matters.

Ding, W. and Zhou, Z. (2004) Minzu diqu ertong zaoqi waiyu jiaoyu lilun yu shijian [Theory and practice of EFL education for ethnic minority young learners]. *Ningxia Daxue Xuebao [Journal of Ningxia University]* 4, 75–77.

Fitzgerald, M. (1978) Factors influencing ELT policies in England with particular reference to children from Pakistan, India and Bangladesh. *EFL Journal* 33/1, 13–21.

Gardner, R.C., Day, J.B. and MacIntyre, P.D. (1992) Integrative motivation, induced anxiety, and language learning in a controlled environment. *Studies in Second Language Acquisition* 14, 197–214.

Gardner, R.C. and MacIntyre, P.D. (1991) An instrumental motivation in language study: Who says it isn't effective? *Studies in Second Language Acquisition* 13, 57–72.

Grosjean, F. (1982) *Life with Two Languages: An Introduction to Bilingualism.* Cambridge, MA: Harvard Univ. Press.

Hamers, J.F. and Blanc, M.A.H. (1989) *Bilinguality and Bilingualism.* Cambridge, U.K.: Cambridge Univ. Press.

Hasen, M.H. (1999)*Lessons in Being Chinese: Minority Education and Ethnic Identity in Southwest China.* Hong Kong: Hong Kong University Press.

Huguet, A., Vila I. and Llurda, E. (2000) Minority language education in unbalanced bilingual situations: A case for the linguistic interdependence hypothesis. *Journal of Psycholinguistic Research* 29 (3), 313–333.

Huss-Keeler, R.L. (1997) Teaching perception of ethnic and linguistic minority parental involvement and its relationships to children's language and literacy learning: A case study. *Teaching and Teacher Education* 13 (2), 171–182.

Jiang, Q., Liu, Q. and Li, Z. (2006) Xibei minzu diqu waiyu jichu jiaoyu xianzhuang diaocha [An investigational study of EFL education in ethnic minority areas of Gansu Province in Northwest China]. *Waiyu Jiaoxue yu Yanjiu* [Foreign Language Teaching and Research] 2, 129–139.

Johnson, B. (2000) The politics, policies, and practices in linguistic minority education in the People's Republic of China: The case of Tibet. *International Journal of Educational Research* 33, 593–600.

Li, D.C.S. (1996) *Issues in Bilingualism and Biculturalism: A Hong Kong Case Study.* New York; Washington, D.C./Baltimore; Bern; Frankfurt am Main; Berlin; Vienna; Paris: Peter Lang.

Liu, Q. (2005) Xibei zangzu xuesheng waiyu xuexi fengge diaocha yanjiu [An investigational Study of EFL learning style of Tibetan Learners in Northwest China]. *Minzu Jiaoyu Yanjiu [Journal of Research on Education for Ethnic Minorities]* 5, 93–96.

Milk, R. (1981) An analysis of the functional allocation of Spanish and English in a bilingual classroom. *California Association for Bilingual Education: Research Journal* 2 (2), 11–26.

Ministry of Education of the People's Republic of China (2001) *Quanrizhi yiwu jiaoyu putong gaoji zhongxue yingyu kecheng biaozhun [English Language Syllabus for Compulsory Full-Time Education and Senior High School Education*]. Beijing: Beijing Normal University Press.

Modood, T. and May, S. (2001) Multilingualism and education in Britain: An internally contested debate. *International Journal of Educational Research* 35, 305–317.

Pedersen, P.B. (1997) Recent trend in cultural theories. *Applied and Preventive Psychology* 6, 221–231.

Pluddemann, P. (1999) Multilingualism and education in South Africa: One year on. *International Journal of Educational Research* 31, 327–340.

Postiglione, G.A. (1999) *Chinese National Minority Education: Culture, Schooling and Development*. New York and London: Falmer Press.

Purdie, N. and Oliver, R. (1999) Language learning strategies used by bilingual school-aged children. *System* 27, 375–388.

Rechards, J.C., Platt, J. and Platt, H. (2000) *Longman Dictionary of Language Teaching & Applied Linguistics*. Beijing: Foreign Language Teaching and Research Press.

Riley, K. (2005) Big change question: Should indigenous minorities have their right to have their own education systems, without reference to national standard? *Journal of Educational Change* 6, 177–189.

Risager, K. (2000) Cultural awareness. In M. Byram (ed.) *Routledge Encyclopedia of Language Teaching and Learning* (pp. 159–162). London and New York: Routledge.

Rollin-Ianziti, J. and Brownlie, S. (2002) Teacher use of learners' native language in the foreign language classroom. *Canadian Modern Language Review* 58, 22–50.

Romaine, S. (1989) *Bilingualism*. Oxford: Basil Blackwell.

Scheu, U.D. (2000) Cultural constraints in bilinguals' codeswitching. *International Journal of Intercultural Relations* 24, 131–150.

Tomlinson, S. (2003) Globalization, race and education: Continuity and change. *Journal of Educational Change* 4, 213–230.

Tucker, G.R. (1991) Cognitive and social correlates of bilinguality. In R.L. Cooper and B. Spolsky (eds) *The Influence of Language on Culture and Thought* (pp. 101–111). Berlin: Mouton de Gruyter.

Wang, B., (2003) *Shuangyu jiaoyu yu shuangyu jiaoxue [Bilingual Education and Bilingual Teaching]*. Shanghai: Shanghai Foreign Language Education Press.

Webb, V. (1999) Multilingualism in democratic South Africa: The overestimation of language policy. *International Journal of Educational Development* 19, 351–366.

Yang, M. and Duan, J. (2003) Jiasu xibu waiyu jiaoyu de junheng fazhan [On promotion of EFL balanced educational development in western China]. *Jichu Jiaoyu Waiyu Jiaoxue Yanjiu [Foreign Language Teaching & Research in Basic Education]* 9, 13–15.

Zentella, A. (1981) Ta bien, you could answer me en cualquier idioma: Puerto Rican codeswitching in bilingual classrooms. In R. Duran (ed.) *Latino Language and Communicative Behavior* (pp. 109–132). Norwood, NJ: Ablex .

Conclusion

Chapter 14
Intercultural Space for Bilingual Education

ANWEI FENG

Introduction

In an overview of two parallel conceptions of bilingual education in China, I conclude that bilingual education for ethnic minority groups has been geared towards the aim of producing bilinguals with native-speaker competence in both his/her home language and standard Mandarin Chinese (*Min–Han Jiantong*), while the aim of Chinese–English bilingual schooling for the majority Han group is often said to be to educate all-rounded talents with sound knowledge in a specialised area and strong linguistic competence in a foreign language (*Zhuanye Waiyu Fuhexing Rencai*, often *Fuhexing Rencai* in short) (Feng, 2005). While both strive for bilingualism, the purposes of the two differ greatly in political and cultural terms. The aim of the former is to develop 'perfect' bilinguals with bicultural identities – own minority identity and cultural identification with the Han majority and more importantly political allegiance to the nation state – whereas the latter is not intended to add or change to any extent cultural identities of the learner and his/her political allegiance to the state but simply to create an effective way for learners to acquire a foreign language. These conceptions or aspirations are determining factors in designing bilingual programmes and in defining the position of mother tongue language and culture in relation to the target language and culture for both minority and majority bilingual education provisions.

These seemingly conflicting aims of bilingual education for the majority and minority groups demonstrate a close relationship between bilingualism and politics and reflect common concerns that many countries have in bilingual education. It is often hoped that culture and language can be easily manoeuvred according to political, social and economic needs of the country. For minority education it is seen, at least initially, as desirable that both minority and majority languages are used as media of instruction and, as a result, both languages and cultures are acquired by minority pupils who can then fit into the mainstream society while maintaining their own identities. When the outcome does not meet the expectation, minority languages and cultures are usually blamed and assimilation prevails. This tendency is clearly exemplified by Proposition 227 passed in 1998 in California, U.S., that resulted in the elimination of the use of bilingual pupils' mother tongue as a medium of instruction (Cummins, 2000). In other cases where linguistic competence in an economically powerful language is desired, the culture embedded in that language is often seen as a threat to national identities of the learners and to sociopolitical stability of the nation state. In these cases, measures are taken by individual states to prevent their pupils from being 'negatively influenced' by the culture of the target language. In the Gulf States, for example, a common objective explicitly stated in the official document of English language education is 'to acquire a good understanding of English speaking people *on the condition that* the above will not lead to the creation of a hostile or indifferent attitude to the students' Arab/Islamic culture' (Byram, 1997: 23, my italics). In China, the content for learning is made ideologically and culturally attuned with the local political and moral context (Feng, 1998). Enough evidence shows that the form of bilingual education taken by a country is rarely dependent upon how it best facilitates the development of linguistic and sociocultural competence of the learners but often upon sociopolitical agendas the country pursues.

Both Min–Han Jiantong and Fuhexing Rencai clearly reflect the sociopolitical agenda in the Chinese context (Feng, 2005). Several questions arise out of the two notions. Do learning outcomes often correspond with these 'political' ideals? How successful is minority bilingual education in terms of creating Min–Han Jiantong bilinguals with bicultural identities? Is it truly desirable if Fuhexing Rencai bilinguals acquire only linguistic competence of the target language without being 'influenced' by its culture? Are culture and language learning and acquisition as manoeuvrable as politicians and educationists wish them to be in bilingual education? Above all, is there an alternative to these conceptions in which the culture of the target language is either expected to be embraced and identified with, willingly or not, as in the case of Min–Han Jiantong, or resisted for fear of influences as in Fuhexing Rencai? To answer these questions, let us first take a closer look at how the two notions are interpreted in the literature.

Bilingualism With Bicultural Identities

In the last few decades, policies and official publications place a high premium on the notion of 'Min–Han Jiantong', mastery of minority nationality home language and Putonghua (Mandarin Chinese), as the desired learning outcome of minority bilingual education. For example, '*Zhuang–Han Jiantong*' (Mastery of the Zhuang language and Putonghua) is stipulated in regional policy documents as the final aim for the largest minority group (Zhuang nationality in Guangxi Zhuang Autonomous Region), '*Zang–Han Jiantong*' for the Tibetans and '*Yi–Han Jiantong*' for the Yi minority group in Sichuang (Dai & Dong, 1997; Chapter 4 in this volume). These policy documents usually state that Min–Han Jiantong suggests prioritising the ethnic minority language in minority education. Local educational authorities in Guangxi and Qinghai, for example, issued official documents stating that pupils in minority schools should master their ethnic minority language first before gradually developing competence in Putonghua (Dai & Dong, 1997). The official documents echo the constitutional position for protecting ethnic minority language rights while promoting nationwide use of Putonghua ([The] *Constitution of the People's Republic of China*, 1982).

The stance of placing Min in the first position in minority education is taken by some educators such as Niyaz[1] (1998). He argues that Min should be prioritised in minority education as it is always the primary means of communication for ethnic minority pupils. To Niyaz, '*Tong*' suggests strong communicative competence in a language and gaining such a competence in Han (Mandarin Chinese), with its sociocultural meaning and embedded modes of thinking, is a long-term task. It cannot be achieved through schooling only but through years of authentic language use. In minority education, Niyaz states that Min should be the major language of learning and teaching and the transition towards Min–Han bilingual education should be gradual. In terms of assessment, he suggests using HSK (Chinese proficiency test) designed mainly for foreign nationals studying Chinese as the means to measure Mandarin Chinese competence of minority pupils.

Surprisingly, however, many openly take the opposite view to Niyaz's even though it clearly corresponds to the official stance. In an article carried by the official flagship newspaper of education, *Zhongguo Jiaoyubao* (2003), an academic cum policy maker states that in bilingual education 'we must put ourselves at the centre and focus our attention on promoting Chinese national identity and national consciousness'. As language is a symbol of a nation, he continues, the dominant language must be Han Chinese for any form of bilingual education, be it Min–Han bilingual education for the minority nationality groups or Chinese–English bilingual schooling in economically developed areas. This Han-first view is shared by many commentators and educators even though many may not assert the view in the same *Han*-as-*the*-centre manner. For example, Amat (2003) states that minority pupils should *first* master Han, the national language, and eventually become masters of two linguistic systems. In the mean time, minority pupils should learn and absorb the 'advanced' Han culture, and integrate and promote both Min–Han cultures. The argument for prioritising Han Chinese teaching is frequently made in the name of developing the economy (Kong, 2003) and of raising the education quality of minority regions (Zhou & Zhao, 2003). Li (2002), for example, states after an overview of an apparently painful process of linguistic and cultural assimilation experienced in the *Bai* minority region in Yunnan that the primary task for addressing many existing issues is to further promote Han culture as well as its language in education. Bilinguals with a strong competence in the Han language and its culture are what are urgently needed for the development of the local economy and for enriching the local language and culture.

Clearly, most commentators cited above see Min–Han Jiantong beyond the linguistic level and take it as an 'idealised' conception of bilingualism with bicultural identities. Min–Han Jiantong bilinguals are expected to be able to speak and think in both Min and Han, identify with both cultures and function easily in interethnic communication. Regions where minority linguistic groups reside are believed to desire these bilinguals for developing their local economies and sustaining their linguistic and cultural capitals. Only when minority pupils master Mandarin Chinese as well as their home language, and think and communicate freely in both languages, Li (cited in Teng, 1996b) states, can they truly maintain and develop their own mother tongue language and culture and be able to keep up with social development. These interpretations not only imply prioritising Mandarin Chinese in bilingual education but also suggest identification with two cultures as the ultimate aim. As indicated in Amat (2003), it is bicultural identities and thus the assimilation into the mainstream society that are embedded in this notion. Bilingualism with bicultural identities is an interpretation adopted by many other authors (e.g. Abliz and Hamdu, 2003; Li, 2002; Yang, 1998), although the cultural dimension is sometimes discussed interchangeably with the term multiculturalism (Teng, 1996b, 2000; Wang, 2004).

Additive Bilingualism

While Min–Han Jiantong is often interpreted as bilingualism with bicultural identities, Fuhexing Rencai, a notion that represents the desired outcome of rapidly spreading Chinese–English bilingual education in major cities and special economic zones, signifies a differing vision of bilingualism. Word-for-word translation of Fuhexing Rencai is 'talents with integrated competence'. Not long ago it was generally defined as graduates with knowledge and skills in two or more specialised areas or more measurably with a combined university degree in these areas (Wu, 1994). In recent years, it is increasingly used to refer to all-round talents with a strong competence in a foreign language and knowledge in one or more specialised area(s). In Luo's (2000) formula, Fuhexing Rencai is basically 'a foreign language + X', in which a foreign language is a constant and X is a variable. The rationale behind this formula lies in its dynamic relationship between the constant, a foreign language desired at all times, and the needs in technological development that vary in the changing society. Hence, Fuhexing Rencai are perceived as bilinguals who have the expertise in most forefront specialised fields and can, when need arises, use a foreign language to communicate with speakers of that language, especially native-speaker specialists and professionals in the fields. The emphasis on the link between specialised knowledge and a foreign language is perhaps the very reason why some authors put a preface Zhuanye Waiyu in front of Fuhexing Rencai to make the semantic implication explicit. In this sense, Zhuanye Waiyu Fuhexing Rencai can be seen as the human capital of the country (Becker, 1964), human resources which can be invested in education and training and converted to economic, social and symbolic assets and benefits for the society.

The linguistic aim for Chinese–English bilingual education as suggested in Fuhexing Rencai is universally agreed by scholars and policy makers of bilingual education. It is the language that is needed by the country for its social and economic development (He & Deng, 2003; Zhu, 2003). Unlike Min–Han Jiantong bilinguals, Fuhexing Rencai are not expected to be bicultural but keep firm with their Chinese identity. This conception is reflected in two interrelated notions commonly used in discussions on Chinese–English bilingual education, namely bilingual teaching (*Shuangyu Jiaoxue*) instead of bilingual education and additive bilingual education (*Tianjiaxing Shuangyu Jiaoyu*). Bilingual teaching (Shuangyu Jiaoxue), Wang (2003b, 2005) observes, may not be a term commonly seen in the literature of bilingual education but it has become widely accepted in China. It differs from bilingual education in that the latter is an all-encompassing term referring to all forms of education provided by the school, society and family environment that have bearings on pupils with regard to moral, intellectual and physical development, whereas the former refers only to inside-class activities. The ultimate aim of bilingual teaching in China is straightforward, that is, to create a more effective way to produce bilinguals to meet the needs of the country, the region and the individual (Wang,

2003a,b). Bilingual teaching thus helps to develop an additive bilingual situation where learners acquire a desired foreign language without any pressure to reduce their mother tongue competence and cultural identity. Additive bilingual education defined as such (strangely 'education' (*Jiaoyu*) is not replaced with 'teaching' (*Jiaoxue*) when additive is added) is echoed in Yu (2006) and Zhu (2003, 2004).

This shared conception of additive bilingual education lays emphasis on positive linguistic outcomes of bilingual education. It is the cultural and affective effects of bilingual education that researchers do not seem to agree on. Jiang (2003) argues that bilingual education can widen learners' views of the world and equip them with intercultural competence to meet the challenges of globalisation. Quite a number of educators such as Liao and Yan (2004) and Xu (2003) blame the decline of learners' interest in Chinese culture and level of the Chinese language on bilingual education and argue for more patriotism, Chinese values, heroes, etc. to be included in the school curriculum. Wang (2003b: 12) asserts that, unlike many other multicultural countries, bilingual teaching in China has little to do with issues such as cultural identity. The issue is linguistic. From the point of view of strengthening China, Wang (2003b: 16) quotes a school principal as saying '... learning English is the saddest thing in China. ... ', but in order to overtake others in science and technology, 'we must learn English well, with our teeth gnashed' (my translation). These words demonstrate not only a utilitarian attitude, that is, to acquire the language in order to access the knowledge in that language and to build the nation state stronger than others (this will be taken up later), but also some sort of resentment in perceiving the need to do so.

Recurrent Issues

The overviews mentioned above present a brief account of two parallel conceptions that coexist in the literature and policy documents on bilingualism and bilingual education (Feng, 2005). The dominant discourse indicates that Min–Han Jiantong is often interpreted as perfect bilinguals with native-speaker competence in both Min and Han and bicultural identities, whereas Fuhexing Rencai signifies a national aspiration for bilinguals with good proficiency in both languages but without any transformative effect in terms of cultural identity. Both notions suggest a very close relationship of bilingualism and politics. Tensions between the political agenda to promote national identity and the perceived risks of bilingual education, therefore, have been evident in the literature on both forms of bilingual education.

In minority bilingual education

In the literature on minority bilingual education, there are reports to show that much has been achieved, particularly in statistical terms (e.g. Hu & Zhou, 2005; *Zhongguo Minzu Jiaoyu*, 2000). The main interest in this type of report is in figures of increased numbers of minority schools, minority students in secondary and tertiary education, government investment in bilingual education and campaigns to eliminate illiteracy and so on. On the other hand, there seem to be more publications addressing recurrent issues in minority education. One of the major issues is the relationship between the home language and Mandarin Chinese in minority bilingual education. It is often found that in many cases minority languages as media of instruction are unavailable because of the following reasons: lack of resources such as textbooks and qualified minority language teachers in remote areas (Li, S.Z., 2003), lack of interest in teaching or using minority languages as media of instruction (Jiayangzhaxi, 1999; Teng, 2000) and vigorous promotion of Mandarin Chinese as the common language in minority or multilingual areas, particularly in towns and cities (Chapter 5 in this volume; Liang, 1994) and in special programmes such as *Neidiban* (Chapter 4 in this volume). In many cases minority pupils have to study school subjects using Mandarin Chinese as the medium of learning. In others, when bilingual education is possible, a minority language is offered in the first few years and quickly gives way to using Mandarin Chinese for instruction, for the simple reason that pupils have no option but to follow the national curriculum and to take high-stakes nation-wide examinations in Mandarin Chinese at such critical times as moving from primary to lower secondary, for some up to higher secondary and for a small number up to tertiary education. Because of unfavourable geographical factors and attitudes and an assessment system that favours pupils with Mandarin Chinese competence, not surprisingly, Min–Han often becomes Han-Min or simply Han as the language for teaching and learning, as in any mainstream school, in schools minority pupils attend. Scholars such as Deng (2000) point out that minority school curricula have predominantly reflected *Ronghe Zhuyi* (assimilationist beliefs) 'out-and-out'.

As many minority children go directly to Chinese-medium schools or transfer too hastily from home-language learning to Chinese-medium learning, they often find it difficult to cope with schooling particularly in cultural terms. They are often found to suffer from 'cultural discontinuity', bewilderment and a fear of learning due to the absence of a familiar home culture in the national textbooks minority children have to use (Li, 2004; Ma & Xiao, 2002a,b). While they may sooner or later acquire grammatical knowledge of Chinese through instruction, cultural meaning in texts is arguably more problematic and it makes minority children feel that they are reading 'Tianshu (heavenly books)', a metaphorical term to refer to textbooks that are too difficult to understand. The 'Tianshu' effect caused by the unsmooth transfer is undeniably detrimental to their motivation and cognitive development (Li, 2004; Li, S.Z., 2003; Wu, 2002). Pupils from linguistic minority backgrounds are usually found to lag behind their mainstream peers in school assessment. Dismal consequences such as children dropping out of school at an early age are often reported (Abliz *et al.*, 2002; Jiayangzhaxi, 1999; Li, S.Z., 2003).

The experience of minority students at the tertiary level can be even more detrimental to their academic and even personality development. As minority children find it hard to follow the school curriculum and to gain access to higher education, most of them, according to Wu (2002), rely on 'favourable policies'[2] for university places. Once in university, these students are placed in the same exam system and their pass rate is found to be much lower than their majority counterparts, so many have to re-sit for exams repeatedly for certification. Qian (2002) observes that teachers usually label minority students as poor learners. Yu (1997) reports that many of her students from minority background consider themselves inferior to others (*Ziren Buru*) in general terms. Lin (1997) observed that minority students undervalued their own culture and languages and took great pains to hide their minority identities by not wearing ethnic clothes and by ridding themselves of their home accents.

Most commentators agree that, despite years of commitment by the government and the efforts of educators, minority education in general faces serious challenges in meeting even basic objectives, for example, to make 9-year obligatory education affordable (Teng, 2004). Li, S.Z. (2003) states that bilingual education for minority linguistic groups is caught in a dilemma, difficult to advance because of practical problems and negative attitudes towards minority languages (Jiayangzhaxi, 1999; Teng, 2000) and impossible to retreat due to linguistic rights constitutionally mandated. In analysing the dilemma, it is common to see 'backward cultures', 'useless minority languages' and 'resistance to otherness or to advanced cultures' used explicitly or implicitly as causal factors. Strangely, however, the notion of Min–Han Jiantong as an ultimate goal of minority bilingual education, as is currently interpreted, is hardly contested.

In Chinese–English bilingual education

Unlike Min–Han bilingual education which has not enjoyed an enthusiastic reception, Chinese–English bilingual education is massively popular and is rapidly developing in cities and other economically privileged areas in the country. Behind this popularity or 'craze' (see Chapter 6), Feng (2005) takes note of sociopolitical, economical and educational factors, the most obvious of which include perceived importance of English as cultural capital for both individuals and the society, observable and hidden forces of globalisation, and the positive outcomes of using English as a medium of instruction in schools as compared with traditional EFL teaching (see also Chapters 6 and 8 in this volume). As a relatively new form of bilingual education, practical problems are often observed, including lack of qualified teaching resources, shortage of appropriate textbooks and lack of coherent planning. These issues sometimes result in students' dissatisfaction with bilingual courses and doubts about effectiveness (Qin, 2005), but, unlike in minority bilingual education, they do not seem to lessen the popularity of bilingual schools or courses and the firm belief that bilingual education is inevitable in today's world and is more effective than traditional EFL teaching (see Chapters 6, 11, and 12 in this volume).

Despite the popularity, fervent debate on the sociopolitical and cultural consequences is evident. Many educators such as Xu (2003) insist that learning English as a lingua franca is a double-edged sword. It eases international communication but at the same time threatens mother tongue language and culture. Therefore, patriotism, traditional values, mother tongue language and culture, etc. must remain at the core of the school curriculum. On legal, political as well as cultural bases, strong opponents of Chinese–English bilingual education, such as Ma (cited in *Nanfang Dushibao*, 2004), have gone further by calling to stop the use of English as a medium of instruction altogether. Ma rejects the use of English as a medium of instruction in schools from the perspective of protecting national sovereignty and national security. He further robustly argues that bilingual education in its strict sense violates the language law promulgated in 2000 by the Standing Committee of the People's Congress.[3] Indeed, Article 10 of the Law of the People's Republic of China on the Use of Language and Script, which came into effect in January 2001, ordains that all educational institutions in China, excluding those of minority groups, must use Mandarin as their primary teaching language and adopt standard Chinese written characters as the written form. Ironically, this legal accusation against using a foreign language as a medium of instruction has not resulted in any official response to clarify the situation. The ambiguous situation clearly demonstrates tensions between globalisation and the political agendas of the country and between various ideological and cultural forces, hidden or overt, which impact on academic discussions and bilingual education practice. The interpretation of the concept of additive bilingualism reviewed before, for example, may well reflect these tensions as political and sociocultural dimensions seem to be deliberately avoided by some advocators in their definition of additive bilingual education.

Impact of English on minority education

Inevitably, the rapid spread of using a foreign language as a medium of instruction in mainstream schools and universities would impact on minority education, particularly in terms of language provision. The last few years have seen a slowly growing literature on the notion of *Sanyu Jiaoyu* (trilingual education). Most of the discussions, not surprisingly, focus on various difficulties minority pupils face in learning English from lack of resources to the cognitive, affective and cultural problems minority children experience (Ju, 2000; Li, Y.L., 2003; Tian, 2001; Wu, 2002; Xiang *et al.*, 2005). Research and discussions on how a foreign language such as English is used as a medium of instruction in schools and universities with minority students and how this impacts on them, however, are rarely existent despite the fact that some schools and universities with a minority student population have started using English as a teaching medium (see Chapters 12 and 13 in this volume).

There are clearly two outstanding issues with regard to impacts of Chinese–English bilingual teaching on minority bilingual education. The first is how Min–Han Jiantong relates to Sanyu Jiaoyu (trilingual education), or more precisely whether the former is made obsolete by the latter. Some commentators such as Yang (2003) take, apparently spontaneously, *Sanyu Jiantong* (mastery of three languages) as the ultimate aim of trilingual education. Luo (2001), on the other hand, comes up with the notion *Duoyu Yitong* (multilingual ability with strong competence in only one language). He argues that in today's world trilingualism or multilingualism is taken for granted. In every region or nation, there is a common or official language, such as Mandarin Chinese in China. It is this language that is the most important for all learners. The second issue is the question of which language is used as the main medium of instruction in Sanyu Jiaoyu. To Luo (2001), of the three or more languages under study, Mandarin Chinese should be the 'leading' language (*Qiantouyu*) in Sanyu Jiaoyu. Guo (2000) also states that in Inner Mongolia Mandarin Chinese should become the medium of instruction for children from kindergarten onwards. Yang (2003), on the contrary, argues that the minority language (Zhuang in her case) should take the centre stage in Sanyu Jiaoyu. She lists as the anchoring points of her argument the importance of children's home language ability for cognitive development and the magnitude of ethnic and linguistic identities. Yu (1997) shares this view for the Tibetan context.

Causal Factors

In view of the nation-wide scale of bilingual education either for the minority or for the majority, it is obviously difficult to pin down the factors that cause the problems or difficulties, as listed above, experienced by different groups in different regions in the country. Many critics point a finger at insufficient investment and shortage of human resources as main reasons for failing to provide adequate bilingual education in mainstream schools or schools in the ethnic minority regions. However, as education authorities at various levels have evidently increased investment in human resources and hardware in both forms of bilingual education (see Chapters 7, 11, and 13 in this volume), lack of resources and hardware and other practical issues such as geographical remoteness, though still issues in some circumstances, are gradually being dealt with and therefore do not give a full account of the situation.

As was implied above, some of the key issues that hinder the development of both forms of bilingual education are evidently theoretical, sociopolitical and cultural in nature. I argue that many of these issues are thoroughly reflected in the current interpretations of the two notions, Min–Han Jiantong and Fuhexing Rencai, I have reviewed above and that there is a need to critique these interpretations from different theoretical and political angles. Let us start with Min–Han Jiantong.

Unattainability of Min–Han Jiantong

The notion of perfect bilinguals denoted in Min–Han Jiantong has long been contested. Scholars such as Baker (2001), Fishman (1971), Grosjean (1985) and Niyaz (1998) argue that rarely can any bilingual be equally competent across all situations. Many research studies conducted internationally and reviewed in Baker (2001) demonstrate that bilinguals can be very fluent in two or more languages but they should be judged, intellectually and linguistically, as complete individuals as they use the languages for different purposes in different domains of language use. These studies reveal that bilinguals in general have advantages over monolinguals in terms of creativity, early meta-linguistic awareness, communicative sensitivity and thinking style. However, it is mistaken to assume that fluent bilinguals possess the same linguistic competence as two monolingual native speakers of the two languages (Skutnabb-Kangas, 1981). For those who are highly proficient in two or more languages, the level of their linguistic competence usually depends on the time when and the context where a language or a variety of a language is used. In most cases, their proficiency in one language or a variety is shown to be stronger than the other in a domain where that language or the variety is predominantly used.

Biculturalism implied in the notion of Min–Han Jiantong is also a concept under debate internationally. Becoming bicultural is by formal definition a process of developing the necessary knowledge of customs, beliefs and values of two different social or cultural groups and the skills to function in both cultures (Richards *et al.*, 1992). Some scholars make affective dimensions and issues of cultural identities more explicit (Edgerton cited in Paulston, 1992; Garret, 1996). Evidence given by Byram (2003) shows that becoming bicultural is possible where there is much commonality between the two cultures, i.e. a high degree of acceptance by each other's social group, and where socialisation into the two cultures starts at a very early age. It would be extremely difficult to become a bicultural holding two sets of values and beliefs and behaviours with ease in two cultures if the two cultures are distant and if primary socialisation, the first socialisation a child has undergone at home through which he/she becomes a member of a society (see Berger and Luckmann, 1966), takes place in a relatively 'monocultural' environment (Byram, 2003; Hoffmann, 1989; Paulston, 1992). This is clearly the case with many students from minority linguistic groups, particularly those living in remote areas where they are rarely exposed to outside cultures.

Another important aspect to take into consideration with regard to being bicultural is the process of ascription by self and others. A bilingual with fluency in two languages and willingness to identify with both linguistic groups may (wish to) ascribe himself or herself a member of either group. Linguistic competence and self-ascription are no doubt important, but not enough. Byram (2003) points out that most members of an ethnic or social group are 'mono-ethnic' and have little tolerance of ethnic 'hybrids'. Becoming bicultural, therefore, depends not only upon linguistic competence and self-ascription but also on other ascription. The process of ascription by self and others explains the feelings of belonging to 'nowhere' expressed by members of European migrant groups who have lived in another European country for generations (Byram, 2003), despite the fact that there is relatively much commonality between their home culture and their host's. When we apply the notion of ascription to the Chinese context, it is clear that the power of ascription by others can be greater in China than in Europe because there is a clearly coercive relationship of power between the majority group and ethnic minority groups. The minority students described in Lin (1997), as mentioned before, might be willing to identify with the majority culture at all costs, but their peers and teachers may still ascribe them as minority students who entered the university thanks to 'favourable policies' and are thus poor learners (Qian, 2002). If such ascription by others is the case, it is theoretically impossible for them to become bicultural.

Empirical evidence presented before proves this theoretical analysis and suggests that Min–Han Jiantong as is currently interpreted sets up a goal that is difficult to attain for most, if not all, minority pupils. As an official catchphrase for bilingual education, it should be critically discussed, reinterpreted or redefined, as Niyaz (1998) tries to do, if not rephrased or replaced. I need to state at this point, however, that Niyaz's (1998) argument that in minority autonomous regions such as Xinjiang, *'Tong'* (mastery) of Mandarin Chinese be assessed with HSK (the Chinese proficiency test) may not stand sociopolitically as it runs counter to the government's aspiration to promote Chinese and national identity among minority groups. His argument may also reduce the value of minority bilingual education, as HSK is essentially designed for learners who study Chinese as a foreign language (*Jiaoyubu* ..., 2002; Niyaz, 1998), which may lead to disadvantages of minority students in the country's job market.

Concealed assimilation

While Min–Han Jiantong sets up an extremely ambitious goal, difficult to attain, in actual practice, an 'assimilation' mindset has been predominant in the history of bilingual education for minority groups (Deng, 2000; Teng, 1996b). People with an assimilation mindset perceive a strong need for minority groups to be 'melted' or absorbed into the mainstream society while loosening and even losing their cultural and linguistic identities in the process (Schmidt, 2000). Unlike minority groups in many other countries, minority linguistic groups in China are not immigrants to a 'host' country but indigenous nationalities whose language rights are constitutionally mandated (Article 19 in [The] Constitution of the People's Republic of China, 1982). Dai and Dong (1997) and Teng (1996a,b) suggest that for about two decades starting from 1958 to the end of the Cultural Revolution, implementation of explicit linguistic assimilation was the most evident in minority education due to extreme leftist ideology predominant during that period. Plenty of evidence, however, suggests that assimilation is not an ideology evident only in that period (Feng, 2005; Jiayanzhaxi, 1999; Jin and Li, 2000; Lin, 1996, 1997; Teng, 2000, Wang, 2004). Even though few people with this mindset are found to argue openly against bilingualism, as mentioned before, minority school curricula have predominantly reflected Ronghe Zhuyi (assimilationist beliefs) (Deng, 2000).

More subtle evidence of assimilation is identified by Hansen (1999) who notes that, while equality of nationalities is preached constitutionally, the so-called deficiencies in minority students' academic achievement are often either explicitly presented in the literature as objective facts or implicitly understood through positive evaluation of cases of cultural change in the direction towards Han. In many other writings, the notion of Chinese first in minority education is found, often in the name of facilitating socioeconomic development in the western regions such as Xingjiang (e.g. Kong, 2003; Luo, 2001). All these reflect what Tosi (1988) calls concealed assimilation by which individual achievement is gauged using majority language criteria, and linguistic and cultural hegemony and ethnic harmony are clandestinely set as the aims in bilingual education.

Utilitarianism in Chinese–English bilingual education

In the case of Chinese–English bilingual education, debates on the purposes mirror a vastly different kind of stalemate in bilingual education, not so much a concern about whether bilinguals with native-speaker or near-native-speaker competence in both languages are produced, but about how to minimise the impact of the target language on learners' mother tongue language and culture during learning. Sociopolitical and cultural consequences of foreign language provisions are, as reviewed before, always given priority by educationists and policy makers all over the world (Byram 1997). As language is a symbol, an emblem or a rallying point of groupness as well as a tool of communication (Edwards, 1985), it appears that tensions always exist between bilingual provisions and political, sociocultural and religious agendas of nation states. China is no exception (Chapter 3 in this volume; Hu & Gao, 1997; Ross, 1992, 1993). Not surprisingly, one can often see in mass media and academic journals such notions as 'putting ourselves at the centre' in all forms of bilingual education (*Zhongguo Jiaoyubao*, 2003), as were presented before, or accusations such as 'to use English as a medium of instruction in classrooms is to advocate English hegemony' (Sun & Gai, 2005) or rhetorical questions such as 'why a huge nation such as China has to use English as a medium of instruction' (Yan, 2004).

The response given by proponents to such a strong current against using English as a medium of instruction is usually the statement of the utilitarian value of English for access to the knowledge in that language in order to facilitate economic development and nation building in general. Utilitarianism defined as such is often reflected in the aphorism *Xixue Weiyong* (Western learning for utilitarian purpose), which has been prevalent for more than a century (cf. Feng, 1998; Ross, 1993). Though the aphorism appears less frequently in the current academic discourse, rationales given to English teaching in general often manifest this ideology. A typical example is seen in Wang (2003b: 16) who makes the call that 'we must enhance our study of English so as to enable us to rapidly grasp the advanced scientific knowledge and technology of the developed countries' (my translation). Following the same ideology, Huang (1997:2) makes this interesting statement in the preface of a monograph on English language education:

> In the opening-up age, we emphatically promote English language education because we wish to acquire stones from other mountains to build our own garden into a genuine place of civilisation for new generations. We hope that our new generations will no long need to spend so much time on foreign languages. They should have more time engaging in creative activities. (My translation)

Huang's hope that future generations will no longer need to spend much time learning foreign languages and the principal's 'learning-English-with-gnashing-teeth' attitude mentioned earlier (Wang, 2003b: 16) show quite an extreme form of utilitarianism that not only rejects all values of learning a foreign language except for its utilitarian worth but also suggests an ethnocentric attitude.

Binary conception

Although the discourse on the two notions, Min–Han Jiantong and Fuhexing Rencai, is mainly sociopolitically motivated, theoretically, it also reflects a binary conception that interprets human cognition, experience, culture and so forth with an emphasis on dichotomous relationships and compacts meaning into a closed either/or opposition between elements or perspectives (Turner, 1990). With this conception, Min–Han and Chinese–English, for example, are seen as mutually exclusive. An emphasis on one inevitably leads to the weakening of the other. With regard to culture and identity, dichotomous oppositions such as Chinese culture and foreign culture, majority culture (advanced) and minority culture (backward), nationalism or patriotism and Westernisation, and so on, are frequently used binary terminology in the discourse on bilingual education and bilingualism. Though taken by many as a natural human trait and basis of perception (Turner, 1990), this conception, according to space theorists, confines our thoughts and actions to only two polarised options (Soja, 1996). People adopting this conception find it difficult to emancipate themselves from binary oppositions that are socially constructed. They would 'take human linguistic capacities as static and quantitative' (Skuttnab-Kangas, 1981: 36) and fail to realise how cultures increasingly transform each other through cultural hybridity in the contemporary society and what 'newness', something that transcends the cultures in contact, can be created for celebration (Bhabha, 1994).

Interculturalism and Bilingual Education

Looking at the causal factors examined above, we can see that the academic discourse and bilingual education practice are interwoven with the sociopolitical, cultural and economic context. The current interpretation of Min–Han Jiantong as an educational goal to achieve 'perfect' bilingualism with bicultural identities is fundamentally concealed assimilation that is intended to blend minority groups into the mainstream society, and the conception for Chinese–English bilingual education reflects a political desire to prevent any 'negative' influence on learners often in a form of utilitarianism. Behind a primarily politically motivated academic discourse is a binary imaginary which is theoretically contentious. On the basis of research and scholarships on bilingual education and bilingualism worldwide, I have argued that 'perfect' bilingualism with bicultural identities has proved to be difficult to attain and utilitarianism misleadingly reduces the educational value of bilingual education.

To address these issues, I now turn to the concepts of interculturalism and tertiary socialisation that are frequently discussed by scholars in foreign/second language education and propose alternative interpretations for Min–Han Jiantong and Fuhexing Rencai. Byram (1989, 1997) and Doyé (1992, 1999, 2003) argue that in learning a foreign language and its embedded culture learners are undergoing what they term a 'tertiary socialisation'. They coin the term on the basis of the socialisation theory by sociologists such as Berger and Luckmann (1966) in their conceptualisation of how children acquire social identities to become members of social groups in a society through primary and secondary socialisation. The former is associated with the family and the latter with 'institutional functionaries', such as teachers at school and the sub-worlds they are subsequently in beyond home. It is through these two stages of socialisation that children internalise or socially construct their subjective realities of the world. When children or adults are learning a foreign language and the culture it embodies, or travelling to or living in another country, they may find some concepts incompatible with those acquired in primary and secondary socialisation. In such cases, learners may re-examine and modify their subjective realities as a result of the new perspectives they encounter. The process of this tertiary socialisation may lead to partial transformation within individuals on three dimensions: cognitive, affective and behavioural, and extend their identities, such as an international identity, which transcend the home and target cultures (Byram, forthcoming). During this process, Byram (forthcoming) and Doyé (1992, 2003) argue, an individual's own set of beliefs and values is not replaced, but new norms are held side by side with existing ones.

Tertiary socialisation thus conceptualised corresponds with the notion of becoming intercultural, which has been increasingly discussed in language education (Corbett, 2003; Hu & Gao, 1997; Kramsch, 1993, 1998), citizenship education (Alred *et al.*, 2006), ethnic minority education (Green, 1999), counselling (Lartey, 1997) and arts education (Bräuer, 2002). Partial transformation at cognitive, affective and behavioural levels is elucidated in the model of interculturalism by Byram (1997), which elaborates the attitudes, knowledge, skills and critical cultural awareness a learner of a foreign/second language should develop. A learner should strive to become an 'intercultural speaker' who possesses an open and curious attitude towards otherness; gains or seeks to gain knowledge not only of his/her interlocutor's culture and his/her own, but more importantly of social groups, social identity and processes of social interaction; develops skills of interpreting and relating events and skills of discovering knowledge and increases critical awareness for evaluating perspectives and practices. It is important to note that an individual who becomes intercultural does not abandon his/her own social group or reject his/her social identities. He/She is willing to step outside the closed boundaries, engage with otherness, bring the two or more than two cultures into relationship and take up different perspectives to view the world.

On the one hand, we need to be aware that human beings desire a sense of security by belonging to social groups and tend to favour insiders of their own groups over others (Tajfel, 1981). On the other hand, once they experience otherness or undergo tertiary socialisation, they are likely to reflect on their own values, beliefs and behaviours and become willing to extend their social identities. In the contemporary society, social identities are increasingly perceived to be negotiated through the process built into the condition of communication in the performative present of interpretation (Bhabha, 1994). Pavlenco and Blackledge (2004: 19), for example, define identities 'as social, discursive, and narrative options offered by a particular society in a specific time and place to which individuals and groups of individuals appeal in an attempt to self-name, to self-characterise, and to claim social spaces and social prerogatives'. In the same vein, Hobsbawm (1996: 1067) points out that 'the concept of a single, exclusive, and unchanging ethnic or cultural or other identity is a dangerous piece of brainwashing. Human mental identities are not like shoes, of which we can only wear one pair at a time'.

Recent theories on identity, interculturalism and socialisation look promising to address the issues related to Min-Han Jiantong and Fuhexing Rencai discussed above. On such basis, I offer alternative interpretations to these two notions though I am aware that as educational aims for a country as huge as China any attempt to reinterpret or re-explain the two notions runs the risk of being accused of as failing to take specific contexts into consideration or missing certain dimensions. As one of the first critical analyses of the two key notions, which aims to trigger more discussions, such a risk is well worth running. To start with, an alternative to conceptualise Min–Han Jiantong as an educational goal could be, for example, to aim for producing bilinguals with strong competence[4] in minority home language and Mandarin Chinese. These bilinguals should be confident in their ethnic identity and at the same time willing to engage with the mainstream society, decentre by recognising their affiliation to the nation state and bringing their personal and local identities into relationship with citizenship at national and international levels (Kubow _et al._, 2000). This definition aims to address the sociopolitical aspirations of the country and at the same time to create intercultural space for individual pupils to reflect on and negotiate identities at various levels, individual, local, ethnic, national and international, in their specific context and become what Cummins (1986, 1996, 2000) terms 'empowered' individuals who are able to challenge patterns of coercive relationships of power in both schools and society, acquire self-esteem and control over their own life and the immediate environment and affirm their identity and further extend it.

Re-conceptualisation of Fuhexing Rencai also entails recognition of interculturalism. Fuhexing Rencai along this line of thinking could thus be seen as individuals with specialist knowledge and intercultural communicative competence (Byram, 1997; Hu & Gao, 1997). This competence includes linguistic competence in a desired foreign language, as well as the mother tongue language, and sociolinguistic and intercultural competence that enable the learners to view the world from different perspectives and bring cultures into relationships productively. The word 'productively' is used here to suggest an alternative to additive bilingualism as currently defined by scholars such as Wang (2003a,b). The concept of productive bilingualism is developed by Gao (1994) with the formula $1 + 1 > 2$. With empirical data, she shows that the process of foreign language learning evidently benefited linguistic development of many highly successful bilinguals in China in both their mother tongue and the target language. Furthermore, because of constant interaction and synergy in their processing and comparing the culture of the target language to that of their own, these bilinguals did not mechanically add a different set of values and norms to their knowledge repertoire but productively constructed new things, things of their own making that transcend the cultures. This productive conception of bilingual education clearly echoes tertiary socialisation and space theory and takes learners as sociocultural and creative human beings who 'engage in relationships with others and with the world', 'participate in the creative dimension' as well as the natural sphere and 'humanise reality' (Freire, 1974: 4–5). Additive bilingualism, as a key concept seen in the academic discourse in China, therefore, needs to take into account the creative or productive dimension and learners' engagement with otherness in bilingual education.

Challenges

Having presented the alternative interpretations of Min–Han Jiantong and Fuhexing Rencai, I am in the position to draw a link between the alternatives with the issues discussed earlier in this chapter. As alternative interpretations offered to the two key notions, they challenge current academic discourse and practice of bilingual education in many ways. In minority bilingual education, three challenges are presented here on the basis of the new interpretations.

- The academic discourse evidently shows an assimilation philosophy and indications of superiority of the majority and inferiority of the minority. Academics and education commentators should be fully aware of the impact of this discourse on policy making, curriculum design and daily educational activities. All stakeholders should demonstrate a stronger consciousness of and commitment to equity of all nationalities and stand firmer against all forms of assimilation, explicit, implied or concealed.
- No matter how difficult and costly it is, ample opportunities should be created for minority children to develop adequate linguistic competence in their home language[5] and knowledge of their own culture so that they can affirm their identity and become cognitively and socio-culturally competent. Only on this basis can minority children avoid 'cultural discontinuity' (Ma & Xiao, 2002a,b) and engage in meaningful bilingual education.
- The practice of using the nation-wide assessment system for all clearly needs re-justification and re-evaluation. This system forces all to fit into one size and leaves little space for meaningful bilingual education

to take place. It may well be the cause of failure of many bilingual programmes and student dropouts. Ideally, there should be specifically designed assessment systems to meet the communication needs of bilingual children (Grosjean, 1985) but the 'political reality' does not usually accept a different system (Baker, 2001: 9). Some pragmatic adjustments, however, could be made to create opportunities for minority students to better engage in bilingual learning and demonstrate their academic capabilities in examination. For example, translation of high-stakes examination[6] papers into the minority *Yi* language proved useful in the *Yi* region in Sichuang (Shen & Luo, 2001). This practice has clear potential for enhancing bilingual education, as minority languages are given equal status as the majority language and for empowering learners because they are given the chance to exercise some degree of control of their environment. However, this practice is sometimes accused of as overemphasis on minority languages at the expense of Chinese (Luo, 2001).

In Chinese–English bilingual education, I see two main outstanding challenges posed by the new interpretation of Fuhexing Rencai and additive bilingualism:

- Bilingual education should be conceived not only as an effective way for a linguistic plus but also as an avenue for sociocultural enrichment (Lambert and Landry *et al.* cited in Baker, 2001) and for overall cognitive and academic growth (Cummins, 2000). This is the very reason why the phrase 'bilingual education' is used throughout this chapter instead of 'bilingual teaching' which is commonly adopted in the literature in China, as the former recognises the educational value of language learning. Deliberate ignorance of sociocultural dimensions and transformative function of language learning could only do a disservice to learners' general development into citizens for the 21st century.
- Fuhexing Rencai by the alternative interpretation means specialist bilinguals with basic understanding of otherness as well as the linguistic system of a target language. Through this understanding, these bilinguals recognise that there are other perspectives and ways of living that are equally sensible and valid. They bring cultures into relationship and develop an open and curious attitude towards other cultural groups, including the minority groups of their own country, and are ready to suspend their own beliefs and critically question prejudices of others and ethnocentricity. The aim of developing such specialist bilinguals clearly suggests rejecting utilitarianism

and the binary imaginary of humanities critiqued earlier in this chapter.

Conclusion

This chapter has argued that factors that affect conceptualisation of bilingualism, Min–Han Jiantong or Fuhexing Rencai, and practice in both forms of bilingual education are context-dependent and sociopolitically, economically and culturally interwoven. Through an analysis of research and scholarship mainly accessible in Chinese, I have identified evidence of several contributing factors to the existing issues under debate. These include utilitarianism in Chinese–English bilingual education and concealed assimilation in minority bilingual education. To address these issues, I have offered alternative interpretations of the two notions as bilingual educational aims and suggested challenges posed by the reinterpretation.

In a report to UNESCO, the International Commission on Education for the Twenty-first Century states that education has to face up the tensions between the global and the local, modernity and tradition, the universal and the individual, as well as the quick expansion of knowledge and human beings' capacity of assimilating it, which are experienced throughout the whole world in the new century. People should gradually 'become world citizens without losing their roots and while continu[ing] to play an active part in the life of their nation and their local community' (Delors *et al.*, 1996: 17). This conception of global citizenship with local and national roots is the very stance this chapter takes with its proposed theoretical framework of bilingualism for both minority and majority groups in China. To achieve the aim of inculcating global citizenship in national or minority education, all stakeholders in education, including policy makers, educators, parents, learners themselves and the larger society, should play an active role in creating sufficient opportunities and spaces for the educated and enable them to become world citizens.

Notes

1. The name of the Uygur author is given in Chinese characters in the original paper. Rather than adopting the usual practice of turning the characters into *pinyin*, thanks to Mr Mamtimyn Sunuodula, a Uygur scholar, I retranslated the name to Niyaz, the English equivalent to the author's original Uygur name which better reflects the author's Uygur identity. The same applies to three other authors, Amat (2003), and Abliz and Hamda (2003) who are also Uygur.
2. 'Favourable policies' refer to preferential measures taken by a regional- or provincial-level government to ensure enrolment of a reasonable number of

minority students into tertiary institutions according to the specific context of that region or province. One of the most important measures is to lower the aggregate marks of the nation-wide entrance examinations in order to give more minority students an opportunity to enter tertiary education. Qian's (2002) paper is an interesting discussion about this issue. He points out that while the policies are politically made in favour of minority students they often lead to biases and discriminations against these students in their own institutions or in job markets because of the 'labelling effect' which tends to tag all minority students as academically lower quality students who are there because of these favourable policies. These policies, Qian argues, are in effect not fair for the minority students and for the society at large. Ma and Xiao (2002b) take a different stance.

3. In fact, according to Chen (2002), many lawyers, policy makers and linguists are aware of the 'unlawful' situation bilingual schooling is in. Most of them argue that bilingual schooling is a very recent phenomenon and regulations or laws governing it will soon follow. So far, however, the 2000 Law is still in effect.

4. It should be noted that the main focus in this context is the dimension of cultural identity that follows the phrase, 'strong competence'. I am aware of the ambiguity of the phrase, but the ambiguous phrase used for an aim statement is intended to imply varied expectations with regard to linguistic competence for different individuals in different regions in the country. A minority pupil studying and living among the majority group, for example, clearly requires native-speaker competence of Chinese while a pupil living in an area where the minority group dominates may require less of Chinese competence and more of the minority language in the school and home, at least at the initial stage of schooling. But in any case, strong linguistic competence in the national language is crucial.

5. This would of course exclude those minority children who in fact speak Chinese or a Chinese dialect as their home or first language.

6. It is commonly agreed that currently the Chinese education system is exam oriented. High-stakes exams are many and the most crucial ones include the pre-secondary school exam, the nation-wide college entrance exam and the post-graduate exam.

References

Abliz, Y. and Hamdu, S. (2003) Shixian 'Min-Han Jiantong', Shizi Shiguanjian [Teachers – The key to Min-Han Jiantong]. *Xinjiang Caijing Xueyuan Xuebao [Journal of Xinjiang Finance and Economics Institute]* 10 (4), 54–57.

Abliz, M., Sadal, M. and Aldan, M. (2002) Saoshu Minzu Xuesheng Shulihua Jiaoyu Xiangzhuang de Yanjiu [A study of the status quo of physics, mathematics and chemistry education for minority students]. *Jiaoyu Tansuo [Education Exploration]* 135 (9), 108–110.

Alred, G., Byram, M. and Fleming, M. (eds) (2006) *Education for Intercultural Citizenship: Concepts and Comparisons*. Clevedon: Multilingual Matters.

Amat, A. (2003) Tan Shuangyu Jiaoxue, 'Min-Han Jiantong' de Yiyi [On the significance of bilingual education and 'Min-Han Jiantong']. *Zhong Guo Min Zu Jiao Yu* 2, 22–23.

Baker, C. (2001) *Foundations of Bilingual Education and Bilingualism*. Clevedon: Multilingual Matters.

Becker, G.S. (1964) *Human Capital: A Theoretical and Empirical Analysis, with Special Reference to Education*. New York: National Bureau of Economic Research.

Berger, P.L. and Luckmann, T. (1966) *The Social Construction of Reality*. Harmondsworth: Penguin.

Bhabha, H. (1994) *The Location of Culture*. London and New York: Routledge.

Bräuer G. (ed.) (2002) *Body and Language: Intercultural Learning Through Drama*. Westport, CT: Ablex.

Byram, M. (forthcoming) *Intercultural Citizenship Language Learning, Political Education and Internationalisation*.

Byram, M. (1989) *Cultural Studies in Foreign Language Education*. Clevedon: Multilingual Matters.

Byram, M. (1997) *Teaching and Assessing Intercultural Communicative Competence*. Clevedon: Multilingual Matters.

Byram, M. (2003) On being bicultural and intercultural. In G. Alred, M. Byram and M. Fleming (eds) *Intercultural Experience and Education* (pp. 50–66). Clevedon: Multilingual Matters.

Chen, S.X. (2002) Language Law Bewilders Bilingual Educators. (Chen Chao, trans.). On WWW at http://www.china.org.cn/english/2002/Apr/31210.htm.

Constitution of the People's Republic of China (1982) On WWW at http://english.people.com.cn/constitution/constitution.html.

Corbett, J. (2003) *An Intercultural Approach to English Language Teaching*. Clevedon: Multilingual Matters.

Cummins, J. (1986) Empowering minority students: A framework for intervention. *Harvard Educational Review* 56 (1), 18–36.

Cummins, J. (1996) *Negotiating Identities: Education for Empowerment in a Diverse Society*. Ontario, CA: California Association of Bilingual Education.

Cummins, J. (2000) *Language, Power and Pedagogy: Bilingual Children in the Crossfire*. Clevedon: Multilingual Matters.

Dai, Q.X. and Dong, Y. (1997) Zhongguo Shaoshu Minzu Shuangyu Jiaoyu de Lishi Yange - 2 [History and development of bilingual education for minority groups in China -2]. *Minzu Jiaoyu Yanjiu* [*Ethnic Education Research*] 1, 50–61.

Delors, J., *et al.* (1996) *Learning: The Treasure Within* (Report to UNESCO of the International Commission on Education for the Twenty-first Century). Paris, France: UNESCO Publishing.

Deng, Y.L. (2000) Shuangyu Jiaoyu yu Wenhua Rentong [Bilingual education and cultural identification]. *Zhongyang Minzu Daxue Xuebao* [*Journal of Central University of Nationalities*] 128 (1) 131–139.

Doyé, P. (1992) Fremdsprachenunterricht als Beitrag zu tertiärer Sozialisation. In Buttjes *et al.* (eds) *Neue Brennpunkte des Englischunterrichts*, Frankfurt a.M.: Peter Lang.

Doyé, P. (1999) *The Intercultural Dimension: Foreign Language Education in the Primary School*. Berlin: Cornelsen.

Doyè, P. (2003) *Foreign Language Education as a Contribution to Tertiary Socialisation*. Paper presented at the Durham Symposium on Intercultural Competence and Citizenship, Durham University, 24–26, March 2003.

Edwards, J. (1985) *Language, Society and Identity*. Oxford: Blackwell.

Feng, A.W. (1998) *A canon, a Norm and an Attitude: Ideological Dimension of Foreign Language Education in China.* Chicago, IL: Central University (ERIC document reproduction service no.: Ed 426 746).
Feng, A.W. (2005) Bilingualism for the Minor or for the Major: An evaluative analysis of parallel conceptions in China. *International Journal of Bilingual Education and Billingualism* 8 (6), 529–551.
Fishman, J.A. (1971) The sociology of language. In J.A. Fishman (ed.) *Advances in the Sociology of Language* (Vol. 1). The Hague: Mouton.
Freire, P. (1974) *Education for Critical Consciousness.* London: Sheed and Ward.
Gao, Y.H. (1994) Shengcanxing shuangyu sianxiang kaocha [An investigation of productive bilingualism]. *Waiyu Jiaoxue yu Yanjiu [Foreign Language Teaching and Research]* 97 (1), 59–64.
Garrett, M.T. (1996) 'Two people': An American Indian narrative of bicultural identity. *Journal of American Indian Education* 36 (1), 1–21.
Green, P. (1999) *Raise the Standard: A Practical Handbook for Raising Ethnic Minority and Bilingual Pupils' Achievement Based on Successful Policy and Practice in Cities Across the European Community.* Stoke on Trent: Trentham Books.
Grosjean, F. (1985) The bilingual as competent but specific speaker-hearer. *Journal of Multilingual and Multicultural Development* 6 (6), 467–477.
Guo, T.X. (2000) Yi Yuyanxue Lilun he Shijian wei Jizhu Zhidao Wochu "Shuangyu", "Sanyu" Jiaoxue Gaige [Reforming bilingual and trilingual education on the basis of linguistic theories and practice]. *Qian Yan* 12, 68–71.
Hansen, M.H. (1999) *Lessons in Being Chinese: Minority Education and Ethnic Identity in Southwest China.* Seattle, WA: Univ. of Washington Press.
He, K.M. and Deng, J. (2003) Dali Tuixing Shuangyu Jiaoxue, Peiyang Quanmian Fazhan de Fuhexing, Guojixing Rencai [Promoting bilingual education to produce international talents with integrated skills]. *Zhongguo Nongye Yinhang Wuhan Peixun Xueyuan Xuebao [Journal of ABC Wuhan Training College]* 5, 55–56.
Hobsbawm, E. (1996) Language, culture and national identity. *Social Research* 63 (4), 1065–1080.
Hoffmann, E. (1989) *Lost in Translation: A Life in Two Languages.* Harmondsworth: Penguin.
Hu, P. and Zhou, X.M. (2005) Zhongguo Minzu Jiaoyu Jiqi Xueke de Lishi Huigu, Chenjiu yu Zhanwang [Retrospect, achievement and prospect of Chinese minority education and its related academic disciplines]. *Hubei Minzu Xueyuan Xuebao [Journal of Hubei Institute of Nationalities]* 23 (1), 84–88.
Hu, W.Z. and Gao, Y.H. (1997) *Waiyu Jiaoxue yu Wenhua [Foreign Language Teaching and Culture].* Changsha: Hunan Jiaoyu Chubanshe. Huang, G.Y. (1997) *Yingyu Jiaoyuxue [On English Education].* Nanchang, China: Jiangxi Jiaoyu Chubanshe.
Jiang, H.D. (2003) Lun Shuangyu Jiaoyu Mubiao Dingwei zhongde Jige Guanxi Wenti [On the relationships of objectives of bilingual teaching]. *Zhongguo Jiaoyu Xuekan [Journal of the Chinese Society of Education]* 4, 34–37.
Jiaoyubu Guanyu Zaiyouguan Shengqiu Shixing Zhongguo Shaosu Minzu Hanyu Shuipin Dengji Kaoshi de Tongzhi (Ministry of Education notification of trial runs of HSK tests in some minority regions and prefectures) (24 Oct. 2002).
Jiayangzhaxi (1999) Guanyu Zangchu Shuangyu Jiaoxue Moshi Xuanze de Sikao [Thoughts on selection of models of bilingual education in Tibet]. *Zhongguo Minzu Jiaoyu* 1, 25–29.

Jin, Z.Y. and Li, X.M. (2000) Guanyu Shuangyu Jiaoyu Butong Guandian he Taidu Zongshu [An overview of different views and attitudes towards bilingual education]. *Neimenggu Shida Xuebao* [*Journal of Inner Mongolia Normal University*] 19 (4), 208–211.

Ju, J.N. (2000) Guoxiao Shaoshu Minzu Xuesheng Diqidian Yingyu Jiaoxue Wenti Tantao [An examination of the problems encountered in teaching beginning minority students at college]. *Qinghai Minzu Yanjiu* [*Nationalities Research in Qinghai*] 11 (3), 76–77.

Kong, J. (2003) Xingjiang Yaofazhan, Hanyu Jiaoyu Yaoxianxing [To develop Xingjiang, Chinese education should take the priority]. *Yuyan yu Fanyi* [*Language and Translation*] 74 (2), 63–66.

Kramsch, C. (1993) *Context and Culture in Language Teaching*. Oxford: Oxford Univ. Press.

Kramsch, C. (1998) The privilege of the intercultural speaker. In M. Byram and M. Fleming (eds) *Language Learning in Intercultural Perspective: Approaches Through Drama and Ethnography*. Cambridge, U.K.: Cambridge Univ. Press.

Kubow, P., Grossman, D. and Ninomiya, A. (2000) Multidimensional citizenship: Educational policy for the 21 century. In J.J. Cogan and R. Derricott (eds) *Citizenship for the 21st Century* (pp. 131–150). London: Kogan Page.

Lartey, E.Y. (1997) *In Living Colour: An Intercultural Approach to Pastoral Care and Counselling*. London: Cassell.

Li, F.J. (2002) Cong Baiyu Shuangyu Jiaoyuzhong kan Shuangyu Shuangwenhua Xianxiang [Bilingual and bicultural phenomena from the perspective of language transfer in bilingual education for *Bai*]. *Yunnan Shifan Daxue Xuebao* 34 (2), 14–18.

Li, H.L. (2004) Wenhua Zhongduan Lilun dui Woguo Minzu Jiaoyu de Qishi [Reflections on cultural discontinuity theory and minority education]. *Guizhou Minzu Yanjiu* [*Guizhou Ethnic Studies*] 98 (2), 149–153.

Li, S.Z. (2003) Shaoshu Minzu Jiaoyu Kunjin yu Duice Sikao [Thoughts on issues and solutions in minority education]. *Zhongguo Jiaoyu Xuekan* 9, 6–9.

Li, Y.L. (2003) Shaoshu Minzu Xuesheng Yingyu Xuexi de Teshuxing Yanjiu [An analysis of the special characteristics of minority students in learning English]. *Xinan Minzu Daxue Xuebao* [*Journal of Southwest University for Nationalities*] 24 (8), 334–336.

Liang, G.Z. (1994) Qianlun Nanningshi Duoyu Xianxiang [Tentative analysis on the multilingual phenomenon in Nanning]. *Guangxi Shiyuan Xuebao* [*Journal of Guangxi Normal College*] 3, 78–82.

Liao, H.Y. and Yan, X.Y. (2004) Woguo 'Shuangyu Jiaoxue' de Wenhua Shengsi [Reflection on the cultural dimension of 'bilingual teaching']. *Heilongjiang Gaojiao Yanjiu* [*Heilongjiang Higher Education Research*] 128 (12), 121–123.

Lin, J. (1996) *Identity and Discrimination: Minorities in China*. Paper presented at the Comparative and International Education Society Annual Conference held in Williamsburg, Virginia, March 5–10.

Lin, J. (1997) Policies and practices of bilingual education for the minorities in China. *Journal of Multilingual and Multicultural Development* 18 (3), 193–205.

Luo, A.Y. (2001) Xibu Dakaifazhong de Yuyan Jiaoyu Wenti [Issues in language education in the development of the West region]. *Zhongyang Minzu Daxue Xuebao* [*Journal of Central University of Nationalities*] 136 (3), 105–109.

Luo, S.P. (2000) Yetan 21 Shiji Fuhexing Waiyu Rencai Peiyang Mushi [A view on models of all-rounded talents with foreign language competence]. *Wai Yu Jie* [*Foreign Language World*] 79 (3), 8–11 and 17.

Ma, Q. and Xiao, L. Z. (2002a). Wenhua Zhongduan yu Shaoshu Minzu Jiaoyu [Cultural suspense and minority education]. *Shaanxi Shifang Daxue Xuebao* [*Journal of Shaanxi Normal University*] 31 (1), 119–124.

Ma, Q. and Xiao, L.Z. (2002b). Lixing de Shaoshu Minzu Jiaoyu [Sensible education for minority children]. *Guangxi Youjiang Minzu Shizhuan Xuebao* 15 (5), 8–11.

Nanfang Dushibao [Southern City Daily] (2004) Muyu Baoweizhan: Paihuai zai Aiyutong de Bianyuan [The fight to protect mother tongue: Meandering on the borders of love and pain], 16 November.

Niyaz, H. (1998) Guanyu 'Min-Han Jiantong' jiqi Biaozhun. [On 'Min-Han Jiantong' and its Criteria]. *Yuyan yu Fanyi* [*Language and Translation*] 55 (3), 62–65.

Paulston, C.B. (1992) *Sociolinguistic Perspectives on Bilingual Education*. Clevedon: Multilingual Matters.

Pavlenco, A. and Blackledge, A. (eds) (2004) *Negotiation of Identities in Multilingual Contexts*. Clevedon, Buffalo, Toronto and Sydney: Multilingual Matters.

Qian, M.H. (2002) Duoyuan Wenhua Beijinxiade Jiaoyu Gongping Wenti [Educational equality under multicultural situations]. *Xibei Minzu Xueyuan Xuebao* [*Journal of Northwest Minority College*] 6, 99–103.

Qin, Q.G. (2005) Tigao Shuangyu Jiaoxue Zhiliang de Diaocha yu Celue Sikao [Survey and considerations for improving quality of bilingual education]. *Dianzi Keji Daxue Xuebao* [*Journal of UESTC*] 7, 130–132.

Richards, J., Platt, J. and Platt, H. (1992) *Longman Dictionary of Language Teaching and Applied Linguistics*. Harlow: Longman.

Ross, H.A. (1992) Foreign language education as a barometer of modernization. In R. Hayhoe (ed.) *Education and Modernization: The Chinese Experience* (pp. 239–254).Oxford: Pergamon.

Ross, H.A. (1993) *China Learns English: Language Teaching and Social Change in the People's Republic*. New Haven, CT: Yale Univ. Press.

Schmidt, R. (2000) *Language Policy and Identity Policy in the United States*. Philadelphia, PA: Temple Univ. Press.

Shen, L.J. and Luo, B. (2001) Tangaoxiao Yi-Han Shuangyu Jiaoyu "Yilei Muoshi" de Shengyuan Wenti [A discussion on the issue of poor student intake for the "First Model" of bilingual education in Yi-Han Tertiary institutions]. *Zhongguo Minzu Jiaoyu* [*Minority Education in China*] 4, 29–31.

Skutnabb-Kangas, T. (1981) *Bilingualism or Not: The Education of Minorities*. Clevedon: Multilingual Matters.

Soja, E.W. (1996) *Thirdspace: Journeys to Los Angeles and Other Real-And-Imagined Places*. Cambridge, MA; Oxford: Blackwell.

Sun, X.Y. and Gai, S.P. (2005) Ying-Han Shuangyu Jiaoxue de Yousi [Worry about English-Chinese bilingual teaching]. *Heilongjiang Gaojiao Yanjiu* [*Heilongjiang Research on Higher Education*] 134 (6), 124–127.

Tajfel, H. (1981) *Human Groups and Social Categories*. Cambridge, U.K.: Cambridge Univ. Press.

Teng, X. (1996a) Zhongguo Shaoshu Minzu Shuangyu Jiaoyu Yanjiu de Duixiang, Tedian, Neirong yu Fangfa [Subjects, features, content and methodology in researching bilingual education for Chinese minority groups]. *Minzu Jiaoyu Yanjiu* [*Ethnic Education Research*] 2, 44–53.

Teng, X. (1996b) "Zhonghua Minzu Duoyuan Yiti Geju" Sixiang yu Zhongguo Shaoshu Minzu Shuangyu Jiaoyu [The structure of pluralist inclusion of Chinese minorities"]. *Minzu Jiaoyu Yanjiu* [*Ethnic Education Research*] 4, 42–49.

Teng, X. (2000) Liangshan Yizu Sheqiu Xuexiao Shishi Yi-Han Shuangyu Jiaoyu de Biyaoxing [Necessity of conducting Yi-Han bilingual education in community schools in Liangshan]. *Minzu Jiaoyu Yanjiu* [*Ethnic Education Research*] 1, 5–25.

Teng, X. (2004) Xiaokang Shihui yu Xibu Pianyuan Pingkun Diqu Shaoshu Minzu Jichu Jiaoyu [On the well-off society and elementary education for the poor minorities in West China]. *Yunnan Minzu Daxue Xuebao* [*Journal of Yunnan Nationalities University*] 21 (4), 148–150.

Tian, J.L. (2001) Xizong Sanyu Jiaoxue de Zuotian, Jingtian he Mingtian [Past, today and future of trilingual education in Tibet]. *Xizong Daoxue Xuebao* [*Journal of Tibet University*] 16 (4), 49 and 75–79.

Tosi, A. (1988) The jewel in the crown of the modern prince: The new approach to bilingualism in multicultural education in England. In T. Skutnabb-Kungas and J. Cummins (eds) *Minority Education: From Shame to Struggle*. Clevedon: Multilingual Matters.

Turner, B.S. (1990) *Theories of Modernity and Postmodernity*. London: Sage.

Wang, B.H. (2003a). Shuangyu Jiaoyu yu Shuangyu Jiaoxue: Zhongwai Bijiao [Bilingual education and bilingual teaching: A Sino-foreign comparison]. *Wen Hui Bao* [Wen Hui Daily], 9 November, p. 11.

Wang, B.H. (ed.) (2003b) *Shuangyu jiaoyu yu shuangyu jiaoxue* [*Bilingual Education and Bilingual Teaching*]. Shanghai: Shanghai Jiaoyu Chubanshe.

Wang, B.H. (2005) Zhongwai bijiao: Shuangyu jiaoyu de jieding, shuxin yu mudi [A Sino-foreign comparison: The scope, form and aim of bilingual education]. *Jiaoyu Fazhan Yanjiu* [*Research in Education Development*] 6, 49–53.

Wang, H.Y. (2004) Shuangyu Jiaoyu, Fazhan Duoyuan Yiti Wenhua de Biranzhilu [Bilingual education: A path to developing a multiculturally integrated culture]. *Zhongguo Minzu Jiaoyu* [*Chinese Nationality Education*] 4, 20–22.

Wu, J.W. (1994) Shilun Peiyang Fuhexing Rencai [A tentative discussion on talents with integrated competence). *Gaodeng Gongcheng Jiaoyu Yanjiu* [*Research in Higher Engineering Education*] 4, 49–52 and 62.

Wu, Y.M. (2002) Yunnansheng Shaoshu Minzu Xuesheng Gonggong Yingyu Xuexi Kunnan Yingsu Qianxi [An analysis of the barriers to learning College English encountered by minority students in Yunnan]. *Yunnan Caijing Xueyuan Xuebao* [*Journal of Yunnan University of Finance and Economics*] 18 (6), 116–120.

Xiang, X.H., Du, H.P., Jia, N. and Chen, J.M. (2005) Zongzu Nuxuesheng Yingyu Xuexi Nandian Poxi [An Analysis of the difficulties Tibetan female students face in English learning]. *Xinan Minzu Daxue Xuebao* [*Journal of Southeast University of Nationalities*] 23 (6), 367–370.

Xu, K.Q. (2003) 'Shuangyu Jiaoxue' Rezhong Yinguanzhu Zhonghua Minzu Wenhua Yishi Wenti [Beware of the loss of Chinese culture in the fervour of 'bilingual schooling']. *Waiyu Jiaoxue* [*Foreign Language Education*] 25 (3), 86–89.

Yan, G.C. (2004) Zhiyi Shuangyu Jiaoyu [Reservation on bilingual schooling]. *Tansuo yu Zhengming* [*Exploration and Argumentation*] 8, 16–18.

Yang, L. (1998) Shixi "Liangzhong Muoshi" de Shuangyu Jiaoyu [An analysis of the "Two Models" in bilingual education]. *Xinan Minzu Xueyuan Xuebao* [*Journal of the Southwest Institute for Ethnic Groups*] 19, 46–47 and 72.

Yang, L.P. (2003) Quanqiu Xinxi Gongxiang yu Fazhan Zhuangying Shuangyu Jiaoyu de Gouxiang [Thoughts on sharing global information and developing Zhuang and English bilingual education]. _Minzu Jiaoyu Yanjiu_ 14 (2), 66–70.

Yu, J. (1997) Feizhili Yinsu yu Shaoshu Minzu Daxuesheng de Yingyu Xuexi [Non-intelligence factors in minority students' learning English]. _Minzu Jiaoyu Yanjiu_ [Nationalities Education Research] 3, 30–31.

Yu, L.M. (2006) Jianada shuangyu jiaoyu he Zhongguo shuangyu jiaoxue de kebixin [Compatibility of bilingual education in Canada and Bilingual teaching in China]. On WWW at http://www.zhuoda.org/cs/64237.html. Accessed 27.7.06.

Zhongguo Jiaoyubao [Chinese Education Daily] (2003) Shuangyu Jiaoyu yu Minzu Jingsheng [Bilingual education and national spirit], 11 March, Section 7.

Zhongguo Minzu Jiaoyu [Chinese Nationality Education] (2000) 'Jiu-Wu' Qijian Woguo Shaosu Minzu Jiaoyu Qiude Jiuda Chenjiu [Great achievements in minority education in the 'Nine-Five' period] 5, 3–4.

Zhou, D.S. and Zhao, X.J. (2003) Tangaoxiao Hanyu Shouke yu Xingjiang Minzu Jaioyu Zhiliang de Tigao [A View on Chinese language education and the quality of minority education in Xingjiang]. _Minzu Jiaoyu Yanjiu_ [Journal of Research on Ethnic Minorities] 56 (14), 56–61.

Zhu, P. (2003) Lun Shanghai zhongxiaoxue shuangyu jiaoxue shiyan [On bilingual teaching experiments in Shanghai primary and secondary schools]. _Kecheng, Jiaocai, Jiaofa_ [Curriculum, Teaching Resources, Methodology] 6, 52–58.

Zhu, P. (2004) Shuangyu jiaoxue de dingwei, fenlei, renwu he mushi [Objective, typology, tasks and models of bilingual teaching]. _Jisuanji Jiaoyuxue_ [Teaching and Learning Through Computers] 3, 13–14.

Index